PHILOSOPHICAL PRACTICE

Other interview books from Automatic Press ♦ VIP

Formal Philosophy
edited by Vincent F. Hendricks & John Symons
November 2005

Masses of Formal Philosophy
edited by Vincent F. Hendricks & John Symons
October 2006

Political Questions: 5 Questions for Political Philosophers
edited by Morten Ebbe Juul Nielsen
December 2006

Philosophy of Technology: 5 Questions
edited by Jan-Kyrre Berg Olsen & Evan Selinger
February 2007

Game Theory: 5 Questions
edited by Vincent F. Hendricks & Pelle Guldborg Hansen
April 2007

Philosophy of Mathematics: 5 Questions
edited by Vincent F. Hendricks & Hannes Leitgeb
January 2008

Philosophy of Computing and Information: 5 Questions
edited by Luciano Floridi
Sepetmber 2008

Epistemology: 5 Questions
edited by Vincent F. Hendricks & Duncan Pritchard
September 2008

Mind and Consciousness: 5 Questions
edited by Patrick Grim
January 2009

Philosophy of Science: 5 Questions
edited by Robert Rosenberger
November 2010

Philosophy of Medicine: 5 Questions
edited by J.K.B.O. Friis, P. Rossel & M.S. Norup
September 2011

See all published and forthcoming books in the 5 Questions series at
www.vince-inc.com

PHILOSOPHICAL PRACTICE
5 QUESTIONS

edited by

Jeanette Bresson Ladegaard Knox

Jan Kyrre Berg Olsen Friis

Automatic Press ◆ VIP

Automatic Press ♦ $\frac{V}{I}$P

Information on this title: www.vince-inc.com

© Automatic Press / VIP 2013

This publication is in copyright. Subject to statuary exception and to the provisions of relevant collective licensing agreements, no reproduction of any part may take place without the written permission of the publisher.

First published 2013

Printed in the United States of America and the United Kingdom

ISBN-10 87-92130-45-3 paperback
ISBN-13 978-87-92130-45-7 paperback

The publisher has no responsibilities for the persistence or accuracy of URLs for external or third party Internet Web sites referred to in this publication and does not guarantee that any content on such Web sites is, or will remain, accurate or appropriate.

Typeset in $\LaTeX 2_\varepsilon$
Cover design by Vincent F. Hendricks

Contents

Preface		v
Acknowledgements		vii
1	Lydia Amir	1
2	José Barrientos-Rastrojo	15
3	Dries Boele	33
4	Vaughana Macy Feary	43
5	Fred Gebler	61
6	Horst Gronke	77
7	Finn Thorbjørn Hansen	89
8	Leon de Haas	109
9	Henning Herrestad	123
10	Jos Kessels	131
11	Dieter Krohn	149
12	Ran Lahav	159
13	Anders Lindseth	171
14	Lou Marinoff	183
15	Peter Raabe	203
16	Shlomit Schuster	221
17	Helge Svare	237
About the Editors		243
Index		245

Preface

Philosophical Practice: 5 Questions
Preface by Jeanette Bresson Ladegaard Knox

―――――――――――― ♦ ――――――――――――

Philosophical practice is rooted in the Greek understanding of philosophy as linked to the actual experience of man, placing the philosopher in the market place armed with a Socratic state of mind that facilitates critical, comprehensive and creative thinking. It reconnects with the Platonic idea of wonder as a starting point for philosophizing and the Aristotelian idea that human beings by nature seek wisdom, truth and meaning.

Since antiquity and up through the centuries philosophy has stood for the passionate yet rational engagement in questions about oneself and the world around. The recent descent of philosophy in the 20th century into becoming a highly specialized professional discipline within the universities has left philosophy in general with an air of impracticality and a reputation of being irrelevant to the lives of people. Such specialization, which we have also observed in many other academic fields, obviously has great value by its mere contribution to multifaceted perspectives on philosophical issues and ongoing discussions on abstract concepts. But at the same time it seemed as if philosophers, as this specialization increased, strayed away from the original pursuit of philosophy. Philosophy somehow got lost in philosophy. The academic turn of philosophy in modern times spurred some philosophers to explore the appeal of philosophy to everyday life and began to conduct philosophical discourse with non-philosophers. At one point in this process Philosophical Practice was coined. Philosophical practice expresses a renaissance of that ancient spirit of making philosophy matter to others than just a brotherhood for the inaugurated few playing out various forms of seemingly endless self-referential mind-games.

Philosophical practice is, however, both a theoretical and empirical discipline. The scope is not to glorify experience at the expense of theories. Philosophical practice encompasses the scrutinizing of fundamental questions relating to existence, knowledge, reason, language, mind, body, etc., the reflection on the application of these fundamental questions and the actual application of them both with oneself and with others. The way it does this has great importance because it does not attempt to simply glue a theory on to a concrete issue. Rather, it aims for a dialectic synthesis of theory and practice showing the necessary and mutually enriching interplay between them.

Preface

Philosophical practice is a fast developing movement and community within philosophy that is working with pressing issues in hospitals, prisons, schools, organizations, businesses, etc. by using philosophical reflection. The focal attention is on the practice of dialogue which can take on various frameworks and be carried out in groups or between a philosopher and an individual. Philosophers within Philosophical Practice are a part of a critical and engaged tradition that tries to situate philosophy in the public debate, in society, culture and politics; it encourages the positioning of philosophy within a concrete context to clarify and amplify the relevance of philosophy to everyday life by revealing predicaments, dilemmas, choices, and challenges and proposing ways of reflecting on and resolving them. Philosophical practice attempts to reunite with the world outside of academia, forcing philosophy to be concerned with the problems of man and not just the problems of philosophers, as once stated by John Dewey. It encourages the Socratic tradition of leading an examined life.

Over the past four decades, philosophers have developed this ancient idea of philosophy. National and international societies of Philosophical Practice, journals and conferences have seen the light of day and a long list of books have been published. There are many different understandings of Philosophical Practice and new ways of exercising Philosophical Practice are continuously being developed. The authors in this volume of 5 Questions are philosophers from the pioneering generation of practitioners. They individually show how rich and diverse and yet similar these different understandings and practices are. The contributors actively work with philosophy in practice, some hold academic positions, some do not and some have a foot in both worlds. They have all helped define the character of Philosophical Practice as a distinct philosophical discipline and greatly contributed to the enhancement of Philosophical Practice as a practice.

Acknowledgements

We are particularly grateful to the contributors for devoting time to writing such erudite, enlightening, and often thought-provoking interviews, and grateful to the philosophical community in general for showing interest in this project. In addition, we would like to thank editor-in-chief Vincent F. Hendricks and editor Henrik Boensvang of Automatic Press ♦ $\frac{V}{I}$-P.

Copenhagen, June 2012
Jeanette Bresson Ladegaard Knox & Jan Kyrre Berg Olsen Friis
Editors

viii   Acknowledgements

1

Lydia Amir

Senior Lecturer in Philosophy, Head of Humanistic Studies
School of Media Studies, College of Management Academic
Studies, Rishon Lezion, Israel

---

1. Why were you initially drawn to Philosophical Practice?

I have always considered philosophy the most practical of disciplines: sustained and educated thought about one's life was helpful as nothing else was. Together with the world religions, philosophy was to me the deposit of wisdom of previous generations, who had struggled with similar problems we face today. As early in my career as the composition of my Ph.D. dissertation on *Personal Redemption according to Spinoza and Nietzsche*, I added a chapter that detailed the path leading to the realization in one's life of the redemptions proposed by Spinoza and Nietzsche. I shared the vision of philosophy as a practical discipline when taken seriously with my dissertation supervisor, Prof. Joseph Agassi, who insisted that I should personalize Spinoza's and Nietzsche's philosophies and make them more palatable for readers by shunning jargon and exemplifying their doctrines with everyday life problems, and who assured me early on that philosophy could fulfill not only my intellectual needs but my existential and emotional desires as well.

Equipped with this vision of philosophy and a native propensity for sharing everything I know, and driven by circumstances to find for a while additional work on the margins of academe, I introduced the first Israeli course of philosophy for non-philosophers (most of them retired professionals) at the Popular University in Tel-Aviv, and fulfilled a friend's desire to learn about Spinoza by giving ten lectures about his philosophy in an apartment in Tel-Aviv. This was soon followed by ten lectures on Nietzsche and more on the Hellenistic philosophers, and as the course on philosophy at the Popular University, for which I had to fight initially, turned out to be a great success, I was swamped with offers of this kind.

When listeners attending these courses approached me to discuss personal matters enlightened by philosophy, I suggested to meet privately.

Once, a friend of mine told me that what I was doing was called Philosophical Practice. When a journalist approached me to write about my private philosophical meetings with clients, I presented my activity in the article as Philosophical Practice. Other philosophical practitioners, such as Ran Lahav, learned about me by reading the article and contacted me. Ran suggested I join him in the first international conference on Philosophical Practice he was organizing with Lou Marinoff in Vancouver. I have been a part of the movement and have never missed a conference.

Twelve years before the publication of the newspaper article on Philosophical Practice, I proposed teaching philosophy to gifted children, but my offer was rejected.

I have always taken philosophy seriously and believed in the importance of befriending it at all ages; but were it not for circumstances that led me to seek work outside departments of philosophy for a while, I may not have had the opportunity of implementing these ideas. Once I put these views into practice, however, I considered it my duty to continue sharing philosophy's benefits with the general public by using ever new forms of communication, such as the radio program I air weekly on a popular radio station in Israel (106fm).

2. What does your work reveal about Philosophical Practice that other related academic fields typically fail to appreciate?

There is no discontinuity between academic philosophy and Philosophical Practice. Taking philosophy seriously means valuing the transformative power of its theories instead of reducing them to a barren academicism. The difference between academic philosophy and Philosophical Practice is a difference in degrees of abstraction and generalization, leading from a condensed thought in academic philosophy to an implementation of its contents in practical matters in Philosophical Practice. The academic lecturer of philosophy is already a practitioner because he has to appropriate the theory in order to fully understand it in order to effectively teach it (Amir 2006a). On the other end of the spectrum, the philosophical practitioner is just a good teacher of philosophy, who is able to tailor for the client/student a private tutorial that fits her interests or needs and level of understanding, with the explicit purpose of imparting to her the knowledge and skills needed for using philosophic tools in order to continue her philosophic education (Amir 2006b, 2003).

Second, philosophy has always been a discipline oriented toward practice as well as theory, mostly for the few and sometimes for the many. I refer to philosophy in its former capacity as perfectionist and in its later capacity as meliorist (from the verb meliorate). The Greek Philosophers provided both paths—a good example is Aristotle's two ways of reaching happiness, one for the many (expounded in most of the chapters of the *Nicomachean Ethics*), and the other for the rare few (Chapter 10)—the Hellenistic Philosophers addressed the many, especially in Roman times. Yet the role of philosophy as provider of worldviews leading to the good life was taken over by Christianity at the end of Antiquity and jealously held for a millennium. By this token, Christianity had reduced philosophy to the role of a servant of faith and disqualifying it as a path leading to truth, happiness, and wisdom. Slowly, however, Modern philosophy disengages itself from this influence through the work of Spinoza, Schopenhauer, Kierkegaard, Nietzsche, Santayana, the Existentialist philosophers, and recently through the movement of Philosophical Practice (Amir 2006c, 2009b, 2006a).

Third, Philosophical Practice does not provide a therapy. As a perfectionist endeavour, it aims higher than therapy, at ideals such as freedom, happiness, peace of mind, and wisdom. As a melioristic endeavour, it aims lower than therapy, at the virtues and skills needed for better citizenship. It might prove beneficial to differentiate between these two traditions within philosophy: one tradition might be called perfectionism or radical philosophy; the other, meliorism or democratized philosophy. Both traditions survive today in academic philosophy, and are practiced in a variety of forms of Philosophical counseling. Both are valid and important, yet ignorance of the differences between them results in tension among counselors and between counselors and academics. Those who are familiar with Oriental philosophy will recognize the Western analogue to Buddhist schools, the Hinayana school or small vehicle leading to liberation, on the one hand, and the Mahayana school or large vehicle, on the other. Other descriptive terms could be radical versus piecemeal philosophy, elitist versus democratic, philosophy oriented towards liberty more than towards equality.

The perfectionist tradition represents the revolutionary face of philosophy, in the following ways. Philosophy presents itself as an alternative to established religion, and to any other establishments. It is highly critical of society's values—it dismisses the common-sense, non-critical views of people, urging them to question their lives and not to take appearances at their face value; it presents itself as an alternative to the common views of happiness: riches, pleasure, and power or fame. It requires a conversion to forms of thought and allegiances foreign to most men. It assumes that radical change is possible through sole understanding and practice. It is total, keeping touch with other disciplines but in a supervising and critical stance, perfectionist and ambitious in answering all worthy needs, including spiritual ones. It prescribes the highest ideals in morality and ethics: it aims at nothing less than liberty, happiness or peace of mind, and even at philosophical redemption. It is for the few. Rare are those who live according to its requirements and even fewer dare claim that they do.

By meliorism I refer to those philosophies which are less ambitious, more in conformity with common sense, with ordinary psychological needs and social goals, more skeptical of perfectionist ends and means. For example, Aristotle's *Nichomachean Ethics* might qualify as meliorist, if we exclude its tenth chapter; other philosophers in this tradition, to mention a few, would be Hume, Locke, Russell, and Popper. This is the tradition that requires further development in Philosophical Practice. If meliorism and perfectionism are both loyal to philosophy's aims and methods, the same virtues championed in perfectionism will also predominate in meliorism. The difference would be that the very high ethical ideals of perfectionist philosophy, as well as its demand of a radical break with society's presuppositions, would be avoided.

Whether under its perfectionist or the melioristic guise, Philosophical Practice does not offer therapy, as it aims either higher or lower than that. It addresses the human being who is plagued by problems related to the human condition, or who is attracted to philosophic issues by other motives. Moreover, there is no diagnostic in Philosophical Practice, as it leaves to health professionals the care of acute anxiety, deep depression, and mental illnesses. It can successfully work in conjunction with psychologists, however, either before or after the treatment and in coordination with psychiatrists as well.

Fourth, philosophy and psychology are both necessary for human well-being, because psychologists are trained in emotional education, yet emotional education needs a frame of values to evaluate emotions, which only philosophers can provide. Psychology has taken over moral questions in the last century: theoretically, it has incorporated moral views into its various theories; practically, psychotherapists use moral discourse in their practice even when not substantiated by theory, as there seem to be a gap between what the theory can offer and the clients' needs. The theories of morality that form part of psychological theories are lacking in depth and scope. Yet therapists are now asked to serve as moral authorities, filling the vacuum left by the loss of older sources of guidance. Because of this demand placed on therapists, a central part of what goes on in helping people in the modern world consists in addressing questions about what constitutes the good life and how we can be at home in the world. These are clearly moral questions in the broad sense, where morality includes not just questions about right actions, but questions which touch on the issue of what kind of life is worth living, or of what constitutes a rich, meaningful life, as against one concerned with secondary matters or trivia. Therapists are ill-equipped for this task. The practice of psychotherapy necessarily makes use of moral discussions, and as the theory is insufficient, these discussions are in most cases unsubstantiated by theory. After examining the historical and social reasons for the situation that led psychologists into doing what they have not been trained for, we might conclude that the role of discussing moral questions should be taken over by philosophical counselors.

Effective moral education involves emotional education. Philosophers' views of emotions tend to be reductive, and when they are not, they point to an irreducibility of affectivity which is not amenable to philosophical investigation. While emotional and moral education should go hand in hand, philosophers seem poorly equipped for the former. Psychotherapists are trained in educating emotions and in attending the irreducible affectivity of individual emotions. Interested as we might be in psychotherapists' specialization in emotional education, we cannot dissociate it from moral education, as emotional education is not value-free. Recalling that psychological theories involve views of morality which do not withstand critical examination, we are reluctant to entrust psychotherapists with moral education. Turning once again to psychology, we realize that we have added a new complexity to the initial problematic status of psychological moral education. While emotional and moral education should go hand in hand, the untenable situation that obtains is that philosophers educate us morally while psychologists educate us emotionally. Moral education is impaired whether it is left to psychotherapists or to philosophers.

Moral education, successful living, and happiness include a normative component, which makes philosophy indispensable for the good life; yet, without addressing the affectivity that determines our emotional lives, all philosophical theories are fruitless, and the normative aspect determining the values and ends of our lives is impotent. Thus, philosophy and psychology are both necessary for human well-being, and should find a way of cooperating to further that worthy goal (Amir 2005b, 2009d, 2006c).

3. What, if any, practical and/or social-political obligations follow from understanding philosophy from the point of view of Philosophical Practice?

Philosophical Practice is the offspring of the Enlightenment, an epoch in which practical philosophies as represented by Socrates and Hellenistic philosophers were predominant. Philosophical Practice expresses a belief in human rationality, in the importance of critical thinking, and in the autonomy of each individual to think for himself. These tenets are the Enlightenment's principles, which are still relevant today for implementing the ideal of living autonomously in liberal democracies. Philosophical Practice should provide the necessary tools to fulfill this ideal in order to help minimize the tension between equality (everyone can) and liberty (you are on your own, we cannot help lest we impinge on your liberty), which plagues every democratic and liberal society (Amir 2009b, 2006a).

To begin with, legal rights are insufficient without the means to exercise those rights. The right to the pursuit of happiness is an empty one, for example, if we lack the tools to develop and harmonize our intellectual and moral capacities. In attaining intellectual and moral integrity we become autonomous not only *de jure* but also *de facto*. Philosophical Practitioners should assist the client in becoming an autonomous individual.

Second, only the philosopher can provide the non-authoritarian, pluralistic, and critical moral education, which is necessary for young adults in liberal democratic societies, but which is left unattended. In contradistinction both to scholarly and religious education, the moral education provided by philosophers is non—authoritarian; it is necessarily pluralistic, moreover, because it involves the acquaintance and even-handed assessment of a variety of moral theories; finally, it is critical, because choosing a morality and abiding by it necessitates the capacity to reflect critically on one's values, and to sustain one's choice by arguments and reasoning (Amir 2009d, 2005, 2004b, 2002a.).

Third, critical thinking is at the very heart of Philosophical Practice and is a key to our freedom in any society, provided we understand that intellectual lives are not devoted exclusively to acquiring beliefs, but also with maintaining, communicating and applying our beliefs to practical affairs. Critical thinking provides us with the means of defending ourselves against manipulation and control by others. When we become self-critical in this way, we are no longer simply at the mercy of whatever others tell us to believe and we no longer take things at face value. We can critically weigh up the positions being presented to us to see whether there are good reasons for believing them. Given that we continue to be subject to various social and cultural influences, critical reflection continues to have a role to play in adult life. In the face of influences from advertising, the mass media, cultural pressures, and political propaganda, along with the seductive messages coming from all manner of experts, gurus, and demagogues, a capacity to be critical, to critically weigh up the claims and arguments we are presented with, remains vital if we are to maintain a degree of independence (Amir 2011a, 2009a, 2006a.).

Fourth, philosophy should once again fulfill its role as teacher of wisdom in order to fight complacent New Age mysticism. I suggest that the New Age movement is not primarily the new locus of mystics who have always accompanied the growth in rationality; rather, the eclipse of philosophy on matters of wisdom, happiness, meaning, and alternative spirituality has led many rational persons to New Age theories for lack of an accessible alternative (Amir 2009a). The New Age movement is relevant for philosophers because of its popularity, its possible confusion with philosophy, and the dangers for adequate thinking that the movement's views represent—almost the sole danger this otherwise peaceful and love-oriented movement represents. It is important for practical philosophers, then, to present clients with comprehensive, rational, and viable worldviews that provide meaning, even alternative rational spiritualities, and especially paths leading to wisdom and happiness, as philosophy has always done (Amir 2009a).

4. What do you see as the most interesting criticism against your own position in Philosophical Practice?

I never heard of any sustained criticism of my views, unfortunately, but I assume that from the point of view of potential critics my position's strengths are also its weaknesses.

First, my take on the necessary relation between academic philosophy and practical philosophy, which I consider crucial for Philosophical Practice and potentially revolutionizing for academic philosophy (Amir 2004a) may be perceived as not aggressive enough toward academic philosophy and certainly at odds with those practitioners who wish to establish Philosophical Practice as a new profession.

Second, the respect I have for psychology and psychiatry, and the emphasis I put on the necessity of Philosophical Practice to be philosophical instead of (pseudo-)psychological, may not appeal to philosophical practitioners who conceive of Philosophical Practice as a substitute to psychology or psychiatry or both (see Amir 2004b). Psychiatry and psychology have been pioneers in studying and sometimes helping abnormal psychological states, including anxiety and depression. They should be applauded for that and encouraged to pursue their research. There is no need for philosophers to compete with their work, as philosophy has always addressed the normal, more or less rational, person, who struggles with the ordinary problems of the human condition instead of with an individual extreme psychological disorder. Philosophical practitioners should take philosophy seriously and avoid selling it short, misrepresenting it, or passing it for what it is not. To take philosophy seriously is to be loyal to its objectives. The philosophical counselor who thinks that philosophical theory is not important does not trust his own discipline, *philo-sophia*, to display a love of wisdom or be a fruitful reflection on life. He might emulate forms of counseling taken from other disciplines, such as psychology or New Age theories, believing that his being a philosopher brings something new to the discussion.

Yet, not every conversation with a philosopher is philosophical. Reflecting adequately is the seal that differentiates philosophy from psychology and New Ages theories. The difference with psychology lies in the emphasis on reflection: philosophical reflection is abstract and derives its power from that. The difference between philosophy and New Age thought lies in the emphasis on adequacy: adequacy stems from rigor of thought, from arguments that establish the reliability of conclusions. This locates epistemology and logic at the heart of Philosophical Practice, with moral and ethical education as the professed goal that directs the enterprise of thinking well, for intellectual virtuesas also moral virtues.

Some philosophical practitioners believe, however, that the birth or re-birth of Philosophical Practice is an opportunity for rethinking the value of psychological counseling, and re-evaluating the help psychologists and psychiatrists bring to patients suffering from abnormal psychological states. And some philosophical practitioners are against psychiatry and psychology altogether. I imagine that they might not like my lenient view of both disciplines and practices.

Third, my emphasis on rationality with the aim of distinguishing between mysticism and religion, on the one hand, and philosophy, on the other, may not appeal to mystical and religious philosophical practitioners. I conceive of philosophy as a rational enterprise that represents an alternative to organized religions. Some philosophies are also spiritual endeavours, but they offer rational spiritualities rather than mystical practices such as accompany the main religions.

Fourth, my call to revive Western philosophies' practical aspects and create Western conceptual frames and somatic practices is at odds with the current importation of Eastern philosophies and practices to the West with alterations to fit Westerners. Emphasizing differences between Western and Eastern philosophies and persons seems at variance with the contemporary *bon ton*. It is not popular today to criticize the way yoga and Buddhist meditation are practiced in the West, as exercises torn from their spiritual aims and metaphysical frames of thought (Amir 2009a). Urging Westerners to develop their own contemporary somatic practices, like the Feldenkrais or Alexander methods, to fit philosophical theories, may not be a commonplace thought.[1]

Finally, the important role I allot the philosopher and the philosophical practitioner as teachers of skills and virtues necessary for bridging the gulf between the ideal citizen of democratic liberal societies and the *de facto* tension between equality and liberty may be at odds with relativistic views of morality, laissez-faire visions of happiness, and views of education as necessarily authoritarian.

5. With respect to present and future inquiry, how can the most important problems concerning Philosophical Practice be identified and explored?

It is important that philosophical practitioners be philosophers. The status of Philosophical Practice has undergone a change in the past twenty years: from an estranged practice, Philosophical Practice has become so appealing that many non-philosophers call themselves philosophers, write and counsel as if they were professional philosophers. As a provider of wisdom, philosophy has relinquished its role in favor of the new age movement; as the locus of theories of happiness, Philosophy is forgotten, leaving happiness without a normative component in the hands of researchers of the social sciences, such as political scientists and positive psychologists; as counsellors to other disciplines, philosophers have been eclipsed from bio-ethics and professional ethics by more down-to-earth professionals. Philosophical practitioners should be set apart from other practitioners by their being professional philosophers: they should be informed by wide and thorough knowledge both of the history of philosophy and of its methods, they should use in the practice a method, a systematization that mirrors philosophy's techniques, and most importantly, they should have a pluralistic attitude, a non-dogmatic approach to problems, and an even-handedness in handling various theories that allows the client to find its own way in the maze of theories and practices (Amir 2001a, 2003, 2006c) Allow me to explain.

To deserve the title philosophical and thereby differentiate itself from psychology and New Age theories and practices, a Philosophical Practice should be faithful to philosophy's objectives and methods. This means that Philosophical Practice should take philosophy seriously. The forms of teaching or tutoring may be different, among the consultancy, the groups outside the university, and the classes at the university, but

---

[1] For somatic devices, such as using music for implementing abstract philosophic ideas, listen to my weekly radio program on the internet, Diotima: Thought in Practice, which uses music to help clarify philosophic concepts that are relevant for everyday life (www.106fm.co.il). For my theoretical innovations, see my forthcoming book, *Humor and the Good Life*, and Amir 2012, 2010, 2002b.

the objectives have to be the same, otherwise the endeavor cannot deserve to be qualified as philosophical. The way I see it, philosophy has three interrelated objectives. The first objective is truth, at least by *via negative*, that is, by eradicating our errors as taught by Karl Popper's critical rationalism; this further involves choosing truth over happiness, if they do not coincide, because truth is the philosopher's happiness. The second objective is liberation, even if partial, from illusions, preconceptions and self-centered intelligence; and the third objective is wisdom, even if negative, in the humble sense of realizing my ignorance and finding out that which I do not want to know, which results in better understanding or comprehension. The relation that holds among these objectives seems to be the following: liberation from untruth is the path to wisdom.

These inter-related objectives, truth, liberation, and wisdom, should be approached through adequate reflection on experience, which is ensured through the use of philosophical methods, such as abstract thought, logic and epistemology. To fit non-philosophers' needs and capacities, however, logic and epistemology should be constructed as applied disciplines and taught in that way, and abstract thought should be supplemented by a movement from the concrete to the abstract and back.

In order to ensure transparency *vis-a vis* the client and loyalty to philosophical goals and means, first, a view of philosophic advancement should be transposed into a method of work to be adopted and followed in the practice For example, the method I found is the method I use in writing and in reading whenever the text is written according to my requirements. First, one formulates the problem at hand in a question, preferably one with multiple answers. Second, one presents the alternative answers to the question. Third, one assesses each answer critically. One is ready, then, to formulate a second question, which has usually some connection (logical or other) to the first one. And so on. The questions and alternative answers determine very clearly what we are doing at each moment of the counseling, and allow the counselee to evaluate what we have done till now. Though the client can leave the counseling sessions at any time, the method of questions and alternative answers allows for easily detectable exits, usually accompanied by a feeling of satisfaction because one recognizes what has been achieved (Amir 2003; 2006b).

In order to ensure transparency *vis-a vis* the client and loyalty to philosophical goals and means, the goals one attempts to reach in the practice should be clarified as well. For example, my goals in the Philosophical Practice are the following. First, I attempt to further thinking by the movement from the concrete to the abstract and back. Philosophy is an abstract discipline; rather than being a hindrance, the abstract as an inward space where thought can be expanded and freedom gained without the tyranny of personal fear is one of the great therapeutic inventions of philosophy. But any solution to any problem that would remain at the abstract level is useless. Hence the necessity of coming to the abstract from the concrete and returning to the concrete after incorporating the abstract's general knowledge. By subjectively appropriating the insights gained in the abstract, I am faithful to philosophy's means (abstract thought) as well as to practical philosophy's goals (the concrete) (Amir 2006c).

Second, I attempt to promote intellectual virtueswith the ultimate goal of furthering intellectual courage and autonomy. I believe intellectual virtuesare what philosophy is about, and I relate them to the questions and alternative answers method by the following argument: knowledge, as intelligent development is connected to the capacity of adopting additional or different points of view both in Jean Piaget's psychology and the history of sciences. Adopting different points of view further such epistemic virtues as impartiality, or openness to the ideas of others, assessing critically different answers further intellectual sobriety, or the virtue of the careful inquirer who accepts only what is warranted by evidence, and the whole process of Philosophical Practice that is faithful to philosophy furthers the virtue of intellectual courage, which includes perseverance and determination (Amir 2011a).

Third, I attempt to promote moral virtueswith the ultimate goal of furthering one's solidarity, for wide thoughts are not sufficient for wisdom; wide feelings are needed too. Promoting moral virtuesis not a separate endeavor from promoting intellectual virtues: feelings are involved in intellectual virtues, and intellectual virtuesare involved in handling feelings. Spinoza made understanding, which is an intellectual virtue, the key to all the virtues, and understanding different points of view brings forth pluralism, tolerance, acceptance, which further solidarity with our fellow human beings (Amir 2004c).

These three goals serve the major goal of philosophy and its practice, which is autonomy, as both a moral and an intellectual virtue. The virtue of autonomy is a mean state of character with regard to reliance on one's own powers in acting, choosing, and forming opinions. Autonomous moral thinking is closely parallel to autonomous theoretical thinking, the one being concerned with what should be done, the other with what is the case. The virtue of autonomy is closely allied to courage, as well as to humility, and it shows the connection between cognitive and volitional processes, for, to be autonomous in one's thinking calls for intellectual skills, including the ability to judge when someone else knows better than you. But it calls also for the ability to control the emotions that prevent those skills from being properly exercised.

The three goals proposed above together with their subsequent greater autonomy for the counselee help minimize the tension between freedom and equality, which is the ultimate objective of a democratically oriented Philosophical Practice (Amir 2006a).

Another problem of importance regarding Philosophical Practice that should be identified and explored concerns the relations between philosophy and psychology. I suggest these should be clarified through the relations between Philosophical Practice and psychological therapies (Amir 2005, 2009d). An individual cannot be dissociated by the two disciplines. Psychologists should be used by philosophers as highly-trained technicians who can work locally on an irrational matter. They should be acclaimed for their work in abnormal psychology. For normal psychology they need philosophers, however, as both the dependence of positive psychology on philosophical theories and therapists' use of Eastern and New Age wider visions of life testify.

Last, but not least, Philosophers should diffuse their power, and shun guruism as anti philosophical. True, philosophy has had its share of gurus (Amir 2009b), and the relationship of teachers and apprentices in philosophy is plagued with problems that are potentially dangerous (Amir 2009c); yet philosophers have devised means to avoid or reduce these dangers (Amir 2011b). In addition to these means, I suggest that humor and especially the counselor's self-referential humor can help diffuse power and minimize self-importance in Philosophical Practice, as well as prove in other ways helpful in philosophic education and philosophic transformations. When used correctly, humor is one of the most useful tools available to a philosopher for furthering philosophic ideals, such as self-knowledge, truth, rationality, freedom, virtue, happiness, and wisdom; it is helpful for furthering the awareness of intrapersonal conflicts, deliberating over them, living with unsolvable conflicts, and for strengthening both our acknowledgement and tolerance of ambivalence and ambiguity that characterize life and human relationships (Amir, forthcoming *Humor and the Good Life*, 2012, 2010, 2002b).

Bibliography

Amir, Lydia.B. 2002a. The Role of Impersonal Love in Everyday Life. In Philosophy in Society, H. Herrestad, A. Holt and H. Svare (eds.), 217-242. Oslo: Unipub.

Amir, L.B. 2002b. Pride, Humiliation and Humility: Humor as a Virtue. International Journal of Philosophical Practice, vol. 1/3: 1-22.

Amir, L.B. 2003. Philosophical Practice: A Method and Some Cases. Practical Philosophy, vol. 6/ 1: 36-41.

Amir, L.B. 2004a. How Can Philosophy Benefit from Philosophical Practice? Practical Philosophy, vol. 9/2: 3-12.

Amir, L.B. 2004b. Three Questionable Assumptions of Philosophical counselling. International Journal of Philosophical Practice, vol. 2/1: 1-32.

Amir, L.B. 2004c. The Affective Aspect of Wisdom. Practical Philosophy, 7/1: 14-25.

Amir, L.B. 2005. Morality, Psychology, Philosophy. Philosophical Practice, 1/1: 43-57.

Amir, L.B. 2006a. Taking Philosophy Seriously: Perfectionism versus Meliorism. In From Theory to Practice, J. Barrientos Rastrojo, J. Ordonez Garcia, F. Macera Garfia (eds.), 11-32. Sevilla: Ediciones X-XI.

Amir, L.B. 2006b. More Philosophy, Less Counseling. In From Theory to Practice, J. Barrientos Rastrojo, J. Ordonez Garcia, F. Macera Garfia (eds.), 33-39. Sevilla: Ediciones X-XI.

Amir, L.B. 2006c. Søren Kierkegaard and the Practice of Philosophy. In Philosophers as Philosophical Practitioners, J. Barrientos Rastrojo (ed.), vol. II, 31-45. Sevilla: Ediciones X-XI.

Amir, L.B. 2009a. Rethinking Philosophers' Responsibility. In Creating a Global Dialogue on Value Inquiry, J. Yan and D. Schrader (eds.), 21-56. Lewiston, NY: The Edwin Mellen Press.

Amir, L.B. 2009b ¿Que Podemos Aprender de la Filosofía Helenista? (What Can We Learn from Hellenistic Philosophy?). Sophia: Revista de Filosofía, 5: 81-89. Much longer English version in www.revistasophia.com.

Amir, L.B. 2009c. Plato I Love, but I Love Truth More. In Philosophische Lehrjahre: Beiträge zum kritischen Selbsverständnis Philosophischer Praxis, T. Gutknecht, T. Polednitschek, T. Stölzel (Hg.) (eds.), 151-172. Münster: LIT-Verlag.

Amir, L.B. 2009d. Philosophers, Ethics, and Emotions. Philosophical Practice, 4/2: 447-58.

Amir, L.B. 2010. Humor and Time. In Proceedings of the first conference on Time, Transcendence, Performance, Melbourne (Australia, October 1-3, 2009), 1-31.

Amir, L. B. 2011a. Epistemology as a Practical Activity. Haser, 2:

41-65.

Amir, L.B. 2011b. The Role of the Teacher in Philosophers' Self-Education. Die Sprache der Freiheit: Philosophische Praxis und Kunst und Religion, T. Gutknecht, T. Polednitschek, P. Morstein (eds.), 143-183. Münster: LIT-Verlag,

Amir, L.B. 2012. Philosophy's Attitude towards the Comic—A Reevaluation. The Israeli Journal of Humor Research: An International Journal (forth.).

Amir, L.B. Forthcoming. Humor and the Good Life. Albany, NY: SUNY Press.

2

José Barrientos-Rastrojo

Professor of Philosophy & Philosophical Practitioner
University of Seville, Spain

MY INVOLVEMENT WITH PHILOSOPHICAL PRACTICE[1]

1. Why were you initially drawn to Philosophical Practice?

I started simultaneously to study nursing and Philosophy in 1999. I finished my studies in nursing in 2001, but I had been planning to dedicate my whole life to philosophy since 1999. I was considering starting a career that could help people to better understand their lives and lead a worthwhile one. Furthermore, philosophy as I saw it and still see it, could assist in reaching this goal by means of encouraging people to a more harmonious existence.

What I found in Philosophy helped me a lot and it helped me to understand and (dis)solve some of my personal problems. If my ethical, metaphysical or epistemological reflections gave me insights to enlighten personal issues, could it be useful for other men and women? Could it really be a practical field or was it just a discipline confined to its "Ivory Tower"?

In 1999-2000, I was invited by the ETOR group to one of their first group of lectures on Philosophical Practice. The ETOR group was part of *Asociación de Estudios Humanísticos y Filosofía Práctica X-XI* (*Humanistic Studies and Practical Philosophy Association X-XI* or *X-XI Association*). X-XI Association aimed at bringing philosophy to all people. One of their working groups had created workshops to be developed in centers that belong to Town Hall. Another group that belong

---

[1] This will be a summary of some of my activities inside the field of Philosophical Practice. In addition to the activities here summarized, I have published more than 20 books on Philosophical Practice, more than fifty articles and chapters on this topic and more that sixty speeches at universities located in New York (USA), Leusden (Holland), Sardinia (Italia), Lisbon, Port (Portugal), Morelia (México), Medellín (Colombia), etc Besides, our work has been explained in books and articles that appeared in the U.S.A., Germany, the UK, France, Italy, Portugal, Israel, Ecuador, México, Argentina and so on.

to X-XI Association was formed by members that were reflecting on a framework for promoting participatory democracy. Finally, the ETOR group wanted to create a theory within a philosophical counseling framework and put it into practice.

At that time, ETOR group hadn't read Professor Marinoff's or Gerd Achenbach's books. On the contrary, they started to work in seminars dedicated to Heidegger's *Being and Time*. Some people will think that Philosophical Practice and Heideggerian hermeneutics are very different or even opposite. In spite of that opinions, Heideggerian analysis of Dasein and its hermeneutics path is the first step to create a kind of a solid theory about understanding current human problems. With these roots, ETOR (we) built our own method of Philosophical Practice. I published this early version in my book *Introduction to Philosophical Practice* (*Introducción al asesoramiento y la orientación filosófica*) in 2003 and the last version was included in the book I edited in 2010 *Philosophical Practice and University* (*Philosophical Practice y Universidad*).

When the ETOR lectures (1999-2000) finished, I began my own first research on Philosophical Practice. I thought that Philosophical Practice existed in a lot of Spanish Universities when I started to look for similar activities to the ETOR group. I was shocked when I discovered that I was wrong. There was just one Philosophical Practice desktop (http://www.gabinetepharos.com/) in Spain and they weren't linked to any university. The called *Gabinete Pharos* had no training or official course on Philosophical Practice or anything like that. That means that ETOR was the first official research and training group on Philosophical Practice at any Spanish University. In some sense, I felt excited because I had discovered a new field to research, a new challenge for philosophy.

In 2002, my first research on the history of Philosophy Practice in foreign countries became an article. A friend asked me to include it in his journal and that was the first publication on the History of Philosophical Practice in Spanish and one of the first in the world. Today, that publication can be read on many websites on the Internet[2], because copy and paste is a normal way of living in E-life. Of course I don't mind. I always considered that diffusion is essential for our profession.

Meanwhile, I discovered that philosophy practiced and studied by ETOR was what I was looking for while I was studying nursing. So, I started to work with ETOR in 2000. I remember how excited we felt with lots of projects: a journal on Philosophical Practice, creating a

---

[2] For example, it can be read at
http://www.monografias.com/trabajos11/filap/filap.shtml.

Master's Degree, an official conference, some seminars and so on. I felt delighted to start to work on these important ideas.

We created the ETOR journal in 2003. It was the first journal on Philosophical Practice in Spanish. It released five issues that gave voice to some of the most important counsellors in the world, such as Peter Raabe, Shlomit Schuster, Trevor Curnow, Lydia Amir, etcThe ETOR journal brought together those people interested in Philosophical Practice in our country.

But we had a long road ahead of us. We needed a place where Spanish and outstanding foreign philosophical counsellors could share their (and our) visions of this new profession. The ETOR group started to talk about a university meeting, but I proposed an international conference. It was November or December 2003 and I didn't know if there were any International Conferences. I found there was an *International Conference on Philosophical Practice* that started in 1995. The Seventh International Conference would be celebrated in Denmark in 2004. Therefore, it wasn't possible at that time to celebrate the International Conference in Spain. Anyway, I put forward the *First Iberoamerican Conference on Philosophical Practice*. ETOR backed that idea and we opened the conference in April 2004.

First Iberoamerican Conference on Philosophical Practice had more than 350 participants. It was the first time that the Assembly Hall of our Faculty was full. We invited the most important Philosophical Practitioners and Counselors in the world, people such as Lou Marinoff, Peter Raabe, Shlomit Schuster, Oscar Brenifier, Trevor Curnow, Lydia Amir, etc.

As a result of that success, a couple of colleagues and I flew to Copenhagen in August of that year with an idea to propose the University of Seville as candidate for the next International Conference. Another strong candidate had been proposed by a good friend. There was a public vote and our arguments were more persuasive. Some participants of the International Conference had been at our Iberoamerican and agreed that we had done a good job. Hopefully we could have another success.

I became director of the *8 International Conference on Philosophical Practice* in 2006. Obviously, I had great help from many colleagues, mainly Professor Ordóñez, Francisco Macera, Fernando Gilabert, Gabriel Arnáiz or Francisco Barrera. People stressed a spirit of friendship at the conference. I have to confess that I enjoyed it. Again, we had many participants. We had more that 400 people; we had to close registration two months before the conference started because we were sold out.

After that, there were a couple of important projects on our minds that demanded our attention: an official research group on Philosophical Practice and a Master's degree in Philosophical Practice with a university certification. The first official research group became a reality in 2006 thanks to the efforts of Ordoñez, Macera and myself. It was the first official research group on this topic in the world (now, there is another one in South Korea). I have developed four annual seminars within this research group. Philosophical Practice is now related to specific topics, such as Spanish Philosophy, University, Methodologies and Concrete Practice. All of these topics gave birth to collective books: *Philosophical Practice for Persons and Groups* (2008), *Philosophical Practice and Spanish Modern Philosophy* (2009), *Philosophical Practice and Academy* (2010), *Methodologies in Philosophical Practice: Education, Business and Prisons* (2011). Some information about them can be found at http://filosofia-aplicada.blogspot.com

Second project was a Master's degree in Philosophical Practice. This was offered for the first time in 2007. It was the first one in Spain that took place at a university. Since then I have developed another one with online training at the University of Mexico (2009) that is still going on[3]. The ETOR has been organizing university courses since 2002. In spite of this, the Master's degree was the most relevant and complicated challenge for us.

In 2008 Professor Ordóñez assembled a collection of books on Philosophical Practice (in Comunicación Social S.L. Publishers). I shared the work with him. At this point, I thought that if we wanted to be considered a serious branch of Philosophy, we needed to create a Ph. D. in Philosophical Practice and an academic journal.

Peter Raabe developed a Ph.D. in Philosophical Counseling some years ago but nobody had attempted the experience in Europe. Professor Ramón Queraltó, a full professor (catedrático) from our university, wasn't a Philosophical Counsellor or Practitioner but he trusted me and my works from the very first day. I received one of the fourteen Ph.D. scholarships (offered by Spanish Research Council to Ph.D. candidates in my country in 2005). I developed my research on this topic with helpful assistance from Professor Queraltó and Professor Peter Raabe (directors of my Ph.D.). It received the Extraordinary Doctorate Award (Premio Extraordinario de Doctorado) in 2009. My Ph.D. dissertation analyzed a new path in Philosophical Practice. It takes its readers from a rationalistic and logical view to an existentialist and poetical perspective. Maria Zambrano's thought was the tool to develop such perspective. Today, it can be downloaded from the Internet[4].

---

[3] See http://www.uvaq.edu.mx/index.php/maestrias-distancia-edist/165-maestria-en-filosofia.html

[4] See http://fondosdigitales.us.es/tesis/tesis/1010/vectores-zambranianos-para-una-

2. José Barrientos-Rastrojo 19

During the years I was working on my Ph.D., I continued giving lectures and writing books and articles. Some of those works tried to offer tools to new philosophical counsellors. They were the tools I would like to have had before I started to work as a Philosophical Counsellor. My latest book could be very useful because of these tools. It is called *Conflict Resolution from Philosophical Practice and Mediation* (part of it can be downloaded at Google books[5]). It was born when I was finishing a Master's degree on Mediation between 2008 and 2010 at the University of País Vasco. It links Philosophical Practice and Mediation. Those two subjects have some points in common.

The ETOR journal published its last issue in 2005. Since then, I thought of publishing an academic journal peer-reviewed and to be included in the most significant index (see below). I started to work on it when I finished my Ph.D. in 2009. We called *HASER. Revista Internacional de Filosofía Aplicada* (*HASER. International Journal on Philosophical Practice*). First issue came out in 2010. Today, it has been included in *The Philosopher's Index*, *Proquest*, *Ebsco*, DIALNET and some other important places as an official journal[6]. It is a place where academics and specialists can publish their research. In addition, it includes interviews with important philosophical counsellors, reviews of national and international conferences, book reviews and the like. It can be downloaded freely by issue or a hard copy can be asked for at haser@us.es. One of its aims is to have a place where people with academic ambitions can research these issues and where they can see published their researches in an official academic journal. Professors and researchers find difficult to publish on Philosophical Practice and Counseling because it isn't a classical topic of Philosophy. Thus, this is one good journal on Philosophical Practice indexed in established indexes.[7]

Anyway, ETOR wasn't just a group for research but also for action. Concerning areas where my group is working, I would like to mention my experiences with four prisons in Spain, with hospitals, with libraries, consultations, businesses, primary and secondary schools and, of course, with the university. In that sense, I proposed a spin-off business in 2010 that won an award at the *5th University Awards for Business*

---

    teoria-de-la-filosofia-aplicada-la-persona/

[5] See http://books.google.es/books/about/ResoluciondeConflictosdesdelaFiloso. html?id=DovhHEPpF-sC&rediresc=y

[6] See number 1 at http://issuu.com/jbbr/docs/haser12010oct. See number 2 at http://issuu.com/jbbr/docs/haser22011020915x21c

[7] In 2011, *Philosophical Practice. Journal of the American Philosophical Practitioners Association* was indexed in EBSCO. Today, I am Editor-in-Chief of its Spanish version..

Ideas[8]. Specifically, I have worked professionally as a philosophical counsellor since 2004 (actually, I started to work, without charging, in 2002) and Francisco Barrera and I started a Philosophical Wine in 2005[9]. However, Philosophical Wine was mainly a Barrera achievement.

Last year, I got a tenured position at my University as Professor, so I am able to follow all these projects on Philosophical Practice. Joan Méndez and I have published the proceedings of the *1 Spanish Conference on Philosophical Practic*e with Joan Méndez (President of the Catalonian Philosophical Practice Association) this year. This event takes place in Catalonia and gathers between one and and two hundred participants.

Last summer (2011), I received a research fellowship at Princeton University with Professor Peter Singer. My work looked for links between Ethics and Philosophical Practice and, now, I am proofreading a book on his ideas and life. In addition, I am starting to work with *Academics Stands Against Poverty*, whose leaders are Prof. Thomas Pogge (Yale University) and Prof. Luis Cabrera (University of Birmingham). Finally, I have a couple of projects to fly to Harvard University (to work on Prof. Amartya Sen's ideas) or to the Massachusetts Institute of Technology (to work on Prof. Nicholas Negroponte's project One Laptop per child) this summer and I have been invited as Visiting Fellowship at the University of Cambridge to research on the relationships between Philosophical Practice and wisdom (that is my present field).

Returning to Philosophical Practice, I have to say that nowadays, I have the opportunity to give more academic time to this topic. I am directing six Ph.D. candidates on Philosophical Practice in Spain and Portugal and students want me to explain how I work as a Philosophical Counsellor. Besides, I have been required to give training in different countries in Europe and America but that is another history.

To sum up, I got interested in Philosophical Practice for several reasons. First, it gave me the opportunity to work in a non-explored field in Philosophy. I wasn't interested in creating a new interpretation on Plato, Aristotle, Descartes, Kant or Heidegger. Rather than that, I wanted to research a new field. Clearly, Philosophical practice is a new version of an old tradition as said by Professor Lahav; however, it was a field that needed approaches, methods and a profound reflection on its issues. That was the aim of my Ph.D. dissertation. I offered an analysis

---

[8] See http://filosofia-aplicada.blogspot.com/2010/06/entrega-de-premio-la-empresa-de.html

[9] For further information see our website: http://vinofilosofico.blogspot.com/2007/09/qu-es-vino-filosfico.html

of basic concepts for consultation such as time, space, word, silence, and the anthropology of the counsellor and counselee.

Second, I thought that Philosophy would help people when they have problems. It had been very useful in my own life; so why not repeat it with counselees? It was a quest: could we get our proposal?

Third, when I started to my research, Philosophical Practice was being developed outside the University. However, Philosophy was its topic as it was the topic of Philosophy degrees. Therefore, I wanted to reconcile both universes.

Forth, I discovered that Psychology (in my country) had forgotten existential, logic or ethic problems. So, when a counselee had a problem regarding this topic, psychologists couldn't manage it rightly. These people needed a philosopher. Unfortunately, our profession wasn't developed in Spain and in most Spanish-speakers countries.

Therefore, we had some quest and I decided to face it. I hope I have resolved at least part of it.

PHILOSOPHICAL PRACTICE AND PHILOSOPHY.

2. What does your work reveal about Philosophical Practice that other related academic fields typically fail to appreciate?

In 2007[10], I compared *the activity* carried out by a philosophical counsellor to the one accomplished by a philosopher who writes a paper. There are some similarities. Both have a philosophical topic that could come from the counselee (counsellor) or from a philosophical mind (philosopher). Both have similar or identical tools: logic, dialectics, conceptual analysis or ideas from the history of philosophy. Both of them want to understand and/or resolve (or dissolve) a problem or question.

Needless to say that there are differences, too. The most important is the relationship concerning the topic. A, so to say, philosopher puts forward problems and solutions by himself; a philosophical counsellor helps a person understand his/her own problems. The latter pursues a maieutic method. Philosophical practitioners help people to discover their own truth. He just prevents logical fallacies, he encourages thought (and he takes a counselee to the Heideggerian and Zambranian, clearing when they can't go on by themselves).

Furthermore, Philosophical Practice guides people from a superficial and unthinking and careless speech to a profound and critical one. A

---

[10] That comparison was part of a lecture given at University of Oporto. Then, it was included it in my tesina and in the book *Idea y proyecto. La arquitectura de la vida* (see Barrientos, J—Dias, J.H.: *Idea y Proyecto. La arquitectura de la vida*, Visión, Madrid, 2010).

philosophical counsellor assists his counselee to analyze ideas and concepts that are at the basis of their behaviour, their feelings, worldviews and, finally, their whole lives. Our activities let them know how most of these ideas don't belong to them but to tradition and/or, society. So they are part of an ideology or, in a Gadamerian sense, they are prejudices. I don't mean that they are bad or good. Of course, some of them depend on economic authority interest in Foucaultian sense. The problem is that many citizens are unaware of how these ideas shape their lives. Philosophy and Philosophical Practice will try to uncover this hidden veil. We won't tell people what to do. We just help them to open minds and philosophical eyes.

3. What does your work reveal about Philosophical Practice that other philosophical practitioners fail to appreciate?

When I started my Ph.D., I discovered Philosophical Practice as Critical Thinking. Authors such as Peter Raabe or Tim Lebon were working on that approach. That was also the approach of some national Philosophical Practice associations. This way of doing Philosophical Practice was useful for most of my counselees.

However, I have had problems with some counselees using this method. They show an abyss between what to think and what to do, what to feel, or most importantly, between what to think and its real being. They say: I know what the right answer is but I can't involve myself in it, I can't carry out that rational and ideal solution. Obviously, as soon as I was working just with logical arguments, I could transform in any occasions their whole existence because human existence is wider than logical reason.

I needed another kind of reason, more wide, if I wanted to achieve more effective outcomes. Therefore, I started to research Blaise Pascal's heart reason, María Zambrano's experiencial reason (razón o saber de la experiencia), Miguel de Unamuno's cardiac/heart/paralogic reason (razones cardíacas/paralógicas) and so on. My research on María Zambrano's (1904-1991) thought and its relationship with Philosophical counseling was very exciting. She had worked with a teenager who tried to commit suicide and helped him recover his zest for life. Zambrano's writings gave me more useful insights: I discovered that the environment of consultation is not just a place for critical thinking tools but one that can transform counselees; I discovered how peculiar consultation time was (different from daily time), how powerful words could be (if we differentiate them from everyday words), I discovered silent meanings or a specific way of seeing. Finally, I worked on a method based on Zambrano's concept abismamiento. It would be very long to explain it but it can be read at my Ph.D.

Today, I am still working on it. However, I am working on understanding (Gadamer's verstehen). I want to use my research and would like to serve as a philosophical counsellor for faculty members. I would like to link these research ideas with an alleviation of poverty and with how academics can answer this urgent situation.

Last, I am relating Philosophical Counseling to wisdom. I think that Philosophical Counseling is not just a way to solve problems by means of logic or dialectics but a road that takes a person from a problematic worldview to wiser one. This means that Philosophical Practice is not an activity related just to cognitive or logical areas but to ontological ones. That journey, carried out by Philosophical Practice, is analogous to the one that takes us from childhood to maturity: problems for a child and a man can be similar, but how they face them is different. What was a problem for a child might not be for a man because their ontological positions are different. According to my research, Philosophical Counseling should aim to provide this development. Thereby, it doesn't *solve* problems but *dissolves* them.

Philosophical Practice as Critical Thinking is based on what Heidegger has termed the Age of Image, or the Age of rationality. By going on our approach, we regain an ontological way of Philosophy. That situation is wider and it is related not to a rational part of human being but to whole human beings. Therefore, I believe, this is a more philosophical way to develop Philosophical Counseling and we touch our counselees' thoughts, feelings, doings and inner being in a holistic way.

4. What do you see as the most interesting criticism against your own position in Philosophical Practice?

I don't know of any formal criticism against my position. However, a couple of colleagues have warned me about the possibility that Philosophical Counseling beyond Critical Thinking could not be considered *Philosophical* Counseling but as Psychoanalysis or as some kind of Psychology.

As I have explained above, Philosophy is more than a field devoted to Critical Thinking. It is true that this is its mainstream since Descartes. However, the last century has discovered that Philosophy is a way to research (inside and) beyond Logic. For example, María Zambrano said that Philosophy is to decipher (or figure out) inner feeling (Filosofar es decifrar el sentir originario). Gadamer and Heidegger argued that there is a sort of thought (denken) (and word) that precedes rational thinking (or ordinary speech). To work on this point is a task for Philosophy. Besides, to work on this in a consultation means to work from the ontological part of human beings, because we go beyond rationality. Furthermore, a mere rational philosophy is part of the age of the image of Philosophy (Heidegger). Tradition of human science (Geistewissenschaft) and debate between them and natural science (Naturwissenschaft) started this discussion. The XX century discovered how naïve it is to work from a simple objective and logical approach without any consideration of who, where and when a theory was built. If we want to understand (verstehen) a person, we need to go beyond a logical game of questions and answers. We should open a dialogue where that game is complemented with living strategies (some of them can be consulted in my Ph.D. dissertation) in order to discover (1) what counselee is living through (his very real experience) and (2) what the spirit (das Geist)[11] that created his thoughts and wor(l)ds.

A beyond-logic view doesn't criticize a rational consideration of Philosophy and Philosophical Practice as being useless just as being incomplete. I work in my consultations with rational insights but they are not enough for some occasions because persons are more than sheer logical reason.

Secondly, when I started to work on Philosophical Practice, some friends said that Philosophical Counseling wasn't Philosophy. Today, I can say that I don't understand their position. We (philosophical counselors) work with philosophical tools, with philosophical texts, from philosophical questions and towards philosophical answers. We have books that help people to reflect on their everyday life and conferences where we try to understand the philosophical grounds of our discipline. Some of my Ph.D. candidates work on how to link Philosophical Practice to the thought created by Gabriel Marcel, Julián Marías, Hannah Arendt and Schopenhauer.

To be sure, we develop a specific field in Philosophy, but it is a Philosophical branch as is Aesthetic, Ethics, Logic, Political Philosophy, Philosophy of Science and the like. Some colleagues have said to me that Philosophy of Science wasn't considered Philosophy some decades ago. Nowadays, it is different. Maybe we need time, hard work, and understanding as it was the case for the Philosophy of Science. Maybe.

Some academics have tried to compare Philosophy to consolidated philosophical subfields such as Hermeneutics or Phenomenology. By means of that comparison, they conclude that Philosophical Practice is not Philosophy because it hasn't got a strong body of knowledge. Nevertheless, Philosophical Practice is a young field compared to other

---

[11] Spirit is more that psyche as we can see with Dilthey, Gadamer or María Zambrano. It involves the whole tradition that give birth (among other things) to counselee mind and ideas.

fields. So we can't ask for a big and whole body *yet*. The Philosophy of Science didn't have this body of knowledge a couple of decades ago but today only a few people would say that it isn't a distinct branch of Philosophy.

We have to confess that Philosophical Practice underlines a different way of philosophy from most traditional philosophies. To *do* Philosophical Practice needs a specific relationship between a philosopher and his counselees or groups. Therefore, a counselor usually doesn't capture his work in a book but through life itself, I mean, his writings are within the consultation process and the interaction created in a philosophical group. In conclusion, it could be a more *lively* activity than ordinary Philosophy, but, as I have explained above, this doesn't mean that it is less philosophical.

There is another criticism: some Philosophical Practitioners try to distinguish their practices from the one carried out in Academia or at the University. I described two ways of lecturing at the University in the introduction to *Filosofía Aplicada y Universidad*[12]. The Classic one can be different from Philosophical Practice because the professor creates a unidirectional speech, so there are few contacts with his students or their life concerns. However, new lecturing approaches understand that the professor is not just someone that provides information to students but somebody that facilitates their students' paths to find subjects and themes by themselves. Even facilitator, a word that comes from Philosophical Practice, is part of new pedagogical jargon. Information is available on the Internet, books, encyclopedias and the like; therefore, students are trained to look for that. They have to pose their interests and questions and professors help them to search information that will resolve them. It could be stated that this is very similar to Philosophical Practitioners and Counselors work. Furthermore, the University is opening its doors to Philosophical Practice as I explain above.

---

[12] Cfr. Barrientos Rastrojo, José: *Filosofía Aplicada y Universidad*, Visión, Madrid. 2010. It is possible to download part of it at http://books.google.es/books/about/Filosof%C3%8DaAplicadaYUniversidad.html?id=PBFSbfW24EC, last viewed December 25 , 2011.

Past, Present and Future of my Research on Philosophical Practice.

5. With respect to present and future inquiry, how can the most important problems concerning Philosophical Practice be identified and explored?

The answer is clear: by practicing. Practice will identify new fields to be researched in Philosophical Practice. A practical field like Philosophical Counseling needs insights coming from outside of divagations far away from real concerns.

After finding new problems, it is essential to explore them in a rigorous way. In that sense, I have to stress one of the biggest tasks for Philosophical Practice: assist its practitioners and counsellors to develop abilities to do research. During the last four years, I have been running HASER (International Journal on Philosophical Practice). HASER needs good articles in order to create a journal that is well considered as a solid academic journal. At the moment, we are in some of the most important academic indexes like The Philosopher's Index. To accomplish that task wasn't an easy road. The most difficult thing on this road was to get good articles (in an academic sense). Authors of most of them don't have the basic skills that enable them to create footnotes, an admissible abstract, to know how and when an affirmation needs to be grounded on a quotation or they haven't got a deep philosophical knowledge to reflect on specific issues and, so, they made important mistakes concerning the history of philosophy.

I understand that at present there aren't a lot of people that develop academic *and* practical profiles inside our field. But this is changing, at least at the University of Seville, because Philosophical Practice is becoming an academic branch. In addition to our Ph.D. candidates on Philosophical Practice, some undergraduate students want to devote their undergraduate thesis to our discipline. I am sure that this dynamic will change the picture soon.

What are main challenges for Philosophical practice in the future?

I think that we have to consolidate our position as a distinct field in Philosophy, inside and outside academia.

Based on my experience in Spain, University is a highly considered institution by society. University is thought as the highest educational and research institution by citizens. Obviously, there are good knowledge and trainings outside University. However, University is said to be a social guarantee for quality knowledge. Most present philosophers have studied at a Department of Philosophy. Almost all present Philosophical Practitioners or Counsellors have spent their first philosophical years in those institutions. A lot of them have hung their official university degrees on the walls of their office and they include that information in their CV. They have said that they are philosophers because they have a degree in Philosophy from a specific university. Who would hide that he/she has a Ph.D. after years of hard work? This means that University is important to Philosophical Counsellors.

In spite of these studies, if we want to see Philosophical Practice as a distinct field in University, we need our Philosophical Practitioners improve some of their academic abilities. A distinct field needs Philosophical Counsellor who can develop academic articles or books where they expound with rigour their discoveries. Today, we have good philosophical practitioners, but we haven't got a lot of Practitioners and/or Counsellors who can explain their outcomes in a academic article. This is crucial for developing a profession.

To sum up, we need to involve our research inside this university framework. By doing this, we could answer the repeated question: Where is scientific evidence that Philosophical Practice works? At the University of Seville, we have completed three studies on that issue. I finished one in 2006 and another in 2009 based on more than three thousand sessions of Philosophical Practice. One of my Ph.D. candidates, Francisco Barrera, developed another one in 2007 on his work with the Fibromialgia Association, where he has been working for five years. Outcomes are being published in issues 2, 3 and 4 of our Journal HASER. Finally, some students are preparing more studies in our research group.

Concerning theory of Philosophical Practice, I think that Philosophical Practice needs to show more faith at its core: life. As I explain above, Philosophical Practice is a profession related closely to lively issues, the ones that concern our counselees or groups. Therefore, we have to look for life. This is the reason why I went from a Logic Philosophical Practice to an Ontological one without negating the first one.

PHILOSOPHICAL PRACTICE AND SOCIO-POLITICAL COMMITMENTS.

What, if any, practical and/or social-political obligations follow from understanding philosophy from the point of view of Philosophical Practice?

Some philosophical practitioners understand their work as a socio-political commitment. That is the case of Christopher Phillips, author of *Socrates Café*, for example. According to his pragmatic point of view, a philo-café is a space to create democracy, as pointed out by John Dewey some decades ago. That was one of the aims of Matthew Lippman too when he started to work on Philosophy for Children. Maybe we could say the same of Paul Richard who is working on how to introduce Critical Thinking inside Universities and secondary schools.

My latest research has a socio-political commitment. It links Philosophical Practice, the university and poverty. I try to show how Philosophy can be useful to alleviate extreme world poverty. In that sense, Professor Thomas Pogge (Yale University) and Professor Luis Cabrera (University of Birmigham) have created, among others, an interesting proposal through *Academics Stand Against Poverty*. They claim that academics have achieved special abilities and skills to advise institutions, legislators, and the general public because of their long training in the academic world.

I think that professors have a more important challenge: they will be the last step in studies made by our futures prime ministers, leaders of companies, judges and a lot of people that tomorrow will lead society. Therefore, the future is in the hands of professors in some sense. If those future prime ministers, leaders, and judges aren't compelled by big problems in our society (one is extreme global poverty) they won't do anything tomorrow. One of the most important causes of extreme poverty is provoked by institutions. Most of them are directed by people who yesterday were students at the university.

How am I linking this issue to Philosophical Practice? Some professors have problems introducing the topic of poverty in their lectures and courses Poverty should be a continuing thread not a specific subject in all careers. My project is to help them on that issue. Before giving them ways to include this issue (poverty) in their courses, we have to research the concept understanding. I am working on understanding (in German verstehen; in Spanish comprensión) because I would like to know how academics understand and create their mental and cultural images. By means of this research I could help them extend their ideas on poverty. Then, they could use their knowledge to open their students' mind to severe poverty concerns. Then, they could use that theory to help them understand this problem or another. I think that Hermeneutics is a great field to start this research.

In addition, why not develop Philosophical Practice for prime ministers or leaders? It is a way to change what we think is not good. Furthermore, is it not true that Aristotle was the teacher of Alenxander the Great?

Ortega y Gasset said that one of the goals of philosophy is to learn to live. I hope that Philosophical Practice can help people to live a good life in wealthy nations but that means that they shouldn't close their eyes to people who are suffering right now. To close one's eyes to this situation is not just an attack against Ethics but against Truth.

Bibliography

Barrientos Rastrojo, J.: *El quehacer de la filosofía aplicada en la contemporaneidad* (The task of Philosophical Practice in contemporaneity), Universidad de Sevilla, Sevilla, 2012. En prensa. Video on Philosophical Practice.

Barrientos Rastrojo, J.: *Resolución de conflictos desde la Filosofía Aplicada y desde la Mediación* (*Conflict resolution from Philosophical Practice and Mediation*), Universidad Católica Portuguesa—Visión Libros, Lisboa, 2010.

Barrientos Rastrojo, J.: *Vectores zambranianos para una teoría de la Filosofía Aplicada a la Persona* (*Zambranian vectors for a theory on Philosophical Practice applied to the person*), Volúmenes 1 y 2, Vicerrectorado de investigación, Universidad de Sevilla, 2009.

Barrientos Rastrojo, J. (ed.): *Metodologias aplicadas desde a desde a filosofia: Estabelecimentos prisionais, Empresa, Ética, Consultoria e educação* (*Metodologies applied from Philosophy: prisons, bussinessm ethics, Consultations and education*), Universidade Católica Portuguesa—VL, Lisboa-Madrid, 2011.

Barrientos Rastrojo, J. (ed.): *Filosofía aplicada y universidad* (*Philosophical Practice and University*) Visión libros-FILOSOFARTE, Madrid (España) -Medellín (Colombia), 2010.

Barrientos Rastrojo, J.—Dias, J.H.: *¿Felicidad o conocimiento? La filosofía aplicada como búsqueda de la felicidad y el conocimiento* (*Happiness or knowledge? Philosophical Practice as a quest of happiness and knowledge*) Gabinete Project, Quarteira (Portugal), 2009.

Barrientos Rastrojo, J. y otros: *Filosofía aplicada y circunstancia española* (*Philosophical practice and spanish circumstance*), Universidad Vasco de Quiroga (Centro de Estudios Sociales y Humanos Vasco de Quiroga)—DOSS ediciones, México—Sevilla, 2009.

Barrientos Rastrojo, J. y otros: *Filosofía aplicada a la persona y a grupos* (*Philosophical Practice to Persons and Groups*) DOSS Ediciones, Sevilla, 2009.

Barrientos Rastrojo, J. (Ed.): *Dominios de Aplicación Práctica de la Filosofía* (*Practice Domains of Philosophy*) Ediciones X-XI, Sevilla, 2006

Barrientos Rastrojo, J. (Ed.): *Philosophical Practice*, Ediciones X-XI, Sevilla, 2006

Barrientos Rastrojo, J. (Coord.): *Philosophers as Philosophical Practitioners*. Volume 1 & 2 Ediciones X-XI, Sevilla, 2006

Barrientos Rastrojo, J.—Ordóñez García, J. (Eds.): *From Theory to Practice*. Papers. Vol 1st & 2nd, Asociación de Estudios Humanísticos y Filosofía Práctica X-XI, Sevilla, 2006

Barrientos Rastrojo, J.: *Introducción al asesoramiento y la orientación filosófica. De la discusión a la comprensión* (*Introduction to Philosophical Practice. From dispute to understanding*) Editorial Idea, Santa Cruz de Tenerife, 2005. Segunda edición aumentada y corregida.

La paradoja de la moderación ideológica en la ética singeriana, *Themata*, número 45, 2012.

La fisiología del saber de la experiencia y los frutos de su posesión, *Themata*, número 44, 2011. Págs. 79-96.

Análisis de la eficacia de los intercambios de la Filosofía Aplicada a la Persona en Internet: Raabe, Schuster y Sherry Turkle, *Apuntes Filosóficos*, número 20, Universidad Central de Venezuela, 2011.

Resolución de conflictos, mediación y filosofía aplicada en Cabrera Izquierdo, L.E.—Díez Jiménez, A.F. (dirs.): *Mediación intercultural, convivencia y diversidad*, Instituto de Estudios Sociales del Mediterráneo, África y Latinoamérica-Junta de Andalucía-Háblame, Almería, 2010. Págs. 45-61.

Projecto, felicidade, escola e filosofia aplicada, en AA.VV.: *Projectar a felicidade na escola. O novo paradigma da Filosofia Aplicada*, CFAEBN, Bragança, Portugal, 2010.

2. José Barrientos-Rastrojo 31

Investigación sobre las concomitancias entre el zambraniano filosófico y la Terapia de Aceptación y Compromiso, *Revista límites*, Revista de la Universidad de Tarapacá (Chile), 2010.

Crítica de la justicia social singeriana en el orbe de una propuesta liberal moderada (Critique of sigerian social justice inside of a moderate liberal proposal), *Dikaiosyne*, número 24, 2010.

Horizontes españolistas para una filosofía aplicada europeísta: consultante, filósofo aplicado y consulta, *Antígona*. *Revista oficial de la Fundación María Zambrano*, número 3, Málaga, 2009. Págs. 17-34.

Itinerarios de la filosofía española moderna y contemporánea en relación a la filosofía aplicada, *Bajo Palabra*. *Revista de Filosofía*, número 3, 2008. Págs. 185-188.

Filosofía Poiética Aplicada a la Persona. El espíritu zambranista en la FAP en DIAS, F. (ed): *Encontros Portugueses de Filosofia Aplicada*, Apaef, Albufeira (Portugal), 2008. Págs. 47-63.

Corrientes actuales europeas del pensamiento y filosofía aplicada, *Revista Tales*, número 1/2008, Universidad Complutense de Madrid. ISSN: 2172-2587. Págs. 135-150.

Philosophy applied in-deph en *Revista de la Facultad de Filosofía y Teología, volumen 3, número 4*, Colombia, Abril 2008.Págs. 79-106.

El atardecer del Pensamiento Crítico. Disquisiciones poético-zambranistas sobre el *Critical Thinking* en *Proyectos de Vida*, N3/2007, SOFIAM, México. Págs. 22-27.

Orientación Filosófica, Democracia y Sociedad Tecnológica, *Revista Alfa*, N19-20/2007. Págs. 223-241.

Husserl y la orientación filosófica en *Philosophers as Philosophical Counselors*, X-XI, Sevilla, 2006. Págs. 75-90.

Philosophical Counselling as Poietic Philosophy en *Philosophical Practice* N3/2006, New York (USA). Págs. 17-27.

Philosophy, Reason and Poietics (ed. Ran Lahav), Vermont (USA), 2006.

Orientación Racional: Una aplicación real del *Critical Thinking* a la Orientación Filosófica en DÍAS, J. H.(ed): *I Encontro Português de Filosofía Prática*. Lisboa, Portugal, 2005. Págs. 91-118.

Definiciones terminológicas y conceptuales del *Critical Thinking*. *Critical Thinking* (1) en *Revista ETOR* N4/2005. Págs. 35-43.

Hacia el Agujero negro invertido ¿Orientación filosófica vs. Psicología? en Ordóñez García, J—Barrientos Rastrojo, J.—Macera

Garfia, F. (eds.) *La filosofía a las puertas del tercer milenio*, Fénix, Sevilla, 2005. Págs. 239-256.

L'insurrezione del poietico nella consulenza filosófica en Pollastri, N. (ed) *Phronesis* N3/ Junio 2004. ISSN: 2038-1263. Registro Tribunale di Firenze n. 5282 del 3 de Julio de 2003. Págs. 11-29.

Filosofía práctica (o aplicada) en la revista de filosofía *El Foro nuevo* (ISSN 1697-0225) en www.geocities.com/elforonuevo Septiembre de 2002 (también publicado en www.monografias.com Septiembre de 2002)

3

Dries Boele

Practical philosopher
Amsterdam

Practical philosophy has been my field of interest for almost three decades now. I started as an art student and continued to study philosophy, in Amsterdam and Paris. I have been involved in the Dutch movement of practical philosophy since 1983. As a self-employed person I work with several forms of Philosophical Practice, such as Philosophical counseling, Socratic dialogue and dilemma training, and give workshops on the philosophy of the art of living.

In the field of practical philosophy, different goals and frameworks are possible. Some colleagues put forward practical philosophy as an extra tool in training for companies, or as an alternative for psychotherapy. I also work with philosophy in different professional settings. However, I prefer to put practical philosophy in the context of the art of living.

From the beginning of the 1980's, my interest in practical philosophy has been in the first place existential: how to live in this confusing world? How can philosophy be helpful in conducting my life? How can questions of choice and meaning be clarified? How can philosophy contribute to a flourishing life? These questions didn't come from an academic interest; they were first of all urgent issues for myself. I learned to be helpful to others by taking my own questions seriously and to translate them into activities that could be worthwhile for others.

By studying Foucault in the mid 1980's, I came across the art of living as one of the major topics in classical philosophy. I welcomed it as a necessary complement, to put practical philosophy in perspective,—although I didn't know yet exactly how to connect both. It was a nice surprise to me to discover how philosophy was basically practical, at least in Antiquity.

Working with philosophy

After several years of training with colleagues, I opened my practice as a philosopher in 1990. I worked as a philosophical counselor, as a facilitator of Socratic dialogues and as a dilemma trainer. With private people and in companies, with management teams, civil servants, police officers, doctors, nurses and prisoners. In addition, from 1994 on, I was and still am the moderator of a philosophical café once or twice a month on a Sunday afternoon, in Hotel de Filosoof in Amsterdam.

At the end of the 1990's, I intensified my studies of the philosophy of the art of living. It's a rich field with a lot to discover: from the old Greeks to Spinoza and Nietzsche, from Zen and Taoism to Foucault and Sloterdijk, and a lot more. I started to give courses on this subject in education centers and as philosophical summer weeks (in Holland, France and Egypt).

I still work in both fields and I am happy to be able to combine them. I am more and more convinced of the intimate connection of practical philosophy and the art of living. Their relationship can be mutually very fertile. Without practices the philosophy of the art of living will remain very theoretical. Without a broader, philosophical context practical philosophy will easily be reduced to some techniques. So they need each other. And the connection is not new. The history of philosophy offers good examples of such a relationship, especially in Antiquity. I plead for a renaissance of it.

The art of living and a new concept of philosophy

For me the art of living is a form of secular spirituality. It has a long history. The art of living is not a modern invention. For Greek and Roman philosophers it was already a theme. As Pierre Hadot shows, in Antiquity philosophy was a way of life[1]. The art of living covered the answers to the question 'how to live'. This question was intimately related to that other question: how to live together? These two questions dominated the activities of philosophers.

However, philosophy did change a lot since then. As it was a total package in Antiquity, in the Middle Ages philosophy became something completely different: it served as 'maid' of theology. It offered auxiliary service to the evangelical truth, in order to clarify difficulties in interpretation and to develop arguments that might convince infidels. And in modern times philosophy again got a totally different role. It became the mother of modern sciences and the guardian of certain knowledge. Also in that period the question 'how to live' was not a philosophical one, but stayed mainly a religious affair. With existentialism in the second half of the 20 Century, philosophy regained little by little its role as an inspiration for everyday life. As a last chapter in the Renaissance,

---

[1] Pierre Hadot, *Philosophy as a Way of Life. Spiritual Exercises from Socrates to Foucault*. 1995. Blackwell Publishers, Oxford.

philosophy has seen the rebirth of an ancient task: its redefinition as a way of life, with the art of living as its ethics.

That's how I would like to situate my work as a practical philosopher: in the context of the art of living as renewing subject of philosophy. Of course, we can't just copy the way philosophy was practiced in Antiquity. We have to find a contemporary way. The human condition has changed. The cultural circumstances are different. Our way of life is strongly individualized, compared to life in a Greek polis or in the Roman Empire. In a long historical process the individual has become the last resort in matters of morality and worldview, as Charles Taylor has shown[2].

We live in a spiritual supermarket with an abundance of choices and tastes. All kind of courses and workshops, books on every subject, multiplied by what is available on the Internet: there is so much and everything is presented as something you should not miss.

On the one hand this is an attractive situation. But there is a downside to it: how to know what is appropriate or good for me? It is not always easy to find out. When I studied philosophy, I was myself overwhelmed by the wealth of different visions. Can they all be true? Also in workshops I meet people who get confused by the sheer number of the spiritual options that are around at the moment. What to do with it? When you are on a search for something meaningful and you don't know exactly what you're looking for, it is not easy to find your way.

This is why the contemporary art of living cannot do without an art of choosing. Practical philosophy may play its role in this process, helping people to clarify their questions, needs and desires.

In order to know what I want, it is important to express myself. By doing so, I invite response from others, including criticism and recognition. Taylor calls this process 'expressivism'. This is probably one of the reasons for the growing interest in forms of dialogue. One of the providers of such a dialogue is practical philosophy. It is particularly suited to do so, because it combines self-expression with critical thinking.

Practical forms of philosophy, such as Philosophical counseling and Socratic dialogue, I consider to be 'spiritual exercises'. Or in terms of Foucault: 'practices of the self'. The Socratic dialogue, for example, shows to be an effective tool of empowerment: participants learn to trust their own capacity to reason, to investigate their experiences as a source of wisdom and to develop their power of discernment.

To see practical philosophy *for myself* in the context of the art of living

---

[2] Charles Taylor, *Sources of the Self. The Making of the Modern Identity*. 1989. Harvard University Press, Cambridge, Massachusetts.

is one thing. How practical philosophy is seen *by others*, and especially by clients, is another thing. One of the reasons is that philosophy is still seen by many in a 'modern' way, namely as a discipline that is primarily concerned with knowledge. Certain and scientific knowledge. Or for those who do not like the subtleties of this research: to make easy things difficult and incomprehensible. So I learned, it's better not to start with an exposé on the changing self-definition of philosophy. Fortunately, times are changing. Thirty years ago, when I started my studies, philosophy was seen as an obscure discipline. Nowadays philosophy enjoys growing popularity, especially because it has shown itself to be a source of inspiration for daily life.

However, it is clear to me that there is still work to do with respect to the self-definition of philosophy. With the renewed interest in the art of living, together with the development of practical forms of philosophy, a new paradigm in philosophy is breaking ground. At the university the old paradigm is still predominant. The practical interest in philosophy is mostly seen as a pale shadow of the original, as it is cultivated in study rooms. It will take some time, and probably a generation shift, to see the renewal of philosophy expanded on university grounds.

What will be the new task of philosophy? To say it is a way of life is too meager. Philosophy is also an atelier for thinking, evaluating and analyzing current thought patterns and creating concepts that make something new thinkable. How to combine both: this is the challenge that will open new horizons. Important is the grounding in everyday life, with a revaluation of experience. Philosophy is not a world apart, but has always to do with humanity, with our adventure called 'life'. Somehow there must be a connection, even if a philosophical text is very abstract at first sight. It is self-defining for philosophy that it has something to offer for our understanding of human questions, needs and desires.

In workshops I try to put into practice this principle, by experimenting with a mixture of dialogue and the input from philosophers. Starting point is a philosophical question that concerns us all. For example: How free am I to change my life? Or: Does life have a purpose? And: How far reaches my responsibility? Participants investigate the topic first. What is their initial answer to this question? They can bring in their experiences, exchange and debate views, formulate their own points of view. From there I introduce the thoughts of philosophers on the subject, in order to challenge the opinions of the participants and to feed them with other points of view.

Although I don't believe in the occurrence of an 'ideal world' or a 'perfect life', it is worthwhile and even necessary to have ideals: striving for better is pushing me as a human being into a flourishing life.

In other words: the enhancement of the quality of life is possible, both individually and collectively. And as a practical philosopher I can contribute to it. The way we think is important for personal wellbeing and for cultural life: ideas, concepts, frames of reference,—it's material for a philosopher; working on it can make a difference. Personally I would like to translate this commitment into the formula: working on a world that I wish for my son to live in. Is it too ambitious? Maybe, but at least it is worth trying.

A few implications

What does it imply to put practical philosophy in the context of the art of living? I want to consider two implications: the role of exercises and the role of the philosopher.

PHILOSOPHICAL EXERCISES

Experience shows that insight is not enough. I may have understood something, but that doesn't mean that my life has changed accordingly. Philosophers of the art of living have been aware of this difficulty. Most of the philosophical schools in Antiquity developed a range of exercises. Such as forms of meditation and contemplation, for example, in order to remind oneself of important insights and rules of life. Reading, writing and holding conversations were also considered as an exercise, just as friendship. And all the schools, like the Epicureans and the Stoics, had their particular exercises, geared to the goals and ideals of that school.

So, we cannot abstain from exercises, also in philosophy. A recent book of Peter Sloterdijk shows brilliantly how human life is basically a practicing life[3]. Work, religion, sport and also philosophy have more in common than might seem on first sight: they all are set in the modus of exercises. I think, it is worthwhile to consider practical philosophy in this light. What kind of exercises is necessary for a flourishing life? What kind of exercises can we develop in order to make insights fruitful?

What are philosophical exercises? I will give a few examples. The Socratic dialogue I consider an exercise, in which participants learn from their own experiences in a systematic way, and by doing so they sharpen their sense of discrimination,—which is key to practical wisdom (in Greek terms 'phronesis'). Also reading, writing and discussing can be turned into an exercise. These daily activities can be done in

---

[3] Peter Sloterdijk, *You Must Change Your Life. On Human Engineering*. (In German: Du musst dein Leben ändern, 2009. Suhrkamp, Frankfurt am Main.)

various ways. Result-oriented, for example, or just for distraction. They become a philosophical activity, if we do it in a reflective and critical way, in dialogue with ourselves, with a text or with others, questioning the relevance of a thought or theory for our understanding. I experience teaching as an exercise: by presenting a philosopher I actualize his or her relevance for my own art of living. By doing so I hope something similar will happen to participants of the workshop or course. For me personally, meditation is an important exercise as well, to interrupt being absorbed in trains of thought and mind bubbles, to become aware of patterns in thought and behavior, and to look afresh at a situation.

THE ROLE OF THE PHILOSOPHER

Another implication concerns the role of the philosopher. Who am I when I work as a practical philosopher? Am I a *counselor?* A *teacher?* Am I an *expert* in the meaning of life or in decision making? How am I involved in the process that is taking place? As a practical philosopher I prefer the model of *friendship*. Sure, a workshop is not a network of friends, but I would like to see it as a temporary community of like-minded people, who are doing research together. And sure, in a counseling session friendship is not really the case; the client and I are not friends. Nevertheless, the way we discuss the issue, brought in by the client, anticipates friendship: we investigate the issue together, and although I have some philosophical expertise, I try to relate to the client on a level of equality and to see him or her as a whole person, and not as a 'case'. I am not going to 'diagnose' his or her situation, neither will I prescribe a 'remedy'. We are involved in a process of investigation, in which I will put myself at stake as well (psychotherapy, by contrast, seems to be rather modeled by the doctor/patient relationship). I am not the expert who will put himself outside the arena.

For me this attitude is typical for philosophy: all the participants put themselves at risk, including the so-called philosopher. I don't see how you can philosophize by staying an outsider. This means as well that I constantly have to work on myself, when I want to work as a philosopher. The art of living is an ongoing process, as life itself is. When I fixate my ideas, I will miss the point, in my own life and towards client or discussion partners as well. So I am grateful for all I have learned from sessions with clients in the different forms of practical philosophy! Not only did I get acquainted with other worlds and professions (I really didn't know how it was to work as a doctor, as a police officer or as a civil servant at the tax department, for example), but they (the clients) did also disturb all kind of ideas that I took for granted. I learned that the question 'Is that so?' is one of the most philosophical questions.

Hadot revealed that in Antiquity one was considered a philosopher when he *lived* as a philosopher, and not because he wrote a book or a treatise. And a philosopher who did write a book, but didn't live accordingly, was not taken seriously any longer. I think it is a good criterion, not only for writing on philosophy (and it would make a big difference on the shelves in bookshops, and rightly so), but also for the work of practical philosophers. Let us refrain from philosophical assertions that we did not verify with our own life. Anyway, it's a guideline for my own approach. Not-knowing is a philosophical virtue indeed.

WHO IS MY COLLEAGUE?

I realize that the connection of practical philosophy with the art of living is not common to all practical philosophers. It's my preference, and I think I have good reasons for it. But I am not in the position to say that every practical philosopher should subscribe this position. More important is that we ask ourselves how we situate what we are doing. What justifies the adjective 'philosophical'?

Who is my colleague? Am I a philosopher who works by putting his approach to life into practice? Or am I a teacher, facilitator or coach with philosophy as one of the options I have to offer a client?

The term 'practical philosophy' covers a variety of methods. A method is not something in itself, but is an instrument that is used in order to bring about a goal or experience, — something that goes beyond the method. So, what is that goal?

There is nothing wrong with working in the field of psychotherapy or management training. The risk is, however, that Philosophical Practice will become just another tool, without any philosophical horizon. It will be incorporated in the world of psychotherapy or in the world of management training. 'Philosophical' will be just another taste, as long as it lasts, — probably till the next fashion. It will lose its vitality, drawn from a wealth of ideas and theories, built up in centuries. Philosophy is such a rich source of inspiration and critical questioning. It would be a pity if we had to miss this input, not only in personal life, but also in organizations and businesses.

Some will say, why is this a problem? Why should one keep in touch with his philosophical roots? Indeed, there is no problem, as long as it is a choice. I prefer to put my work in a philosophical perspective. In my experience it is inspiring. It enables me to grow personally and professionally at the same time. I practice philosophy because I feel at home in the philosophical approach of life, with its very rich and divers range of traditions and individuals. Therefore I am glad of this late renaissance of philosophy as a way of life, with the art of living as its ethics.

Moreover, I welcome philosophy as an important surplus in a world that risks being colonized by efficiency, profit and usefulness. These 'values' are okay, as long as they are not dominating. They need some counterforce. If not, humanity will be in danger. It's important to preserve enough space for other dimensions of life, both in our personal and professional life.

To provoke result-oriented people (some managers, for example) I sometimes introduce philosophy by saying that it is useless, but meaningful. By saying this, I know the contrast is too black and white, also concerning philosophy, but it is to underline that usefulness and meaningfulness are not the same thing. Philosophy cultivates a free space, for reflection and questioning, by suspending the concern for immediate or tangible results. I think, it's indispensable for a balanced life. Therefore I would like 'philosophical' to be more than just another option in the toolkit of a random professional. It's worthwhile to preserve philosophy in its own right, also when it goes practical.

Bibliography

Dutch:

Dries Boele, Het socratisch gesprek. Een oefening in levenskunst. In: Olga Crapels & Edgar Karssing (red.), Filosoof in de praktijk. 2000. Van Gorcum, Assen.

Dries Boele, Bij wijze van gespreksleiding. Over visieontwikkeling, zich inleven en levenskunst. In: Jos Delnoij en Wieger van Dalen (red.), Het socratisch gesprek. 2003. Damon, Budel.

Dries Boele, Opgeruimd gemoed. In: Prana, tijdschrift voor spiritualiteit en randgebieden der wetenschappen. Nummer 142, april/mei 2003/2004. 29 jaargang nr 4.

Dries Boele, Openbaar filosofisch spreekuur in het café. Een goed gesprek over gezonde problemen. In: Deviant. Tijdschrift tussen psychiatrie en maatschappij. Nummer 43. Jaargang 11. December 2004.

Non-Dutch:

Dries Boele, The Training of a Philosophical Counselor. In: Ran Lahav and Maria da Venza Tillmanns (ed.), Essays on Philosophical Counseling. 1995. University Press of America, Lanham.

Dries Boele, The Benefits of a Socratic Dialogue. Or: Which Results Can We Promise? In: Inquiry. Critical Thinking Across the

Disciplines. Spring 1998. Vol. XVII, No 3.

Dries Boele, Une autre façon de philosopher. In: Eugène Calschi (dir.), Philosopher au café. 3 Colloque international. Ouverture et recherche de sens. 2003. La Gouttière.

3. Dries Boele

4

Vaughana Macy Feary

Program Director
Excalibur Center for Applied Ethics, Stockton, NJ

---

1. Why was I originally drawn to Philosophical Practice?

I became a philosopher because a child in my family was a victim of violent crime. At a very young age I became, to use Emily Dickinson's telling phrase, a "mourner among the children both in the literal sense of grieving over the death of someone I loved, and also in Dickinson's metaphorical sense, setting aside beliefs implicit in childhood innocence.[1] I became skeptical about the possibility of goodness and justice in the world, the existence of a benevolent deity, and the role of choice in determining human destiny. From the start, my interest in philosophy was a passionate desire to understand my own existential condition.

Later as an undergraduate, I became fascinated by abstract philosophical issues with little direct application to daily life. My academic training was largely in analytic philosophy and originally focused upon epistemology and philosophy of mind. Later the influence of my anti-war and civil rights work during the '60s, together with the exigencies of the job market at that time, lead me to specialize in moral, social, political and legal philosophy. By the time I completed my Ph.D., I was married to a man already employed in a high paying position, and we had three children so it was not possible for me to become an academic nomad, but the universities and colleges where we resided were not hiring new faculty. Although I was frustrated by the dual career impasse, my logistical problems turned out to be serendipitous. Per force, I worked in other fields and familiarized myself with philosophical problems endemic to those areas. Without realizing it, I was laying the groundwork for becoming a philosophical practitioner. Eventually a tenured faculty member died, and I was hired to teach philosophy at Southern University in New Orleans.

My work in Philosophical Practice crystallized after I began teaching

---

[1] Emily Dickinson, 378 (959), *Final Harvest: Emily Dickinson's Poems* (Little Brown and Company.1961).

philosophy at Fairleigh Dickinson University (FDU) in Madison, New Jersey. How this happened may suggest how new practitioners might build practices of their own. FDU has many adult students from the corporate sector and a very interesting graduate program and yearly conferences in corporate communication. As a consequence, I did a great deal of academic work teaching and writing about philosophical issues in business and made numerous contacts within the business community.[2] Soon my corporate consulting work was a great deal more extensive and lucrative than my work in the academy. Fairleigh Dickinson also had a new program in women's studies for which I did courses in feminist philosophy. Devising and delivering workshops centered on women's philosophical issues then became a substantial portion of my practice as well.

As a consequence of teaching courses in the philosophy of law and criminal justice, and the contacts that I made as a result, I was soon asked by our local sheriff's department to design and deliver programs for inmates in Morris County Correctional Facility which would be consistent with upcoming changes in sentencing guidelines. I attended conferences in correctional education, gave workshops on the role of philosophical counseling in correctional contexts, and soon was being contacted by wardens around the country to set up programs for their adult and juvenile facilities.[3]

In order to teach my FDU students the role of philosophy outside of academia, and to build bridges between the university and the community, I began holding a few collaborative class sessions each semester with my inmate classes at Morris County Correctional Facility and my business ethics, feminist philosophy, and philosophical counseling classes at Fairleigh Dickinson. As part of the class work, I helped FDU students who participated in these sessions to create a small non-profit, Excalibur: A Center for Applied Ethics. These students became dedicated Board members. Excalibur's mission was to forge alliances between key sectors of society and to design and deliver philosophy-based programs to assist in resolving social problems. We began by creating alliances between the academic, corporate and criminal justice sectors

---

[2] See for example, Vaughana Feary, " Sexual Harassment: Why the Corporate World Still Doesn't Get It (*Journal of Business Ethics*, 13, 1994), "Crime, Business Ethics and Corporate Communication in Michael Goodman, ed. *Business Communication for Executives* (New York, NY: SUNY Press 1998). " The Right to Freedom of Commercial Communication ", Journal of business Ethics II, 1992.

[3] See, for example: Vaughana Feary, "The Role of Philosophical Counseling in Rehabilitating Criminal Offenders,. *Inquiry Critical Thinking Across the Disciplines, Vol. XVII, No.3, Spring 1998 .and* " Feminist Perspectives on Virtue Cased Counseling, *Practical Philosophy (Vol.6) 2005.*

in our community in order to reduce crime and substance abuse. With the help of students and corporate volunteers recruited by them, I designed and delivered numerous programs for adult and juvenile offenders over a ten-year period. It was not uncommon for Excalibur to have forty trained volunteers working in correctional facilities each semester. In effect, this work served as a kind of internship in Philosophical Practice for FDU philosophy students and it taught them more about social justice, corporate philanthropy, inequality of opportunity, and the role of philosophy in resolving social problems than they could ever have learned in the classroom.

Due to a health crisis, I retired from teaching, but Excalibur is still in existence and beginning to address the problems of medical patients. Soon we hope to design and deliver philosophy-based programs in day retreats for cancer and heart patients and to design programs for the blind here on my seventy-acre "philosophy farm" in New Jersey. We have already run successful pilot projects of this sort and these programs mesh very nicely with my existing "Philosophy and Nature" workshops.

I have been drawn to Philosophical Practice and became a founding Board member and vice-president of the American Philosophical Practitioners Association (APPA), in part because of my desire to help young philosophers and to enrich my discipline.[4] There are still not enough academic jobs available for new Ph.D.s in philosophy, and there is still little flexibility in a system established long before the difficulties of balancing two careers became commonplace. As a consequence, in today's uncertain economy, there are fewer and fewer students choosing philosophy as a major, much less as a career. This results in funding cuts for many philosophy departments which are now frequently merging with other departments in order to survive. If allowed to continue, this state of affairs can ultimately only impoverish our discipline and diminish its influence in the world. The antidote for these difficulties is to create jobs for philosophers outside the academy and to show students that philosophy can be a good career path.

For the most part, departments of philosophy have been slow to defend the turf they already occupy. With increasing regularity, we see professors in other disciplines colonizing applied philosophy courses. When these sorts of courses are turned over to non-philosophers to teach, the philosophical component is often diluted and badly taught. As a consequence, the role philosophy plays outside of the academy is further diminished. The recourse for this state of affairs is to begin

---

[4] For the history of philosophical practice see, Lou Marinoff, Philosophical Practice (San Diego, California: Academic Press, 2001).

developing graduate programs centered on applied philosophy and Philosophical Practice. Such programs would make internships available which would be directed by philosophers experienced in practicing philosophy outside the narrow confines of the academy.

In sum, my desire to see philosophy enrich every profession as well as the personal lives of students continues to draw me to Philosophical Practice. My interest in Philosophical Practice is, at base, an interest in the renaissance of philosophy, itself, as a guiding force in the contemporary world.

2. What does your work reveal about Philosophical Practice that other related academic fields typically fail to appreciate?

A brief description of my own methodology will demonstrate how Philosophical Practice can create new dimensions for philosophy and counseling. For brevity, I will focus on individual counseling, but these phases of counseling are easily adapted for group and organizational work. The four phases of counseling are: the analytic, the synthetic, the critical, and the comparative.

In the *analytic* phase of counseling, I try to understand the initial problems the client (an individual or corporation) wants to resolve and to identify the deeper philosophical problems which may underlie them. At this stage I also ask clients about their priorities and make referrals where necessary. In assessing the problem, I try to understand the client's beliefs about the problem and any connections between these beliefs to relevant emotions, behaviors and relationships. I employ techniques of conceptual and logical analysis to clarify what a client thinks about key concepts under discussion and the reasons given in support of beliefs about the situation the client confronts. I also try to ascertain whether the client is exhibiting any barriers to critical reasoning such as denial, projection, etc. or demonstrating emotions such as anger, guilt anxiety, shame, depression, etc. which are like to impair it. Particularly when I am working with adult and juvenile offenders or clients in substance abuse programs, I listen for cognitive deficits: poor consequential reasoning, egocentricity, cognitive rigidity, and fallacious reasoning. These sorts of problems with thinking may occur with people who ordinarily reason quite well, but who are operating under profound stress in new and frightening situations.

In the *synthetic* phase of counseling, I work with clients to examine what they have said about their issues and to begin, based solely on that data, to help them construct or make explicit relevant provisional personal or organizational philosophies. This work is necessary; without it, clients will not recognize later changes in perspective or regressions to unproductive patterns of thinking.

In the *critical* phase of counseling, I help clients to subject their informal philosophies to philosophical scrutiny. Clients are assisted in identifying informal fallacies in their thinking, together with any contradictions in beliefs or inconsistencies in values. They are also helped to consider the impact that their belief systems may have upon emotions, behaviors and significant relationships. Depending upon the context in which I am practicing and the problems being addressed, specific techniques learned from colleagues may be used for individuals or groups: Philosophical Midwifery, The Peace Process, Socratic Dialogue, Dilemma Training, etc. At the end of this phase, clients should be in a better position to identify, understand, and resolve personal problems as well as to recognize any sources of potential conflict between personal philosophies and other belief systems, organizational philosophies, etc.[5]

During the *comparative* phase of counseling, I invite individuals or groups to compare their respective philosophies with selected theories from the philosophical tradition. The objective at this phase is to enrich and enlarge the vision of the individual. For example, clients with relationship problems might be invited to examine their beliefs in terms of various philosophical views of love, marriage or friendship. Organizational groups might explore the relevance of Aristotle's theory of virtue to business ethics and leadership.

The artistry of Philosophical Practice involves adapting methods and theories for particular clients. The approach that works in one context may not be equally suitable for other individuals, groups, or organizations. Some clients may merely wish to engage in philosophical conversation with a competent philosopher about a particular issue or question (e.g., the justice of a war, the mission of a given organization). In such cases, the sessions are open ended philosophical explorations. Other clients may want help in finding meaning in a changing or traumatic situation (e.g., illness, retirement, corporate downsizing, being a crime victim, etc.). Here a more directive approach is justified because of some expertise that has been acquired by the practitioner which can be deployed to help the client chart a course in unfamiliar terrain. Still other clients like psychiatric patients, substance abusers, and adult and juvenile offenders may need to radically deconstruct unproductive philosophies which lead to harming self or others and to construct more productive world views. Here the goals of the session are therapeutic,

---

[5] Pierre Grimes and Regina l. Uliana, *Philosophical Midwifery: A New Paradigm for Understanding Human Problems with its Validation* (Costa Mesa, California, Hyparxis Press, 1998) and Marinoff for discussion of these techniques, pp. 67-173.

as in attempting to reduce management problems, relapse, recidivism, etc. In sum, Philosophical Practice, like Wittgenstein's games, consist in a variety of activities with overlapping similarities, but no real common thread uniting them.

Enough has already been said to suggest how varieties of Philosophical Practice, including mine, have unique contributions to make to philosophy and to clinical practice. Differences between Philosophical Practice and most fields of academic philosophy seem to depend upon at least three related issues. The first is that Philosophical Practice, like psychotherapy, emphasizes the importance of listening and responding to the needs of clients. The second is that in responding to the needs of clients, the practitioner must often deal not merely with belief structures but also with feelings, behavior and relationships in so far as they are representative of personal or organizational philosophies. A third related difference is that Philosophical Practice encompasses concern with the informal philosophies (outsider or vernacular philosophies) to which clients already subscribe. As a consequence, Philosophical Practice often exposes philosophical problems which are not currently being examined by other fields of philosophy, and represents a return to practical interests common to ancient philosophy and the tradition of philosophy as care for the soul.[6]

Philosophical practice is a form of applied philosophy, but Philosophical Practice does not merely apply a theory to a particular context. Instead there is always a kind of dialectical interplay between theory and practice, and between philosopher and client. As J. C. Murphy pointed out in an interesting article on punishment years ago, theories can be formally correct, but materially deficient.[7] A theory is formally correct if it is consistent and coherent, but it is materially deficient if it makes assumptions about human beings and the world which turn out to be wrong. Philosophical practice forces us to assess the material adequacy of our theories. Theory informs practice, but Philosophical Practice enriches theory.

Clearly, Philosophical Practice makes unique contributions to clinical practice because it is unlike psychotherapy in a variety of ways. First, Philosophical Practice, unlike most psychotherapy, always uses philosophical methods (e.g., conceptual, logical, and phenomenological analysis), together with the riches of the philosophical literature, as a basis

---

[6] See works by Pierre Hadot for a discussion of this tradition, especially: Pierre Hadot, *What is Ancient Philosophy?* Cambridge, Mass. (2002); *Philosophy as a Way of Life*. Malden, Mass, 1995; *The Present Alone Is Our Happiness, Conversations with Jennnie Carlier and Arnold I Davidson*, Stanford, California, 2009.

[7] J. C. Murphy, "Marxism and Retribution" in J. Simmons, M. Cohen and C. Beitz (eds.) *Punishment: A Public Affairs Reader,* Princeton, NJ: Princeton, NJ (1995).

for counseling about questions of meaning, value, moral duties, etc. which are not within a psychotherapist's legitimate scope of expertise. Second, Philosophical Practice is education rather than treatment; as such, irrespective of its instrumental value, it always has intrinsic value. Third, prolonged psychotherapy often encourages individuals to have a narcissistic and ultimately boring focus upon the particulars of their own lives and feelings. By contrast, philosophical counseling leads individuals to broaden their vision by considering universal questions and ideas of concern to everyone.

Despite the differences to which I have just alluded, the attempt to make a sharp bifurcation between philosophical counseling and psychotherapy is doomed to failure if only because psychologists have borrowed so freely from philosophers. REBT and Cognitive Psychology have borrowed from logic and the Stoics. Existential and feminist psychotherapy borrow from their philosophical precursors. Positive psychology is only the most recent type of psychology to borrow from philosophy, finally jettisoning the emphasis on psychopathology to which Philosophical Practice has long objected, replacing it with an Aristotelian concern with eudaemonia. However, as I have pointed out elsewhere in spelling out differences between feminist philosophical counseling and feminist psychotherapy, contemporary Philosophical Practice usually makes its own philosophical assumptions explicit, inviting clients to consider them critically. In this sense, Philosophical Practice is transparent where psychotherapy is opaque. By encouraging clients to consider alternative perspectives, contemporary Philosophical Practice departs from much Hellenistic philosophical therapy (care for the soul) as well as most types of psychotherapy.

As the brief outline of my modest contributions to the methodology of Philosophical Practice illustrates, Philosophical Practice identifies individual and institutional philosophical problems which traditional academic philosophy and psychotherapy leave untouched. It also develops new horizons for individual and group counseling, as well as for organizational consulting.

3. What if any practical and&or social obligations follow from understanding philosophy from the point of view of Philosophical Practice?

Since the first international conference in Philosophical Practice, I have talked to numerous philosophers about their conceptions of Philosophical Practice. I have concluded that there are at least three working models for a philosophical practitioner, each with an emphasis upon quite different correlative obligations, all of which merit attention. These models are: The Professional Model, The Social Political Model, and The Classical Model. These models are not mutually exclusive. In fact, as we will see, the professional model and the Ethics Code of the American Philosophical Practitioners Association(adapted from the American Society for Philosophy, Counseling, and Psychotherapy Code of Ethics), provides some accommodation for all three sets of obligations.[8] The Professional Model is the most fully developed and widely accepted. Never-the-less the emphasis in each model is different. Ignoring such differences can only lead to confusions between descriptive and honorific conceptions of a philosophical practitioner, as well as about the obligations practitioners should discharge.

1. THE PROFESSIONAL MODEL

While there is considerable variation in Philosophical Practice in different countries, there is widespread agreement that philosophical practitioners have the following obligations if they wish to be regarded as professionals in this field: (a) they must obtain a graduate degree in philosophy or its equivalent; (b) they must also obtain education, training, or experience in individual counseling, group facilitation, and organizational consulting from philosophical perspectives; (c) they must be able to demonstrate familiarity with the corpus of basic literature pertaining to Philosophical Practice and related fields: and (d) they must show a commitment to a code of ethics approved by some relevant national organization associated with Philosophical Practice. Once these criteria have been satisfied, it is also widely recognized that philosophical practitioners have professional obligations to keep current with the literature and developments in their field and to conduct their practices in accordance with an ethics code which contains the sorts of standards included in the American Philosophical Practitioners Association (APPA) Code of Ethics. Certification by a professional association provides some assurance to clients that the certified practitioners they retain satisfy these widely recognized criteria necessary for being regarded as a professional philosophical practitioner and can reasonably be expected to live up to their professional obligations.[9]

Philosophical practitioners, as professionals, have further obligations if they wish to function in specialized areas. Standard 22 of the APPA Code of Ethics incorporates recognition of this sort of obligation, but the nature of the multi-disciplinary skills and knowledge needed to perform well in specific contexts has yet to be elaborated. My own practice

---

[8] See Marinoff, *Philosophical Practice*, pp. 221-227.

[9] For APPA standards for certification, see pp. 212-292.

has involved work in correctional facilities, hospitals and corporations, and I would suggest that philosophical practitioners wishing to work in these specialized fields have obligations to acquire the following sorts of knowledge and skills. Philosophical consultants for correctional facilities have professional obligations to learn something about correctional education, prison culture, inmate profiles, prison management, sentencing guidelines, etc. Similarly, philosophers working with cancer patients in hospitals have obligations to learn a great deal about cancer and hospitals. The philosophical problems of stage three lung cancer patients are very different from stage one breast cancer patients, and patients are likely to have quite different philosophical issues as they undergo different forms of treatment. Frequently, cancer patients have problems which are best referred to social workers or oncology nurses so philosophical practitioners need a thorough understanding of how their counseling programs mesh with existing programs and services. Analogously, practitioners serving as consultants in business contexts have obligations to learn a great deal about training (as distinguished from teaching), the specific ethical and legal challenges faced by employees in different areas of business, management theories, the character and missions of specific corporate cultures, etc. As graduate programs in Philosophical Practice are developed, the education of practitioners will undoubtedly encompass internships in these areas of existing practice, and philosophical professionalism in these specialized areas will become more common.

Any criticism of the professional model and the professional obligations emphasized by it, seems to pivot upon a failure to distinguish between different descriptive uses of the term philosophical practitioner, and between descriptive and honorific uses use of the term. For example, one objection to the professional model (which was also a basis for naive objections to certification programs) centered upon claims that philosophical practitioners are not mere professionals or technicians.[10] The response to this objection is that while the professional model may not exhaust our conceptions of what a philosophical practitioner is, or ought to be, defining philosophical practitioner in terms of some favored ideal is not helpful in clarify the obligations emphasized by different existing models. Furthermore, counselors and consultants who do not live up to these professional obligations are unlikely to be a credit to this emerging profession.

---

[10] Pierre Hadot, *Philosophy as A Way of Life*, pp 264-277.

2. THE SOCIAL POLITICAL MODEL

Another popular model for a philosophical practitioner is that of advocate for social justice, social activist, and ethicist. The emphasis for this model is upon social and moral obligations, but the character of these obligations is not all clear. Some professional practitioners do spend a great deal of time as advocates, activists, and ethicists, while some spend very little time. Some are philosophers with graduate degrees in philosophy while others have degrees in other disciplines, but also possess highly developed philosophical skills. Practitioners, in this informal sense, may not have any training in Philosophical Practice as such, but are employed outside of the academy using their philosophical skills to implement or critique social and political policies or to educate the general public.

Do all philosophical practitioners have obligations to be political activists, or at least advocates for social justice? If so, what would this entail? Part of what this might mean is encapsulated in the sixth fundamental canon of the APPA Code of Ethics which says that Philosophical practitioners will, beyond attending to the needs of their clients, endeavor to secure the greater good of the community and society in which they reside. This is a very general professional obligation which can be satisfied by a variety of activities, *e.g.* ,providing pro bono services, giving public lectures, running philo-cafes, etc. In addition, Standard 23 of that Code requires practitioners to comply with existing laws and to, . . . work for change of existing laws where such laws prevent or obstruct ethical practice."

Philosophical practitioners who subscribe to some variant of the social political model might also suggest that all practitioners, and all professional organizations and societies concerned with Philosophical Practice, have social obligations to espouse public positions about such issues as world hunger, human rights, environmental issues, etc. or, at the very least, to protest egregious cases of injustice. After all, the American Bar Association and the American Philosophical Association have both taken public positions condemning the death penalty. Presumably the arguments here would be that philosophers have the expertise to understand competing conceptions of social justice and that some practitioners also have special professional expertise in detecting the ways in which theories of rights and social justice will actually work in particular areas such as health care, criminal justice, et al. Therefore philosophical practitioners (and the associations devoted to practice) may have at least minimal obligations to try to educate the general public about social justice issues. These obligations would certainly be consistent with Fundamental Canon vi of the APPA Code of Ethics mentioned earlier.

Sometimes it appears that involvement as an advocate, activist, or ethicist may impose additional moral, social, and political obligations upon such practitioners. If philosophers publically subscribe to specific social and political theories in the course of their practice, or are employed in social advocacy contexts, such activities seem to generate at least minimal negative obligations to refrain from actions which are inconsistent with these theories or missions. Moreover, because of connections between moral beliefs and action, there is an inconsistency between subscribing to ethical principles or social values of some sort and failing to act upon them. Professing allegiance to specific ethical, legal, and political theories in the course of one's practice, or theorizing and counseling in specialized areas of practice, may generate specific positive moral obligations to act in particular ways. This subject requires a more careful argument than can be provided within the scope of this paper, but the following example suggests how this might occur.

In my own practice, I have concerns about the sorts of moral obligations philosophical practitioners working with cancer groups have to potentially terminal cancer patients who are, or have been, participants in their groups.[11] Contrary to my original expectations, I have found no cancer groups, even those with metastatic problems, desirous of talking about death. A few individuals, however, do desire counseling about death and rational suicide, and I always provide pro bono individual counseling for such clients if they desire it. Sometimes when moral, legal, and practical problems surrounding death are somewhat decided immediately following a cancer diagnosis, patients can more comfortably undertake the challenge of fighting for life. This was so in my case when Lou Marinoff did very courageous counseling with me after my supposedly terminal diagnosis of lung cancer at Sloan Kettering in 1999.

Of course, philosophers have obligations to help clients with cancer explore conditions for a meaningful life in the face of suffering, as well as to sustain hope for eventual remission and good quality of life. However, I also think that philosophers in this area of counseling have obligations to try, if possible, to make useful referrals for patients planning to terminate their own lives when treatment fails or when they conclude (after careful reflection) that life is not worth living. Given my allegiance to the belief that there is a moral right to commit rational suicide and that there ought to be a legal right to physician assisted

---

[11] For a discussion of philosophical counseling with cancer groups see Vaughana Feary, " Medicine for the Soul: Philosophical Counselling with Cancer Patients in *Philosophy in Society*. ed. Henning Herrestad and Helge Sware.(Oslo, Norway: Unipub Forlag, 2002) .

suicide in the U.S., I have concluded that I have correlative moral obligations to be present in a variety of supportive roles (like the followers of Socrates) for my clients should they wish to terminate their own lives. I also have professional obligations, consistent with Standard 23 of the APPA Ethics Code, to marshal support for legal change concerning the issue of physician assisted suicide. However, consistent with Standard 23 of the APPA Code of Ethics, philosophical practitioners should also be diligent in refraining from inadvertently violating laws relevant to Philosophical Practice.

The social political model certainly emphasizes very important dimensions of practice. While the obligations correlated to this model are certainly consistent with the professional model, professionalism can sometimes lead to political conservatism and a needlessly attenuated view of the role of philosophy in not merely understanding the world, but also in changing it. Certainly, philosophers can do much more to emulate Socrates by serving as social gadflies than they do at present. Since the end of the Vietnam War, academic philosophers seem to have abdicated from any role in political activism and one can hope that Philosophical Practice will undertake to play a more Socratic role.

Finally, I would argue that all philosophical practitioners have obligations to be ethicists, or moral educators, and to relinquish any pretense of having the supposed ethical neutrality claimed by most kinds of psychotherapy. This supposed neutrality has often masked tacit support for continuing social injustice, either by accepting the status quo., gender stereotypes etc.) or by smuggling in value judgments in the form of diagnostic categories in the DSM.[12] Worse yet, as many psychologists and social scientists have long recognized, much psychotherapy (and all the popular versions of it foisted on the public by the media) simply assume that ethical egoism is the sole legitimate basis for helping clients reach decisions about their lives.

There are all sorts of problems with the egoistic orientation of psychotherapy. First, there is no good reason to assume that one's own psychological well being should be the sole valid standard of right conduct. Aside from the fact that universal ethical egoism cannot be consistently advocated, taught, or practiced, such an orientation precludes any real consideration of moral issues. Second, the egoistic orientation of much psychotherapy (with the exception of family system approaches) treats the client as an isolated individual apart from communal ties. Third, just as counseling based upon egoism may not produce the best life for the

---

[12] For the latest version, see American Psychiatric Association, Diagnostic and Statistical Manual of Mental Disorders, Washington, DC: American Psychiatric Association, 1994.

individual, so individuals counseled by psychotherapy may not produce the best society, but rather a culture of narcissism.[13] While no doubt Philosophical Practice can suggest how psychotherapists can be more sensitive to moral issues, it is best to leave the bulk of ethics education to philosophers who have the requisite expertise in the field.

Consistent with the third standard of the APPA Code of Ethics, all philosophical practitioners have obligations to educate their clients, to engage their reflective and critical powers, and to refrain from imposing their own philosophical views (including moral views) upon clients, but this last obligation does not imply that practitioners must maintain a sphinx like silence about their own philosophical and moral allegiances. As any philosophy professor who has taught applied ethics knows, it is quite possible to articulate one's own philosophical position on a topic, while simultaneously fostering autonomy and respecting the rights of others to hold opposing views. In fact, thanks to the influence of psychotherapy, clients and the general public may need philosophical counselors to model what it is like to take reasoned moral positions.

The ethics education of clients and the general public must also involve showing them that psychological insight, while undeniably valuable, has its limits, and that the current popularity of both egoism and relativism with the general public is largely attributable to the lamentable trend of individuals and the media to psychologize every issue. By contrast, practitioners can show clients that many life problems are philosophical problems to be resolved through philosophical dialogue and moral reflection rather than through endless examinations of one's own feelings. Especially in a world where, The best lack all conviction, while the worst/ Are full of passionate intensity practitioners have obligations, at least, in this minimal sense, to be ethics educators as well as critics of psychotherapy.[14]

3. THE CLASSICAL MODEL

A third model of the philosophical practitioner is the practitioner as sage or exemplar for the art of living. As Pierre Hadot has eloquently argued, there is a long tradition bequeathed to us from ancient philosophy which conceives of the philosopher as a role model for philosophical ways of life. Hadot seems to be arguing that Socrates, Plato, Aristotle, the Stoics and the Epicureans were all role models for the art of living who serve to show us not only what a philosophical practitioner was

---

[13] Philip Reiff, *Triumph of the Therapeutic,* Garden City, NY: Anchor Books, 1961; Christopher Lasch, *The Culture of Narcissism* (New York: Warner Books,1979).

[14] William Butler Yeats, *The Second Coming* in *The New Oxford Book of English Verse 1250-1950* (Oxford: Clarendon Press, 1972).

like then, but also what a philosopher ought to be like now.

In ancient philosophy, philosophy is treated as both a way of life and a way of discourse. As Hadot says, philosophy was a mode of existing-in-the-world which had to be practiced at each instant, and the goal of which was to transform the whole of the individual's life; writing of the Socratic and Platonic tradition, Hadot argues that there are two poles of philosophical activity, the choice and practice of a way of life and a philosophical discourse which is at the same time an integral part of this way of life and renders explicit the theoretical presuppositions implicated in this way of life.[15] He reminds us that, for Plato, philosophy is understood as care of the soul and training for death. The individual is lead through philosophy from an individual and passionate perspective to a rational and universal perspective. Similarly, Hadot shows that while Aristotle might seem to emphasize theory, philosophy for him, as for Plato, involves an inner transformation. The form of life the Aristotelian philosopher models is life according to the mind. It is the life of the scholar, a life of both wisdom and virtue. Hadot goes on to discuss both Stoicism and Epicureanism as different approaches to the art of living and the care of the soul which correspond to opposite but inseparable poles of our inner life: the demands of our moral conscience and the flourishing of our joy in existence.[16] Finally, Hadot argues that acting in accordance with justice is an essential element of every philosophical life and that all the schools of ancient philosophy were concerned not merely with the good of the individual, but also the good of the polis.

This is a very old and appealing tradition of philosophy and the role of the philosopher. Some minimal recognition of the claims of this model are embodied in Standard xxi of the APPA Code of Ethics which says: Philosophical practitioners should exemplify those moral qualities of character associated with being philosophical (for example, being open minded, honest, rational, consistent, fair, and impartial). Pierre Hadot's interesting works, like Martha Nussbaum's, *Therapy of Desire*, are important in showing that philosophers in ancient philosophy were practitioners for whom philosophy was also a way of living.[17] Certainly, one could also argue that the ideal of the philosopher as sage and role model for the art of living is the dominant model of a philosopher in Indian and Chinese philosophy.

---

[15] Pierre Hadot, *What is Ancient Philosophy?* (Cambridge, Massachusetts: Harvard University Press, 2002), p.76.

[16] Pierre Hadot, *Philosophy As A Way of Life*, 272-276; 272.

[17] Martha C. Nussbaum, *The Therapy of Desire, Theory and Practice in Hellenistic Ethics*. Princeton,, New Jersey, Princeton University Press, 1994.

At the same time, we need to recognize that not all contemporary philosophical practitioners subscribe to the classical description of a philosopher (much less embody it), nor to the sorts of exacting moral and political obligations associated with it. While I find Tantric images of the union of theory and practice very seductive, the claim that all philosophical practitioners in the descriptive sense, have obligations to be exemplars of the art of living seems overly demanding. Never the less, this is an honorific conception of a philosophical practitioner which can only enrich our notions of what philosophers and philosophical practitioners ought to be.

4. What do you see as the most interesting criticism against your own position in Philosophical Practice?

Philosophical practice is an umbrella term under which many different conceptions and kinds of practice can shelter. As a consequence, I think that the most important criticism that might be made against my own position concerns my working hypothesis that Philosophical Practice usually complements rather than conflicts with psychotherapy and psychiatry and that the boundaries between psychiatry and Philosophical Practice are reasonably well distinguished. In prison settings especially, I work very amicably with psychiatrists, psychologists, social workers and substance abuse counselors on case management. I have found such work very helpful in understanding correlations between problems in those areas and specific philosophical problems; such knowledge is essential for group counseling with those clients.

Some philosophical practitioners are more critical of both psychotherapy and psychiatry. For example, in a recent paper, Peter Raabe challenges biomedical accounts of mental illness and the usual defenses for the necessity of using psychotropic drugs in treating mental illness, suggesting that mental disorders can be treated, if not cured, by means of philosophy.[18] In another recent paper, Kevin Aho challenges the DSM bio-psychiatric model for depression and discusses the value of Existentialism and Buddhism for clients suffering from depression. He admits, however, that clients may also need medication to benefit from philosophical counseling[19] I agree with much of the criticism Raabe, Aho and other critics make of the medical model and its reductionism. Of course, given my areas of practice, I also agree that philosophical

---

[18] 'Mental Illness': Ontology, Etiology, and Philosophy as Cure in Haser, *Revista International De Filosophia Aplicada (International Review of Philosophical Practice)*, Sevilla, Spain. No1 (Vol.1), October 2010.

[19] Kevin Aho, "Rethinking the Psychopathology of Depression, *Philosophical Practice Journal of the APPA,* Vol. 3, Number 1, March 2008, pp. 207-218.

counseling, conjoined with treatment, can be very helpful to patients who have been diagnosed with psychiatric or psychological problems. Critics like Raabe and Aho assist us in expanding our conceptions of the legitimate scope of Philosophical Practice. However, in my work, especially in prison settings, I encounter many clients whose predominant problems do not appear to be philosophical in nature. For example, some have alcohol and drug problems which need to be addressed before philosophical counseling can be successful. In such cases, referrals are essential. The APPA Code of Ethics, Fundamental Canon I, says: Philosophical Practitioners will above all, endeavor to do no harm. I would prefer to err on the side of caution.

5. With respect to present and future inquiry, how can the most important questions concerning Philosophical Practice be identified and explored?

We know that one of the most important overarching questions concerning Philosophical Practice is what it can do further to benefit individuals, groups, organizations, and governments. There are, of course, meta-questions to consider: What are the new philosophical problems in these areas? What counts as a benefit in new areas? If practice has intrinsic value for new clients, how so? If practice has instrumental value, what sorts of evidence will we have to provide to substantiate such claims? In short, the interesting questions will emerge from practice.

The questions which arise from extending Philosophical Practice to new areas and client bases are best explored through the dialectical interplay between theory and practice. As new philosophical issues emerge, new philosophical approaches and theories must be devised, but their efficacy can only be decided by putting them to work. All the really significant questions will always end, as they began, in practice.

Bibliography

Vaughana Feary: "The Right to Rehabilitation", in *Perspectives in Philosophical Practice* (Leusden, Holland, 1997);

Vaughana Feary: "The Role of Philosophical Counselling in Rehabilitating Criminal Offenders", in *Inquiry, Critical Thinking Across the Across the Disciplines*, Spring 1998 Vol. XVII, N. B o 3

Vaughana Feary: "Crime, Business Ethics and Corporate Communication" in Michael Goodman ed.: *Business Communication for Executives* (New York, SUNY Press 1996)

Vaughana Feary: "The Right to Freedom of Commercial Communication", in *Journal of Business Ethics*, 1992. Vol.II, No.1

4. Vaughana Macy Feary 59

Vaughana Feary: "Sexual Harassment: Why the Corporate World Still Doesn't Get It ", in *Journal of Business Ethics*, 1994, Vol. 13, No.8

Vaughana Feary: Corporate Communication and Privacy Rights: Some Ethical Considerations for the Communication Specialist, in *Global Communication*, (Madison NJ: Fairleigh Dickinson Press, 1998

Vaughana Feary: "AIDS Education in the Workplace: Individual and Corporate Responsibility for the Year 2000", in *Approaching 2000*. Madison NJ, ,Fairleigh Dickinson Press, 2000

Vaughana Feary: "Philosophical Dialogue and Multicultural Values in Counselling and Practice" in ed. Trevor Curnow end, in *Thinking Through Dialogue, Essays on Philosophy in Practice*. Oxted UK. 2001

Vaughana Feary: "Virtue Based Feminist Philosophical Counselling" in *Practical Philosophy*. Vol.6 No.1. 2003

Vaughana Feary: "Art and the Good Life: The Role of Literature and the Visual Arts in Philosophical Practice", in *Philosophical Practice*, Vol. 1, No 2 July, 2006.

5

Fred Gebler

Philosophical practitioner
Greifswald, Germany

---

1. Why were you initially drawn to Philosophical Practice?

Mainly three experiences brought me to Philosophical Practice:
1. My early awakened interest in famous philosophers which I found to be exceptional individuals thinking unconventional and genuine thoughts.
2. My disappointment with the theoretic, boringly abstract education at grammar school and at the university.
3. The variety of meanings and values offered by religions, psychotherapies and natural sciences based on principles that cannot be questioned.

The external and internal devastations left by World War II pushed people in Germany as well as in many other parts of the world into an ethical and existential crisis; it seemed like values and contexts of meaning which had been passed down for generations had become doubtful and suspect in the face of the misery that highly civilised and cultivated men and their institutions had caused.

In Western Germany, where I grew up, in the 1950s and 60s people tried to create values and to find the right within the wrong, such as reconstruction, a free market economy or the primacy of science. This materialistic and science-oriented way of coping with life was not satisfying for me.

As a grammar school student, I firstly sought answers in philosophy, then in the diverse currents of eastern religions, mainly in Zen Buddhism. Finally, I immersed myself into Sigmund Freud's and C.G. Jung's depth psychology. However, I considered that depth psychology, psychoanalysis and the other groups of depth psychology as being overly determined by the dogmas and ideologies of the concerning groups as well as their founders.

At that time, many people were seeking alternatives to the materialistically limited possibilities of everyday life, wanting to emancipate themselves from traditional concepts of love and sexuality, property situations and gender relations. People discussed and tried different forms of property and communal life; they experimented with consciousness-expanding drugs, developed new forms of therapy and adopted inspirations from eastern religions.

The kind of psychology which I became acquainted with at the university in the 70s and which I studied until I passed my intermediate diploma seemed too much tied to natural science and restricted to me. The religions, whether Christianity or Buddhism, dictated a predefined conception of the world, they taught and still teach dogmas not to be questioned. Experiences with psychedelic drugs proved to be a possibility of expanding one's horizon of experience and consciousness, but they barely gave practicable advice on how one should live one's life and required an ethical framework of their own.

With its interesting characters and manifold possibilities enabling one to see, to experience, to recognise and to think, philosophy had already intrigued me when I was at school; here, the questions life brought up were approached without the dogmas, taboo restricted thinking and axioms I came across with in the different religions and natural sciences.

Philosophy accepts the unknown in the world, philosophers blazing trails for others to find their way through the unknown and the doubtful so they can freely move within it. In order to render this tradition and impetus of philosophy useful for our materialistic and consume-oriented world, Philosophical Practice has been developed.

Academic philosophy has always been elaborating many theories and still does so. In the meantime, these have been and still are of little importance for each individual's problems and concerns. The teaching and studying of philosophy at a German university were of no help vis-à-vis the students' concrete worries. Seminars dealing with logic, Descartes and Plato, Neo-Kantianism and linguistic analysis: Just about everything was taught and learnt—without really affecting the individual on a personal level. We worked in a scientific manner, but did not think and live in a philosophical fashion.

In the courses, the issue of the individual's own successful, mastered life meaning how one should, may and can live was a purely theoretical one being processed with the likes of Plato, Aristotle or Leibniz à la Happiness in Kant's Moral Doctrine.

But what about my own happiness or sadness? To all appearances, the study of philosophy did not have anything to do with these topics. A theory about the meaning of life does not necessarily make sense to the individual in his or her concrete situation. For this philosophy requires categories that can be utilized, for instance empathy; categories which arise from phenomenological and hermeneutical knowledge. Having the aspiration to concentrate on the individual life by locating the diverse philosophical modes of thought within it and to use the rich tradition of philosophy and, so to say, remind it of its duty, my Philosophical Practice came into existence. Therefore, while being at the university, I provided alternative tutorials where participants presented their personal problems and questions. Based on these, we reviewed the answers or methods of the different philosophers and of their philosophies. Were the philosophers' thoughts useful? Did they prove themselves? How did they prove themselves?

If the philosophies, ways of thinking and theories of the famous and unknown thinkers are nothing but thinking exercises, theory construction and historical science, philosophy is not of great value for the individual. It is indeed a generally accepted opinion that philosophers are unworldly theoreticians, if not cranks.

2. What does your work reveal about Philosophical Practice that other related academic fields typically fail to appreciate?

If we look for the features that distinguish Philosophical Practice from related academic branches, two questions arise:

What does Philosophical Practice achieve that academic philosophy does not, on the one side, and what does Philosophical Practice achieve that human therapeutic disciplines, that medical doctors, physical therapists, and social education workers work with, do not achieve, on the other side?

To start with, philosophy is a serious study in the sense that it follows strict rules and methods with subjects such as logic, propaedeutics, philology, exegesis, language analysis, and the history of philosophy. This important work is taught and studied at universities. At the same time, philosophy is self-contemplation and is not part of the humanities. It encourages independent thought; it is the acquisition of enlightenment and emancipation. Philosophy is a kind of art, the art of thinking: an art that deals with how ways, i.e. scientific methods, are possible: philosophy as the prerequisite for making science possible. Science, no matter whether it be the humanities or natural science, does not think original. It always requires an attitude, a focus, a method. Philosophy is, to quote a famous phrase by Nietzsche Happy Science—La Gaya Scienza, a science that draws from the richness of human nature, from the unity of the freethinker, singer, and creator.

The original philosopher is different from the philosophical scholar like the artist is different from the expert on the theory of art. The painter opens up new perspectives, a certain angle of view at the world.

With his brush, paint, form, and canvas he is the creator of a painting that depicts a certain view and grasp of the world. The expert on the theory of art analyzes and structures views and comprehension and comes to an interpretation of the painting, i.e.: The artist creates a world, the expert interprets this creation.

The philosopher presents his individual view of the world in his works. The philosophical scholar at a university classifies the philosopher's works historically and in regard to its content and tries to understand and criticize it.

The philosopher of Philosophical Practice draws his thoughts from two disciplines. On the one hand, he has gotten to know the works of the philosophical tradition during his academic studies, and on the other hand, he brings to life these works as Philosophical Practice when discoursing with the despairing or doubting, the seeking and amazed guest of his practice. With this discourse the philosopher as philosophical practitioner enters new grounds and is challenged like a detective and explorer: he investigates into the unfamiliar site of this specific case. He is referred to the unknown, uncertain human, which every human has to offer in a unique way and which philosophers and the wise men have been pondering and negotiating about in their own way ever since. The philosophical practitioner is, to use Nietzsche's words once more foreigner in a foreign land.[1]

There is no method in Philosophical Practice. Philosophical Practice just happens as a search for a method in the discourse with the respective guest of the practice. For this the practitioner needs education (arts, music, literature, cultural history, etc.), psychological and sociological knowledge, but above all life experience and awareness for his own life. He needs empathy and a comprehensive knowledge of those parts of the history of philosophy that are concerned with conceptions of human life plans (Lebensentwürfe) and concrete life problems. This history of philosophy is oriented towards a specific reading of the history of philosophy, in which special emphasis is given to preciously minor characters of philosophy, which up until then were given only little attention from the academic side, like, to name just a few examples, the Stoics, the Sceptics, the Cynics and Epicureans, the Early Fathers of the Church of the late antiquity; also philosophers such as Cicero, Seneca, Augustinus, Montaigne, Rousseau, Rosenzweig, or the American tran-

---

[1] Jeder Philosoph ist es in der Fremde: und muss erst das Nächste als fremd fühlen. (Each philosopher is a foreigner in a foreign land, and at first, he has to feel habitual and next things as strange.) 1872—1873; 23 (23), Friedrich Nietzsche Sämtliche Werke. Kritische Studienausgabe in 15 Bänden, Ed.: G. Colli, M. Montinari, München Berlin New York (Deutscher Taschenbuch Verlag, De Gruyter) 1980, vol. 7, p 548.

scendentalists: Emerson, Fuller, Peabody, Thoreau.

Philosophical Practice works closely with an individual's destiny. It addresses the troubles of those who visit a philosophical practitioner. It is challenged as a distinct and proper philosophical discipline. Philosophical Practice does not act in the commonly valid, but in the individually valid. In a way Philosophical Practice brings to life academic philosophy: Dephlegmatisiren—Vivificiren, as Novalis demands[2].

Due to his wisdom and his knowledge, his powers of distinction and his experience the philosophical practitioner looks for the respective method needed: practitioner and guest of the Philosophical Practice get involved in the situation, in questions and in the act of philosophizing.

Academic philosophy and Philosophical Practice are more of less in a productive discourse. Philosophical Practice requires an academic dealing with philosophy and profits from it, as the philosophical practitioner can fall back on thoroughly edited works, for example. Impulses from the field of Philosophical Practice stimulate academic philosophical research, as is reflected in the steadily increasing number of doctoral theses and publications on Philosophical Practice. In Italy courses in Philosophical Practice has been established at universities and something similar is planned for in Spain.

Let us now turn to the two initial questions concerning the difference between Philosophical Practice and related academic disciplines from the field of human sciences. These are disciplines that look into the human being and its needs; disciplines like psychology, sociology, medicine or cultural anthropology, which at the same time have a therapeutic effect due to psychoanalysts, psychotherapists, medical doctors, and social education workers working in the respective field.

People visiting a Philosophical Practice rarely have found sufficient consolation elsewhere, have been given advice too often, and have gone through several therapies with doctors and psychotherapists. Sufferers who visit a Philosophical Practice are not sick. They suffer neither in a medical nor in a psychological sense. They are suffering from the unknown of their lives. The practitioner and his guest try to engage with this unknown of a concrete, subjective past.

Academic disciplines that are concerned with the human being, are looking for an objectivized distance to their object, the human being. In their quest for the universally applicable and the objective truth, they generalize (often using statistical surveys) and create a human model in a way, which can be treated according to a fixed method following

---

[2] Novalis (1798): Logologische Fragmente I, 15, Novalis Schriften, Zweiter Band, Das philosophische Werk, Ed.: R. Samuel, H.-J. Mähl, G. Schulz, Stuttgart Berlin Köln Mainz (Kohlhammer) 1981, p 526.

a set pattern.

Psychotherapy perceives itself more or less as a verifiable pragmatic science, which develops certain methods of treatment in the various schools, with the help of which those seeking help can be diagnosed and treated. Different schools advocate and specialize in different views of man and cures respectively.

The medical doctor works strictly scientifically. He never doubts his fundamental principle, the scientific method in any way, because otherwise he would be guilty of treating his patient unscientifically and irresponsibly.

The social education worker locates the person according to the guidelines, at first to those of the current state of sociological research, then according to those of the society in which he lives. The individual is seen as part of a social environment and is treated in line with the demands of this social environment.

In academic and non-academic therapeutic disciplines the basic philosophical question for what constitutes physical, mental and spiritual health, what constitutes the well-being and the nature of the human being is silently assumed to be already answered. It may be part of the therapeutic method, like in Logotherapy (Victor Frankl), for example, but it is not, like in Philosophical Practice, a characteristic in itself that leads to a specific method. In Philosophical Practice, the individual seeking help does not get caught in the definition of a specific therapeutic method. This path develops throughout the discourse. For Philosophical Practices the human is more than just a scientific and social matrix. Philosophical Practice neither treats nor advises. In Philosophical Practice two or more people are in a discourse that does not necessarily lead to a solution but at least it gets them further.

Just like the study of psychology is followed by a training program for the person wanting to become a psychotherapist, there should be a training program in form of a specific education (Bildungsgang) for prospective philosophical practitioners after they have finished their degree in philosophy, as it is offered by the German professional association for Philosophical Practice (Berufsverband für Philosophische Praxis). Such a program will train the graduate of academic philosophy to deal with individual real-life case.

3. What, if any, practical and / or social-political obligations follow from understanding philosophy from the point of view of Philosophical Practice?

Primarily, there are, in my experience, two particular practical and social-political aspects of Philosophical Practice that contribute to philosophy: Firstly, it astonishes and also disturbs humans with essential questions in order to broaden their view of themselves and their responsibilities. Secondly, Philosophical Practice is obliged to educate, i.e. to give an understanding of the classical human testimonies.

There are a number of general questions that no one has a definite answer for: Who are we? Who am I? Where do we come from, where are we going? What are we living for? What has been, what will be? Philosophizing is a sceptical, astonished questioning, and Kant has phrased those questions in his lectures on Logic in the following way:

What am I able to know?
What shall I do?
What may I hope for?
What is mankind?[3]

Most people aim to escape boredom because boredom holds the danger of being confronted with these questions, with the unknown world and also the unknown Self. So they bury these questions under their daily routines and their often only ostensible duties. In order to function under the expectations of daily life, humans can make use of their perception and attention, their abilities to feel and understand only in a very restricted way.

The task of philosophy in Philosophical Practice is to make people aware of their sometimes monotonous, sometimes complacent and mechanical routines between their jobs, families and media consumption. Just the way Socrates went to the agora to ask inconvenient questions, philosophy should reach out to the public and ask questions—while being prepared to be challenged itself. And just like Socrates, who perceived himself as an irritatingly biting horse fly, that tried to revive the cititzens of Athens, to wake up and open their eyes, the philosopher as a Philosophical Practitioner should awaken people from their habitual thinking patterns.

When Ortega y Gasset said that God needed philosophers to "think things apart so that the other animals don't fall asleep"[4], he meant that even though philosophers produce a lot of ivory-tower thoughts, it's exactly these thoughts that may awaken the humans from their slumber of habits and not-thinking, and also make them rise their heads above

---

[3] 1) Was kann ich wissen?—2) Was soll ich tun? 3) Was darf ich hoffen? 4) Was ist der Mensch?, Kant's gesammelte Schriften, Band. IX, Ed.: Königlich Preußische Akademie der Wissenschaften, 1. Abt. Werke, Berlin und Leipzig (De Gruyter) 1923, p 25.

[4] Der liebe Gott *braucht* die Zerdenker, damit die übrigen Tiere nicht schlafen. in: Martin Heidegger "Denkerfahrungen 1910 -1976", Ed.: Hermann Heidegger Frankfurt am Main (Klostermann) 1983, p 77f.

their blanket of the image they have of themselves to look at things that they took for granted in a new and questionable light. And sometimes, it is this light that opens up a whole new, unknown world.

To demonstrate the opportunities of such new (surreal, romantic) perspectives, Bunuel and Dali cut open a human eye in their famous movie "Un chien andalou" (1929). While the American post-war Beat Generation (for example Allen Ginsberg) strived to expand consciousness by drug use and meditation, philosophy has always tried to inspire people through questions to experience perception and thinking in a new way.

Certainly, a philosopher's thoughts cannot be used to build a car or a house, but you can ask why and if we need houses or cars or to what extend they concern us and how useful and important they really are.

Of course, humans survive more easily, if they go about their lives purposefully and restrictedly. Once in a while, however, they should stop and lift their eyes, not only because their own path of life should be examined from time to time, but also because at some point, it might be too late to do so; an accident, a stroke of fate, a breakup may force them to reconsider their lives and seek a Philosophical Practice in their distress.

A crisis also holds opportunities and people in distress often notice only then that just beyond the worries of every day life there is a mysterious richness, that we all have a hazy sense of and that we all are longing for. This liveliness and fascinating aspect of the living existence lies in front of us but we do not recognize it. The human being resembles a starving man sitting in front of all kinds of excellent food: He does not reach out his hand because he does not see the feast laid out before him. The world in all of its unfathomable richness is inexhaustible. To quote the German philosopher Nicolai Hartmann, real life is "saturated with values and overflowing. It is full of wonder and glory wherever we grasp it"[5]. It is one of the marvels of human existence, that although we cannot understand the reasons of being, being itself holds and creates joy. A medieval verse quoted by Karl Jaspers in "Ciphers of Transcendence[6], goes as follows:

I come, I do not know where from,

---

[5] Denn die wirkliche Welt ist unerschöpflich an Fülle, das wirkliche Leben ist wertgetränkt und überströmend, und wo wir es fassen, da ist es voller Wunder und Herrlichkeit. Nicolai Hartmann "Ethik", Berlin und Leipzig (De Gruyter) 1926, p 10.

[6] Ich komme, ich weiß nicht woher, ich bin, ich weiß nicht wer, ich sterb', ich weiß nicht wann, ich geh', ich weiß nicht wohin, mich wundert's, dass ich so fröhlich bin. Karl Jaspers (1961) Chiffren der Transzendenz", Ed.: H. Saner, München (Piper) 1977, p 12.

I am, I do not know who,
I will die, I do not know when,
I am surprised that I am so happy.

Taking pleasure in the world is as much part of humans as is their plight, the inscrutability of their existence, their melancholy or depression and perplexity. Philosophical Practice draws from both pools—plight and joy of life, melancholy and inspiration. Both are part of life as the laughing melancholic Demokritos lived it, much to the puzzlement of the Abderites.

It is not only about coming to your senses through inconvenient questions, to see and think in new and different ways and to find an alternative path of life, but it is also about taking life into your own hands, to emancipate yourself from the control of others, not letting yourself being lived but to act and to make your own decisions. It means to become aware of your responsibilities and position in your family and your community.

Guests of a Philosophical Practice should learn to live philosophically and take responsibility for themselves and their environment, not only to open their eyes to their own vital and mental richness but also to the richness and the problems of society and the world that surrounds them.

The philosophy of Philosophical Practice does not simply confront disconcerting and essential questions of the human existence but also gives answers. It is the task of Philosophical Practice to cultivate education and spiritual traditions. We are part of a more than ten-thousand-year-old cultural history that has brought forth an abundance of creative testimonies. Testimonies that—according to their time—tried to answer the elementary questions of humanity.

The shaman culture with its tales and paintings conveys another awareness for the world, another self-concept of being part of this world than we today are able to understand. The stories and testimonies of nomadic and pastoral tribes exist right next to the great tales, epics and dramas that came with settlements and the building of cities.

The essence of Western culture is just as important as that of other great and small cultures. Religions, philosophy, literature, music, arts, theater, our historicity—it is important to learn from all these attempts of describing and defining human existence as much as possible or necessary in order to place ourselves and to recognize that we are not alone in this world, that there have been problems everywhere and throughout the ages.

Dicussing spiritual testimonies of the past and present, e.g. antique tragedies, a sonnet by Shakespeare or a contemporary novel, result in a better understanding of ourselves and of our own spiritual and mental inner life.

It is important to me to introduce these testimonies in my seminars on Philosophical Practice, to take them seriously and to reflect on them in regard to our own lives with its problems and possibilities. It is like a treasure chest waiting to be opened.

4. What do you see as the most interesting criticism against your own position in Philosophical Practice?

When something new emerges, it will only just be generally comprehended and accepted once it has proven itself, once it is established and once the change of perspective and paradigm caused by the novelty has become popular. This process is a characteristic of cultural history and can be observed in the invention of writing, the emergence of philosophising, of the telescope, the steam engine, psychoanalyses or abstract art.

However, before a novelty has gained acceptance, the reaction of most people and mainly of the experts is incomprehension and (often rude and inappropriate) criticism. Only with an increasing acceptance of the novelty the criticism reaches a more knowledgeable level and becomes more constructive. Thus, since the 1980s, the understanding and criticism of Philosophical Practice as well as Philosophical Practice itself have changed and evolved from a complete incomprehension towards an academic and general acceptance, academic philosophy having discovered the schools of late antiquity, publications addressing philosophical ways of life and a philosophical art of living now being common and the various groups and societies dedicated to Philosophical Practice working intensively on the evolution and formation of the cause of Philosophical Practice.

At this point, I would like to quote some of the interesting and prolific criticisms I come across now and then:

Everybody can philosophize. I can think enough on my own.

Philosophers are unworldly theoreticians having no clue about the real everyday life.

Philosophical Practice as a retreat for the individual is unpolitical.

Only an elite minority can afford Philosophical Practice.

There are enough forms of therapy, Philosophical Practice is dispensable.

I am fine, so why would I need education and Philosophical Practice?

All of these general points of criticism and certainly more of them are important to me. Their examination is prolific. Hereafter, I would like to relate two episodes from the early times of my Practice. They illustrate how criticism sounded like in the 1980s and how one can make use of it:

It was not long after I had duly and well legibly attached my sign "Philosophical Practitioner" next to the front door of my practice in Bonner Talweg in the Südstadt district of Bonn. One day, I discovered the following words scribbled on the wall next to the sign: "Is that a joke!?"

Is that, namely philosophy as a practice, supposed to be a joke? Does philosophy in all seriousness want to offer a healing doctrine? Much as I understand the bad reputation philosophy has for being out of touch with reality, something in this sentence made me begin to wonder: Of all the wide variety of healing doctrines, why would philosophy be a joke? If there would have been a sign in front of my practice reading: Mathilda Betters, Teacher for Yoga and Reiki or Life Coaching Using the Forces of the Cosmos or Psychotherapy and Healing with Aroma Therapy, it would have been shrugged off with a certain languidness, but not perceived as a joke.

Philosophy can take credit for being a joke. In a time presenting itself as a succession of cynicism and jokes, which it perceives, if anything, as a depression, in a time like this, anyone coming under the suspicion of taking things seriously and reflecting on them becomes a laughing stock—and a danger.

The blindly bustling, cynical lifestyle is a joke to the philosopher, Demokritos laughs at the Abderites who in turn declare him sick and mad.

In the shape of Philosophical Practice, philosophy is given the opportunity to describe what is ponderosity and earnestness in its full consistency. In doing so, it eventually is no bad joke, but a stand in a world that is a joke itself.

Another incident occurred in front of my practice in Bonn as well:

It is late in the evening. A silent observer standing on the opposite side of the street, I can observe three older students walking past my practice sign, glimpsing at it. They proceed a few steps, then one of them turns around abruptly, walks back followed by his friends, in order to thoroughly study the sign and eventually says in incredulous amazement: "This is for real!"

The sentence: "This is for real!" completes the one quoted above: "Is that a joke!?" It goes even further because for one thing, the exclamation "This is for real!" implies the former ("Is that a joke!?") and for another, it can as well be phrased as: "This has to be a joke, they are for real, this just can't be true."

However, as an incredulous amazement, the sentence: "This is for real!" goes beyond the level of a joke: "This is for real!" also means "Someone is doing serious business here!"

A philosophy which is taking itself seriously will apprehend the human being as an action-competent individual. Such philosophy is Philosophical Practice; its work consists in transforming life into an individual one, into a volitional history and an accepted fate. In the deliberate, knowing conduct of life, philosophy concretises as work, namely the work of Philosophical Practice, proving itself as the life of a philosopher.

The only method of criticising a philosophy that is possible and proves anything at all is, to quote Nietzsche once again, certainly one of the ancestors of Philosophical Practice, to see whether one can live by it[7].

5. With respect to present and future inquiry, how can the most important problems concerning Philosophical Practice be identified and explored?

In the future, particularly three fields and questions will determine the assignment of Philosophical Practice.

1 · How is the Philosophical Practitioner able to start and organize the business and service of Philosophical Practice successfully?

Philosophical Practice as both institution and business has to deal with business management. Every person, who opens up a Philosophical Practice, has a need for this particular knowledge as a free entrepreneur. Philosophers are, as well as Philosophical Practitioners, often no businessmen and often insufficiently competent in financial affairs. Insofar, it will be essential to pay attention to the general conditions of such a business: He has to rent rooms at the right spot and arrange them adequately. He has to set prices and fees for his services. Furthermore, it is necessary to acquire knowledge of bookkeeping and the handling of sale tax, tax deductions and how to write a tax computation.

This knowledge is indispensable, if the Philosophical Practitioner is not able to work cost-covering and carefully regards income and cost economically. Otherwise he risks, regardless of philosophical expertise, closing down his Practice, possibly burdened with debt. This can be avoided, if the Philosophical Practitioner can afford a manager and a tax counselor from the very beginning. Besides financial and operative knowledge, the Philosophical Practitioner should know about the

---

[7] Die einzige Kritik einer Philosophie, die möglich ist und die auch etwas beweist, nämlich zu versuchen, ob man nach ihr leben könne, ist nie auf Universitäten gelehrt worden. Friedrich Nietzsche (1874): "Unzeitgemäße Betrachtungen, Drittes Stück: Schopenhauer als Erzieher. 8", in Sämtliche Werke. Kritische Studienausgabe in 15 Bänden, Ed.: G. Colli, M. Montinari, München Berlin New York (Deutscher Taschenbuch Verlag, De Gruyter) 1980, vol. 1, p 417.

judicial terms and conditions, which are defining and limiting his commitment action as Philosophical Practitioner by law, like laws for health and consulting professions. In addition to that, he has to conclude contracts of lawful binding.

2 · Who is representing the Philosophical Practice and promotes its reputation and interests?

To establish a Philosophical Practice, you need to be knowledgeable about organizational and financial aspects of a business. As a business, Philosophical Practice requires local and superregional publicity. During the last 30 years, the idea of Philosophical Practice as an institution and a place, in which theoretical philosophy has to prove itself in practice, has established itself more and more. The opening of Philosophical Practices has increased at a larger scale, and the Philosophical Practice succeeded to build up and claim a particular position beside other institutions, which offer therapies and help. In this context, Philosophical Practitioners have to care for a consistent and extensive significant value, which will be of importance to distinguish themselves from other similar institutions.

Philosophical Practice is what a Philosopher, a Philosophical Practitioner, is making out of it. Every Philosopher is standing for himself. His personality represents the constitution and the direction of his practice. For the future, however, it will be essential that the different philosophical personalities find a common concept in their way of working as Philosophical Practitioners. This concept should give space to the originality of every single Philosophical Practice as well as the mutual consensus that is connecting them. It seems to be indicated, to develop national and international vested interests and professional associations, which care about this mutual consensus of the manifold background of Philosophical Practice.

Those professional associations should additionally promote for acceptance in the public, for example to acquire grant applications and create assignments and foundations. They have to negotiate with social and health insurance agencies, institutions for professional qualification and specific professional institutions, for example for medical professions, psychologists and teachers. Their task is even to effect a broad acceptance and sponsorship of Philosophical Practice.

3 · How does the Philosophical Practitioner optimize his work both in his own Practice and the Philosophical Practice as field of research?

Next to the requirements of a public funding, the more important task of consolidating the Philosophical Practice throughout the work is with Philosophy itself. Philosophical Practice as institution that wants to accompany people helpfully requires an open, astonished and curious mentality. Philosophical Practice is not the result and ending of a course of studies but a process of constant education and constant research. The Philosophical Practitioner is therefore challenged to question himself again and again about his way to work philosophically and to take seriously the Socratic question pos biotéon—how should we live?

One characteristic trait in Philosophical Practice is freedom, and it will be a future challenge that the Philosophical Practitioner will be free. He has to emancipate from common patterns of thought and appreciation in the way that he'll not be corrupted by prosperity, fame and prestige.

If he wants to stay loyal to the idea about his conduct of life and his philosophy, it might be necessary that the Philosophical Practitioner is forced to get along by working in other professions, temporarily or even permanently. As well as Socrates, Spinoza, and other Philosophers kept their freedom of philosophizing and their philosophical efforts working as stonemason, as glass grinder or shoemaker. "It is better to be a beggar than to be uneducated; the beggar needs money, the uneducated needs humanity (humanitas), as Aristippos from Kyrene, a follower of Socrates underlines the priority of philosophical education[8].

In my opinion, Philosophical Practice is not a service enterprise. And it should not degenerate to an arbitrarily consulting practice for general and specific wisdom about life and world. Philosophical Practice is not a new form of therapy among others; Philosophical Practice is not even a philosophical mentoring but a philosophical event or Ereignis in the Heideggerian sense that is oscillating between the Philosophical Practitioner and his guest.

To consolidate Philosophical Practice as an independent institution it will be the essential topic of those professional associations to create adequate education opportunities to a greater extent which enable those who feel called upon to learn about existentialistic, hermeneutic and phenomenological dimensions in the contact with people and the world. He will be stimulated to cultivate the philosophical-practical virtues as attentiveness, vigilance, astonishment(Staunen), radical questioning,

---

[8] Diogenis Laertii Vitae Philosophorum II, 70, Ed.: H.S. Long, Oxford University Press 1964, p 86.

empathy, serenity (Gelassenheit), constancy, seriousness, and firmness. As the Philosophical Practitioner is confronted with various kinds of people and suffering, it is necessary that he engages in medical, psychological, juridical or just social circumstances to develop adequate understanding for the suffering and the needs of his guests.

In the progress of Philosophical Practice and its establishment in both society and science, it will be fundamental to do permanent research that comprises the preparation of client profiles and describes philosophical proceedings. In addition to that, it is necessary to compile studies about Philosophy and its history, in which the requirements, experiences, and cognitions of Philosophical Practice are regarded.

Global problems like climate change or the ecological crisis, turbo charged capitalism and the financial crisis, starvation and war, people are confronted with in everyday live are only on the surface; people are first of all searching for a personal aim in their life.

It will be prior task of philosophical work in Philosophical Practice to support people as philosophical friends and to understand mutually what is going on in the micro- and macrocosm of everyday life. Philosophical Practice is not able to cure or even salvage human beings or the world itself, but it can help to find a better understanding or a new insight and to reconcile human beings with their own fate.

To conclude: The questions to be discussed in Philosophical Practice are the crucial questions of human existence not to be calmed down or eradicated like a toothache: Philosophical Practice will last.

Bibliography

Fred Gebler: Balinesische Medizin und magische Schriftzeichen in *curare. Zeitschrift für Ethnomedizin und transkulturelle Psychiatrie*, Vol. 4 1981, S.232ff, Ed.: Arbeitsgemeinschaft Ethnomedizin Heidelberg, Wiesbaden 1981

Fred Gebler: Die Gottesvorstellungen in der frühen Theologie Immanuel Kants, Königshausen & Neumann, Würzburg 1990

Fred Gebler: Der Philosoph und sein Haus in *Agora. Zeitschrift für Philosophische Praxis*, 14/15, S.28ff, Ed.: Gesellschaft für Philosophische Praxis, Köln 1993

Fred Gebler: Zehn Voraussetzungen Philosophischer Praxis in *Zeitschrift für Philosophische Praxis*, 1/94, S.37ff, Ed.: Gesellschaft für Philosophische Praxis, Sankt Augustin 1994t

5. Fred Gebler

6

Horst Gronke

Director
Pro argumentis, Berlin

Some years ago, in two medico-ethical research projects of the Institute for Advanced Studies in Vienna on ethical issues of xenotransplantation and genetic counseling several groups of researchers observed and evaluated Socratic dialogues facilitated by my colleagues Beate Littig[1], Paolo Dordoni and me. Prior to these dialogues the participants were asked for their expectations for the following dialogues. Given some advance information on Socratic Dialogue the participants set extremely high hopes for the dialogue, e.g. regarding the understanding of the positions of other dialogue partners, the development of their own communication skills or the experience of a clearly structured discussion.

But there was also great skepticism, and even hopelessness among the participants. Even if the dialogues had been very successful, or if the dialogues would have been the best dialogues they had ever experienced in their lives, this would not lead to substantial changes of their minds. And they also thought it would be impossible to reach a consensus on the truth of any assertion by reason of common insight. After the socio-political catastrophes especially of the twentieth century, in an era in which, in view of the new intransparency of the world, of the threat of a climate catastrophe, and of their feeling of being exposed to the imperatives of the international finance markets, people look towards the future more with fear than with hope. And what is more, after the half-truths of the skeptical and postmodern theses as God is dead, the subject is dead, the truth is dead have penetrated the lifeworld, one believes that dialogical reasoning is capable of good understanding at most but not of recognizing the truth.

I see my own Philosophical Practice as a struggle against this fatalism, widespread not only in society in general but also, more or less, in

---

[1] B. Littig, Neo-Socratic Dialogue in Practice. The Xenotransplantation and Genetic Counselling Cases, *Philosophical Practice. Journal of the American Philosophical Practitioners Association*. Vol. 5.3, 2010: Special Issue on Socratic Dialogue, 685-97.

the scene of the philosophical practitioners of today. And I do that simply by trying to prove the contrary by using the Socratic way of common thinking that is fundamental to my own Philosophical Practice.

However, in order to achieve this, a renewal of the Socratic approach against Plato, as well as against its common understanding and use in the 20 century, is necessary. I hope to be capable of clarifying convincingly that the New Socratic offers a particularly suitable way for implementing a search for truth in dialogical Philosophical Practice.

And I am very pleased that I can do this in a Socratic way which in this case means answering five questions instead of telling a story.

1. Why was I initially drawn to Philosophical Practice?

I was drawn to Philosophical Practice by certain moments in my life, such as the first time I took part in a Socratic dialogue (with the happy coincidence to have Gustav Heckmann, one of the veterans of Socratic Philosophical Practice, as a conversation partner) and the feeling and awareness this gave me: this is where I belong. But beyond this it is also recurring experiences that keep me in Philosophical Practice.

For example, I am always excited to support people who are not trained philosophers in the practice of concrete philosophizing, in a way of doing philosophy that engages with aspects of their life and working world. When this is successful, I have the feeling of being able to do what originally drove me to study philosophy.

Furthermore, I realize again and again that through independent Philosophical Practice that is oriented towards problems of life and action, I can, in conversation with others, reach ideas and insights that have a particular personal and motivational quality. It is quite possible that this intensity of insights also emerges from working through philosophical texts and discussing them in university seminars (I find false the usual opposition of oral and written, inherited from the dualism of orality and literality that has lasted from Plato through today). But we should remember that Philosophical Practice did not begin with the study of already-existing philosophical texts. And herein lies one problem of current academic philosophy: it is essentially bound to the study of philosophical texts. Reference to concrete experience, possibly even to concrete *personal* experience, is considered unprofessional. And when a philosophical conversation that is oriented towards everyday phenomena does take place, then it is very often within the framework of so-called competence courses focused on key qualifications (in the sense of training philosophers to lead conversations) and not as something unique to philosophy. Or the philosophical activity relates to the real world of experience only in a secondary instance, as applied philosophy, or applied ethics.

Further, my concentration on philosophical conversation reflects my own strengths: generally success for a philosopher or humanities scholar in the academic world is achieved through appealing speeches and lectures, through their ability to present their knowledge. The ability to have a philosophical dialogue about subjects drawn from life plays a more minor role. In contrast to this, as a university lecturer I have viewed leading philosophical dialogues as the primary task of my work. In the end I also found that Philosophical Practice gave me an opportunity to develop my skill at dialogue outside of the academic context.

2. What does my work reveal about Philosophical Practice that other related academic fields typically fail to appreciate?

As I first gathered my thoughts for this essay, I sat in the park near my office. On a construction site at the edge of the park, a bulldozer was working noisily. *Can I form philosophical thoughts in this setting?* Surely it was not the ideal situation for intense reflection, and so a little later I changed my thinking spot. It seems to me that the situation is characteristic for my understanding of Philosophical Practice, however, because Philosophical Practice does not shutter itself against the noise of the world. It does not withdraw into study halls, houses of thought and rural idylls. It is not pure contemplation. It does not just produce theory onto which the real world is later—if at all—transposed.

But this does not mean that Philosophical Practice stands in an antagonistic relationship to contemplative thinking and philosophical theory. I do not share the hostility towards theory, the rejection of academic philosophy that is occasionally to be observed by practitioners of philosophy. I believe that academic philosophical work is essential for the great achievements of philosophical thinking and thus also for a solid and responsible Philosophical Practice.

I call the situation in which Philosophical Practice gains a foothold in lived reality the Socratic situation. I distinguish this from other situations that can be characteristic for philosophy, in particular the Aristotelian and the Platonic situations, which are, in my opinion, less conductive for Philosophical Practice and in a certain sense also for philosophy in general. Both Socrates' student Plato and Plato's student Aristotle moved from the public site of the lived world (the marketplace or the agora), in which Socrates primarily acted, into the schools that they founded, Plato in his academy, Aristotle, who had refused to follow Plato into the academy, into his Lykeion. On the one hand, the foundation of these schools had significant advantages. Plato, for example, made philosophy teachable. He gave it systematic form and laid the foundation for the development of philosophy as a discipline. Aristotle continued this work by establishing differentiations within philosophy, by making a distinction, for example, between theoretical philosophy, which is concerned with the eternal and unchangeable, and practical philosophy, which is concerned with changeable actions.

On the other hand, Plato and Aristotle set problematic courses, which continue to shape the understanding of reason, thinking and language in a one-sided manner. The most influential course was set place by Plato when he declared that dialectical thinking in dialogue was only an early stage of true knowledge of ideas. According to Plato, the philosopher perceives the ideas that make truth and existence possible through principally solitary looking. Dialectics is merely the stony path towards becoming capable of looking at ideas. This is how philosophical theory (Greek theorein = to look) came into being. Even today, thinking is generally spoken of as looking at an object to be known (= in-sight). Accordingly, in analytical philosophy sentences are written on the chalkboard or on paper and are analyzed as if language was originally something to look at. And many participants in philosophical conversations believe that they arrive at a deeper insight through dialogue, that this insight itself is however not part of the dialogue, but rather simply came into being in their minds through the flash of the light of knowledge (of a spark, Plato says), and is thus personal and may not be communicable through language to others or even to oneself.

This view has consequences for the relationship between theory and practice. In Plato's Republic, for example, the philosopher knows through looking (theoria) with the inner eye of his mind at the idea of the just state. And then he turns to practice, by attempting to first create the state as close as possible to this idea. The philosophical practitioner is here more of a constructor or a craftsman who shapes or creates what he has known or thought before. Speaking of guiding visions that must be realized, as is common today, has much in common with this conception: I have visions—and then I begin working in order to realize them.

Although Aristotle is critical of the Platonic teaching of ideas, he still preserves the idea of knowing as looking, although he reserves it for theoretical philosophy. In the realm of practical philosophy, he emphasizes the social character of human action. On one of Aristotle's greatest achievements was to distinguish this social action, which he calls praxis, from productive action, which he calls poiesis. Aristotle combines this distinction from theoretical philosophy with a reduction of the claim to knowledge in the realm of the practical. Where everything is constantly changing in the social collective, looking cannot lead to exact knowledge. In place of true knowledge comes the differentiated understanding of lived practices, lived values and virtues in an actual community and the training in this practice. The Aristotelian philosophical practitioner, whose sphere of efficacy now solely lies in practical philosophy, is a conservative pragmatist. Criticism of established values and virtues, as the Platonic Socrates was able to carry out because of his orientation towards ideas, is now no longer possible or is only possible to a reduced degree through confronting of established interests, values and virtues with one another.

On the other hand, in Socratic dialogue, both the truth orientation in the realm of everyday action as well as the demand to be accountable in dialogue for one's action and inaction are preserved. Socratic philosophizing refers to the real lived world, reacts to the challenges which emerge from the world of action, tests the principles that guide human action, and supports the demand for harmony between dialogic truth-oriented thinking and social practice.

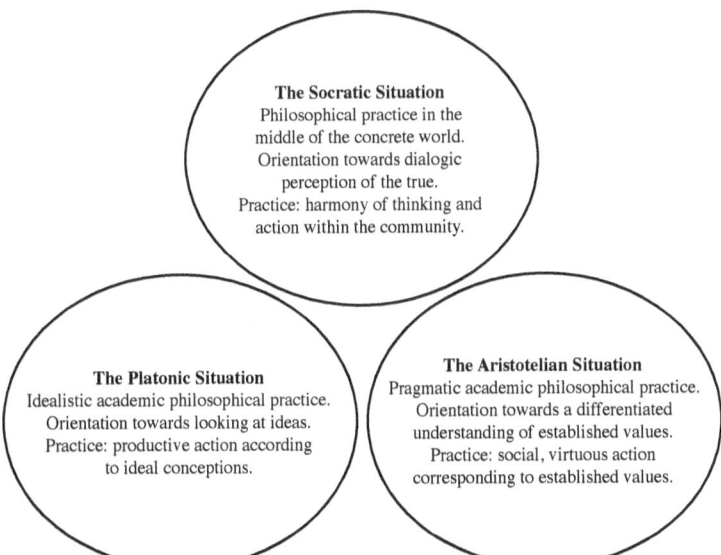

The Socratic Situation
Philosophical practice in the middle of the concrete world.
Orientation towards dialogic perception of the true.
Practice: harmony of thinking and action within the community.

The Platonic Situation
Idealistic academic philosophical practice.
Orientation towards looking at ideas.
Practice: productive action according to ideal conceptions.

The Aristotelian Situation
Pragmatic academic philosophical practice.
Orientation towards a differentiated understanding of established values.
Practice: social, virtuous action corresponding to established values.

The "New Socratic" is an attempt to renew the Socratic perspective on Philosophical Practice, which is oriented towards dialogue and truth under the conditions of the modern world, which is characterized by technology, globalized market economy and a superfluity of information. In a way similar to Chaim Perelman's renewal of ancient rhetoric with the concept of the New Rhetoric, I juxtapose ancient Socratism with the New Socratic.

A characteristic of both the classical Socratic dialogue and the New

Socratic dialogue is the acceptance of and demand for self-responsibility on the part of the dialogue partners. The Socratic dialogue expects *self-determined persons* with *a basic readiness for change*. This is evident in Socrates' conversations, conducted according to the elenctic hypothesis method (checking for contradictions). Socrates asked for the fundamental convictions, the hypotheses, which stood *behind* concrete decisions and aims and which people consider the basis for their present and future life and behaviour. After his dialogue partners had developed their basic convictions, he compared them with their other basic convictions. If there was harmony between the disclosed convictions, they then could be regarded as a safe basis for acting for the time being. In the case of a contradiction it was necessary to further explore the convictions. The characteristic confusion that was caused by Socrates' art of refutation reveals to interlocutors the space for new insights and a change of their acting.

With this, Socrates founded the basic method of truth-oriented Philosophical Practice. It suffers, however, in its interpretation by Plato in precisely the same way that is also characteristic for the initiator of the renewal of the Socratic Method in the twentieth century, Leonard Nelson. Proceeding from the understandable desire to distance itself from the rhetoricians who are only interested in successful persuasion, it devalues the dimension of communication. It is odd: despite the dialogic character of Philosophical Practice, that of the Socratic dialogues of Nelson and his students—from Minna Specht through Gustav Heckmann and a majority of the Socratists who form the German Society of Socratic Facilitators—knowledge is in the final analysis solitary knowledge (in conversation of the soul with itself), or immediate knowledge (Nelson). It emerges from self-observation (Heckmann) rather than from dialogic insight.

The New Socratic understands Philosophical Practice consistently as a conversation of people with each other. Like Socrates, it assumes that Philosophical Practice explains and examines implicite, frequently unarticulated knowledge. But this knowledge is not only individual, but rather—as the discourse ethicists have shown, following Karl-Otto Apel and Jürgen Habermas—also intersubjective. This means: knowledge is only knowledge when it proves to be so in argumentative dialogue of a communication community. The consensus (that is, the consensus of the ultimately unlimited communication community) and not the individual immediate knowledge is the intended idea that regulates the philosophical conversation. Accordingly, the New Socratic is not only characterized by a concrete reference to experience and thinking for oneself, but also through cooperative thinking and through consensus-oriented thinking.

3. What, if any, practical and/or social-political obligations follow from understanding philosophy from the point of view of Philosophical Practice?

Philosophical practice is not something that must be added as a supplement to philosophy. It is not applied philosophy. It is also not merely a part of philosophy. In a certain sense it embodies philosophy in its original form. This is because theory (looking) is not the original form of thought. Thought is a process of action, albeit one that is far from actions that are determined, directly referring to and intervening in the world. This action is reflective, it is oriented in an explanatory way towards the preconditions of our daily action in the world. And this action is dialogic. It can only succeed in cooperative thinking, in intersubjective conversation. Even where thinking takes place as a monologue (something that I am doing in writing this essay), this thinking, if it seeks to be comprehensible and open to critique, must be connected to dialogue with possible other dialogue partners. The requirements for the possibility of dialogue in society proceed from this. Our education system is a long way from meeting this challenge. We need a consistent education in dialogue. It is certainly correct to expand citizen participation in political discussions and decisions, as well as the participation of workers and customers in administrative and economic firms. But all of this will only bring limited results, and will perhaps even be dangerous if the institutions do not open themselves to argumentative dialogue and if people are not educated in argumentative dialogue. Accordingly, Philosophical Practice would also come too late if, as is said of Minerva's owl, it does not begin its flight until twilight, if it is restricted to those people who come into Philosophical Practice with immediate crisis experiences. A dialogic culture of reflection does not come into being through ad hoc conversations. Philosophical reflection should become a constant companion to everyday action. Families, groups, and organizations should make free space for these accompanying conversations. It could become a good model for civilized society if people, groups and organizations regularly took time for Socratic breaks, that is, to clarify foundational questions of their self-understanding in serious dialogue.

To put it in the words of Xavi Hernández, the middle-fielder of FC Barcelona: it is not a question of functioning as a player (as a person) and simply providing corrections for problems, but rather to ask why, that is, the thinking behind the tactics, understanding behind everyday goal-oriented actions.

4. What do I see as the most interesting criticism against my own position in Philosophical Practice?

It is difficult for me to answer this question straightforwardly. It depends on in what respect I could find criticism interesting; for example (1) in the sense that it is characteristic of the postmodern Zeitgeist or for traditional occidental thinking? (2) in the sense that it is not easy to react to this criticism with good arguments? (3) in the sense that it points to possibilities of application and understanding that cannot be covered by my approach to Philosophical Practice? Because I address (1) at other points in this essay, I will concentrate here on (3) and also mention a few counterarguments and counterpoints to (2).

Classically, philosophy distinguishes between the level of validity and justification on the one hand and the level of understanding and significance on the other hand. The New Socratic seeks to connect the two by connecting dialogic understanding with the search for truth. The link between seeking dialogue understanding and seeking truth is its foundation.

In some approaches, this link is not seen as so essential. In them, other aspects are included, not only as supplements, but also—more or less—as replacements. Thus, in some prominent approaches, dialogic understanding is only viewed as an intermediary phase that is replaced by a phase of solitary, completely individual knowledge or through a kind of mystical knowledge that is inaccessible to our linguistic and hence to dialogic thinking. Or the philosophical search for truth is relativized by the fact that it is rooted in the context of rhetoric, in which above all the effects of one's own utterances on the other dialogue partner are emphasized. In the end, orientation towards the truth can be viewed as unproductive or as dangerous and can be replaced by orientation towards understanding. Is—one asks—understanding of oneself and of others not much more significant than the efforts to determine who is right and who is wrong?

What impresses me in these approaches is the satisfaction that can frequently be observed among individual participants or an entire group of participants in this type of Philosophical Practice. The participants feel respected; they feel well understood; and above all they feel relieved from the usual struggle over the truth, which can cause so much inner frustration and irritation. In my participation in these dialogue groups, I have experienced something like a feeling of community or a deeper connection emerging in the participants—and a feeling that the individual perspective is to a degree enriched through having been made comprehensible to others.

The form of Socratic dialogue that was founded in the Netherlands by Jos Kessels and that includes both rhetorical and mystical aspects attempts to bring as many dimensions of understanding as possible into the dialogue through recourse to the trivium of the artes liberales (rhetoric, grammar, and dialectics) and other artes (art, music, etc.). With this, the different abilities of the dialogue partners can be comprehensively addressed. This is certainly a good thing and the success of this method confirms its usefulness for the participants. I fear, however, that the philosophical meaning of Philosophical Practice gets lost here. The participants and presentations that I have experienced so far lead me to doubt whether the characteristic aspect of the Socratic dialogue, the shared argumentative search for true knowledge in reference to fundamental questions, is preserved here and is not superimposed by rhetorical and grammatical (side) effects. Here other narrative, poetic and iconic forms of knowledge are on equal footing with argumentation or are superior to it. What is still philosophical here? In my opinion it is not the practice, which is sometimes not unlike rhetorical and communication training, but rather—undoubtedly—the background conception of a charismatic dialogue expert that guides this dialogue practice. This is not a little, but also not enough philosophizing.

A philosophical background idea is also fundamental to the dialogue approach of Peter Garrett and David Kantor, inspired by David Bohm. What I find truly great about this approach is that it is oriented towards groups, through which the spirit of the dialogue is said to breathe. The trust in a collective's ability to guide itself, a collective which is not already determined one-sidedly by the social imperative, enables a free flow of meaning. And through this it can come to a deep understanding that leaves the usual conventions behind, such as those about values that a concrete community holds. Here I see an important similarity with New Socratic. In both cases, at issue is the binding assumptions *behind* each person's individual assumptions. Thinking in dialogue becomes an open process that is not immediately oriented towards solutions and results. A difference of degree lies in the degree of openness of the process. I have no doubt that the Bohmian understanding of dialogue addresses dimensions that the Socratic dialogue does not reach because of its rather regimented form. But the opposite is also true. The Socratic dialogue is more radical. It does not presume a particular worldview, nor a metaphysics or a system-theoretical concept of the process of development of groups and organizations. In the first place, the participants in a Socratic dialogue remain individuals in a strong sense. They are not subsumed in a collective. They seek the binding element in interaction (inter-subjectivity), not the super-individual (collectiveness). Only in this way is it possible to have a real search for truth and not simply collective understanding, which is often erroneously called truth, e.g. by Heidegger. The Socratic Philosophical Practice ensures that the twoness, the individual within the collective, is preserved.

Marinoff's concept of philosophical consulting approaches the Socratic practice from a different angle. I do regard the proposed consulting process of PEACE (problem—emotions—analysis—contemplation—equilibrium) as extremely promising. Lou Marinoff suggests, however, on the basis of his criticism of the seemingly unending process of psychotherapeutic analysis, that philosophical conversations can lead to the solution of a problem in a short amount of time. I view that as an illusion that is supported by the fact that the philosophical counselor Marinoff (here his charisma plays an important role once again) has a strong influence on the conversation partner.

5. With respect to present and future inquiry, how can the most important problems concerning Philosophical Practice be identified and explored?

One challenge for Philosophical Practice that I see is that it must resist the lure of producing philosophical advice, such as in so-called happiness research or books of wisdom that teach how one should change one's life. This means resisting the corresponding desires of customers seeking orientation from someone to whom they attribute a certain wisdom, who can show them the way. My question, in a somewhat extreme and paradox formulation, is: how can Philosophical Practice be useful and helpful for the lives of individuals without wanting to help and be useful in their current concrete life problems? This conflict is especially inherent in the Socratic situation. Socrates did very often leave dialogue partners who had turned to him with a request for advice in a state of enlightened confusion. Thus it is and will continue to be a problem to convince people, organizations and companies that Philosophical Practice that is far from desires for fulfillment and is associated instead with impositions of an exceptionally concentrated corporate thinking does still represent an important form of understanding. The approaches that are nearer to psychotherapeutic practice than the Socratic conception or that psychologize the Socratic conception (such as in some forms of cognitive behavior therapy) will have an easier time here, because they can more quickly reach an emotional liberation. Similarly, approaches that use reinforced rhetorical structures and advertise their orientation towards results can be attractive to customers who are solution-oriented.

But I find these approaches undesirable in Philosophical Practice. The approaches that are near to psychotherapy, which are, as far as I can see, used by a majority of German and Scandinavian philosophical practitioners, must struggle to clearly distinguish themselves from psychotherapy. They sometimes do this by creating a negative image of psychotherapy. In this image, psychotherapy hem the clients in with a framework of preconceived notions. These philosophical practitioners position the supposed particular degree of consideration and openness of philosophy in contrast to this negative image. In place of psychological conversation, to my mind, they place a philosophical conversation *setting* more than a philosophical conversation *method*. Guests who come in to the Philosophical Practice are supposed to receive the impression of having a particularly open and attentive conversation partner. I also have the impression that here the philosophical conversation is often gilded with the eclectic inclusion of thoughts of existential philosophers from Epicurus to Kierkegaard, Nietzsche and Heidegger, as well as the corresponding literary authors, and—despite all their claims to openness—are steered in a certain direction. These and similarly-minded philosophers are also not infrequently brought in to support the art of living. For me, however, Philosophical Practice is not about engaging the dialogue partner with ideas from the philosophical practitioner's favorite thinkers. Accordingly, what interests me about Socrates is not everything that he thought about, but rather only the model that he gave us for dialogue that is bound to life practice and to truth.

Bibliography

R. Zimmer, H. Gronke, B. Hüsing, *Evaluation of the Neo-Socratic Dialogues in Germany: Increasing Public Involvement in Debates on Ethical Questions of Xenotransplantation*. Karlsruhe: Fraunhofer ISI, 2003 (ISI-B-52-03)

H. Gronke, L. Sparnaay, Feelings in a Socratic Dialogue on Feelings. *H. Mason; P. Shipley (ed.): Ethics and Socratic Dialogue in Civic Society*. London; Münster: Lit, 2004, 169-178.

H. Gronke, First Things First! Analytic and Strategic Elements in Socratic Dialogue. In: *D. Krohn u. J. P. Brune (ed.): Socratic Dialogue and Ethics*. London, Münster: Lit, 2005, 160-186.

H. Gronke, J. Häußner, Socratic Coaching in Business and Management Consulting Practice. In: *Practical Philosophy.—Journal of the Society for Philosophy in Practice* 8, 2006, 28-38.

J.P. Brune, H. Gronke, D. Krohn, *The Challenge of Dialogue. Socratic Dialogue and Other Forms of Dialogue in Different Political Systems and Cultures*, London, Münster, Lit, 2010.

H. Gronke, The different use of Socratic method in therapeutical and philosophical dialogue. In: J. P. Brune u.a. (eds.), *The Challenge of*

Dialogue. Münster: Lit, 2010, 41-54.

J.P. Brune, H. Gronke, Ten years of Socratic Dialogue in Prisons. Its Scope and Limits. In: *Philosophical Practice. Journal of the American Philosophical Practitioners Association*. Vol. 5.3, 2010: Special Issue on Socratic Dialogue, 674-684.

7

Finn Thorbjørn Hansen

Philosophical Practitioner and Professor in Applied Philosophy, Centre for Dialogue and Organization at the University of Aalborg, Denmark

---

1. Why were you initially drawn to Philosophical Practice?

Probably because of my lived experience along with the pedagogical and cultural atmosphere of what we in Denmark call a Grundtvigan Danish *Folkehøjskole*. I think I was around 19 years old and had just finished my college's years when I decided to sign up for one of these special kind of residential colleges where young people from 18-25 years have an opportunity to take a 'thinking pit stop' in their life and educational career.

I especially remember one day in the beginning of the term when all students were invited by the principal (who later became the Danish Minister of Culture for a period) to come and listen to a speech she wanted to give on the life and literature of the Russian novelist Dostojevskij. We were around 100 students who really did not have a clue of who this guy was and to be honest quite a few of us arrived with an impatient attitude of boredom. But, as I remember it today, her obvious heartfelt engagement and inspired and vivid talk about Dostojevskij's life, novels and life view grabbed me profoundly. It opened my eyes and heart for a whole new world, a world of great literature, beauty and wisdom, which seems to shine from these books and stories. I do not think that I really understood the depth of her engaging speech and the dialogue that later followed in her home in front of a fireplace where we were about 15 who had taken her offer to continue the talk after the speech. But the whole atmosphere of the dialogue and love she expressed for his thinking made a great and lifelong impression on me. And I also remember the philosophizing we did together that evening on what Dostojetsky's polyphonic writing was aiming for and what kind of Truth understanding that may follow such a polyphonic writing. I really took in the idea that his greatness as a writer was his ability to touch upon and evoke in the reader deep fundamental and existential and philosophical *questions*. This he did through poetic and literary means without giving us or pointing at *one* truth, *one* answer, but at many very different human voices and answers which all seem equally true or trustworthy and yet, after having read the novel we as readers were *not* left at the edge of a nihilistic and relativistic abyss but rather in an open realm of hope and wonder and a new listening to our own lives and common world as such. This is a way of thinking and indirect communication that I, by the way, later learned also is at play in the writings and thinking of the Danish philosopher Søren Kierkegaard.

This anecdote may also be a kind of similitude [*sindbillede*] for the whole culture or spirit, which pervades the Danish *Folkehøjskole* when it is at its best. After my university studies in philosophy and the history of ideas, and before I became a Professor at the university and a trainer of Philosophical Practice, I had the fortune to become a teacher at such a residential college. Here I learned that to teach at a *Folkehøjskole* is not only a matter of teaching *in* a subject but *with* a subject. Teaching *with* a subject means that the teaching should also give room and point beyond the narrow discipline and syllabus of the subject in order to let the subject be seen in a broader cultural, existential and political context, and through a reflection and dialogue about how this subject may also help us to *live* a more wise, beautiful and democratic life.

These schools for self-cultivation (*Bildung*), democratic citizenship and cultural leisure are a unique Danish educational and cultural invention. They have, since 1844, had a profound historical influence on the development of the Danish educational system and thinking and Danish culture as such. Today there are around 80 different kinds of *Folkehøjskoler*. They are all supported by the Danish government in order to make it affordably for everyone to chose such a break, or 'breath of spiritual or cultural air', in life.

Let me dwell a little bit more on the life on and purpose of such a *Folkehøjskole* because I want to show that *doing* Philosophical Practice has, or can have, a clear analogy to the educational ideas and practices of the *Folkehøjskole*. Or let me say it in another way: To philosophize in Philosophical Practice is not so much a question of knowing a fair number of great philosophers and being skilful in different philosophical methods and ways of analytical reflections. In fact having too much academic knowledge (*episteme*) about philosophy and too much focusing on and skilfulness in philosophical methods (*techne*) may stand in the way of the philosophical practitioner to reach a musicality for the important Being dimension that give him or her an entrance to the practical and existential wisdom (*phronesis* and *sophia*) of Philosophical Practice.

As Kierkegaard once wrote in his diary:

7. Finn Thorbjørn Hansen

"How true and how Socratic was this Socratic principle: to understand, truly to understand, is to be. For us more ordinary men this divides and becomes twofold: it is one thing to understand and another thing to be. Socrates is so elevated that he does away with this distinction."[1]

So Philosophical Practice has much more to do with a special way of being-in-the-world, a wondrous open and listening way where you— as a philosophical practitioner—also put your own life and life view at risk and at play in the dialogue with your visitor or '*philosophical companion*' as I prefer to call the guest in the Philosophical Practice.

Or said with the insight of a Danish Poet, Paul la Cour: *To be a Poet is not to make a Poem, but to create a new Way of Living*. And similar: To be a philosophical practitioner is not to have a reflection and dialogue with another person *over* and *about* this person's life and life view, but to create a new opening and becoming-into-life through what I call a *Community of Wonder*. In this community of wonder both the philosophical practitioner and philosophical companion participate on equal terms because no one can—and especially not a philosopher!—be an expert on what the good and wise life is. Here we meet as human beings in equal and shared ignorance, wonder, longing and vulnerability.

But what does that mean in practice? How do we get a sense of it? How do we train people in such a wisdom-seeking practice? How do we see Philosophical Practice as a life form or way of being and a community of wonder rather than as an academic discipline and theoretical discourse applied on practice or as a therapeutic treatment?

I think I got a sense of that through my living experiences at the Danish *Folkehøjskole*.

The overall purpose of a *Folkehøjskole* is not just to teach in specific subjects or acquire some useful competencies or solve some special professional or personal problems or only to follow some subjective interests or issues. It is to be—as the original founder of the Danish *Folkehøjskole* tradition, the Danish poet, theologian and philosopher N.S.F. Grundtvig (1783—1872) would say—a School *for* Life, or to be more precise 'a School for the Wonders of Life.

Folkehøjskole is therefore a school, which in many respects give us resemblance to the old Greek understanding of the word *scholè*. As we

---

[1] (JP, 4: 4301) *Søren Kierkegaard's Journals and Papers*. Seven volumes, edited and translated by Howard V. and Edna H. Hong, assisted by G. Malantschuk. Indiana University Press, Bloomington and London. (1) 1967, (2) 1970, (3&4) 1974, 5-7) 1978.

know *scholè* originally meant a 'free space' for contemplation and for having cultural leisure time away from the often too bustling, too utilitarian and too calculated working life.

Indeed Grundtvig was very eager for the *Folkehøjskole* to create candidates who had a strong whish to engage *in* society and ordinary life as well as working life by becoming active democratic and visionary citizens.

But he encourage them to do so only if they, so to speak, did it with their hearts and from an experience of a deeper sense of meaning and personal call in life.

Not necessarily from a religious point of view (that might be, but the *Folkehøjskole* should not like a church, he warned us, be a place for preaching!) but from a deeper longing and love for what we long for and experience as being beautiful, true, wise and good in human life.

To direct the students towards these more existential and life philosophical issue and areas of life should not, he said, be done by giving philosophical or political or scientific answers to the grand questions. On the contrary, what the teacher should do, though, was to create a cheerful, playful, experimental and wondrous atmosphere through what he named 'the Living Word' and 'the Living Conversation'.

What should distinguish a good *Folkehøjskole* teacher from an academic teacher is his or her obvious *love* and passion for the subject *and* his or her ability to transmit this love and knowledge or skills in a personal and vivid way to other persons so that common people will also be able to acquire this knowledge or skills and participate in the dialogue.

Thus these schools are free to teach in what ever they want and in the way they want as long as they make it possible for the young adults to comprehend it, and as long as the subjects being taught also are put into a more broadly and wisdom-seeking perspective. 'What might be the deeper meaning of doing for instance drama or economy?' 'Who and where are you in all these reflections, knowledge, skills and actions; where and what is *your* voice?' And 'How can we together create a better world by learning this subject, and what really is a good life and a 'better world'?'

Another feature of the *Folkehøjskole*, which in fact I experience as a positive shock when I started as a student on the *Folkehøjskole,* is that there are no exams!

This fact creates a very special and free and creative educational atmosphere for both the students and the teachers. The only obligation the student and the teacher have is to spend their time on something, which really matters to them in a heartfelt way.

The Danish translation of the verb 'to *teach'* is '*at undervise*', and the Danish word '*under*' can be translated to 'wonder', of having or seeing a 'wonder'(in German: *Wunder*) like a unexpected miracle or breath-taking and beautiful experience. And the Danish word '*vise*' can be translated 'to show'. So one could say that the Danish word for teaching in fact means 'to show the wonder in and of life'.

Not all Danish teachers in the modern ordinary educational system and not all educational researchers will of course agree on this or use this translation. Instead they will just translate the word *undervise* as *teaching* or to *educate*. But at a Danish *Folkehøjskole* the translation 'to show the wonder in and of life' would in fact be a very precise description of what the overall purpose of the teaching and dialogue is all about at a *Folkehøjskole*.

With one important addition, though, that to teach at a *Folkehøjskole* is not only to teach in and with a subject in order to point to the deep wonder in and of life and the enigmatic feature of human life but also to point to the passion and love we have for life as such. Because without that love we would, Grundtvig claims, not be able to reach and get into a wise relation to and understanding of ourselves, the other or the world. As he wrote in a song verse: *"And He has never Lived/ who Wise became/ on Things he didn't Love."*[2]

So one of the main pedagogical principles in teaching at a Danish *Folkehøjskole* is first to 'enliven' the students before you try to enlighten them by your knowledge. And this is typical done by the teacher, when he or she starts the teaching (or better the living dialogue and word) with a song, a poem, a story or a personal lived experience, which authentically have made an impression on the teacher.

So the teacher is asked to be much more personally involved and be willing to open up as a human being than what is the normal custom in academic or educational settings and cultures. But note that if the teacher becomes too personal or too occupied with the personal dimension of the students in a *therapeutic* and too *psychological* sense then we have left the sound ground of the *Folkehøjskole*'s living and wondrous and egalitarian conversation.

And this goes too for the teacher if he or she talks about great life issues and questions in a too *preaching*, *dogmatic*, *asserting*, *knowing* or *professional* way!

As I said you cannot be a 'professional' and have a professional approach when turning towards the great existential questions and issues in life. But you can meet these in an I-Thou-relation, in what I earlier called a community of wonder.

---

[2] Grundtvig, 1834, from the song *Nu skal det åbenbares*, vers 5, song number 88a in *Højskolesangbogen*, Foreningen for Folkehøjskoler i Danmark, Copenhagen, 2006 (my translation).

The Danish philosopher Søren Kierkegaard was a young man when Grundtvig talked about *Life Enlightenment* and *Folkehøjskoler* as oppose to the rational and academic school of Enlightenment. But Kierkegaard's thoughts on love, existential reflection and indirect communication also, indeed, turned out to make a great impact on the way the modern *Folkehøjskoler* understand themselves and how they teach today.

Note also that the Austrian philosopher Martin Buber was very influenced by the educational thinking of Grundtvig and the Folkehøjskole tradition, when he talked about his view on education.

2. What does your work reveal about Philosophical Practice that other related academic fields typically fail to appreciate?

As you now can imagine my later work as a trainer and practitioner of Philosophical Counseling and Socratic Dialogue Groups (Hansen, 2000) and as an educational researcher, Associate Professor and philosopher of education at University of Aarhus, has all been very influenced by my compassion for the Danish *Folkehøjskole* and my former experiences as a *Folkehøjskole* student and teacher.

My doctoral dissertation *Det filosofiske liv—et dannelsesideal for eksistenspædagogikken* [The Philosophical Life—an Educational Ideal for Existential Pedagogy], which was published as a book in 2002 (Hansen, 2002), was the first doctoral dissertation in the Nordic countries that describes and discusses Philosophical Practice and especially the tradition of Philosophical Counseling in the perspective of adult education and especially in the context of existential oriented adult learning theory and practice.

In the book I reflect on thoughts of Late Foucault and Pierre Hadot and their ideas of living a Philosophical Life and a life with Ethical Self-Care and philosophical practices understood as spiritual exercises in the art of living.

I also discuss the educational ideals of the American and postmodern philosopher Richard Rorty when he talks about '*the liberal Ironist*' and of a radical *self-creation*. I continue on to compare his educational thoughts critically to Søren Kierkegaard's educational ideal of *the existential Humourist* and his view on Socrates *as* a humourist and as a 'border existence' between the Divine and human life, the universal and particular, the Eternity and Temporal or contingency and the metaphysical.

What distinguishes the Kierkegaardian Humourist from the Ironist is his ability to see the Grand and eternal *in* the small and temporal things of life, and at the same time see the small and (warm hearted) comic in the human attempt to create grand theories about and a firm grip on existential moments and phenomena of life through rigid definitions and pompous systems and methods of logical arguments and analysis.

So there is in the worldview of the Kierkegaard's Humourist a fundamental trust in life and an experience of a profound beauty, joy and meaningfulness in life (what Kierkegaard called 'the lyrical'), and at the same time a humble acknowledgement and reflection on the finitude of our ability to grasp, control, know and state something systematic or scientific about this ontological Being dimension and experience of meaningfulness. A dimension which Kierkegaard said we could only get in contact and dialogue with through a Socratic not-knowing, or as he claims, what Socrates did was to *grasp the infinite in the form of ignorance* [At fatte Uendeligheden i Uvidenhedens Form][3] or in other words: through a fundamental wonder (*thaumazein*).

Kierkegaard gives a good expression of the attitude of the existential Humourist alias Socrates when he writes in *Concluding Unscientific Postscript*: *"The actually existing subjective thinker, thinking, continually reproduces this in his existence and invests all his thinking in becoming. This is similar to having style. Only he really has style who is never finished with something but "stirs the waters of language" whenever he begins, so that to him the most ordinary expression comes into existence with newborn originality."*[4]

Kierkegaard also writes that whereas the Ironist is egocentric and aristocratic in his haughty better knowing attitude towards life and the grand questions, believing that *he*—in contrast to the others—*knows* that there are really no deeper meaning in life but only the meanings we construct by ourselves—the Humourist, Kierkegaard says, is *lyrical*. He has a deep sense of the meaningfulness and beauty in life, which he discovers or receives when engaging *in* life.

But he—the lyrical Humourist—also has such a great respect and love for this unspeakable meaningfulness that he will be careful not to step over the border between the contingence and metaphysics in order—as a "Metaphysician" would do—to give names to the nameless. Or rather, he will be aware of the danger of this possibility and pitfall when talking about the existential phenomena and questions in a too firm and knowing and lecturing attitude and language. In fact, if he meet such a lecturing approach to the grand questions he would probably come up with a comment or expression that will—in a friendly and warm hearted way—get the lecturing and too knowing person to

---

[3] Kierkegaard, S. (1992 [1846], p. 84) in *Concluding Unscientific Postscript*, Princeton University Press (trans. Howard and Edna Hong).

[4] Ibid., p. 86.

laugh at himself—that is, help him to see with a self-ironical twinkle in the eye that *maybe* Life is a bit more grand and mysterious than his clear assertions and impressing statements and arguments can ever capture.

The Kierkegaardian Humourist therefore also has a special partiality and respect for the arts and poetry because the artist or the poet seem to have a peculiar ability (or divine gift?) to sing out or show what cannot be said in direct proportional knowledge and clear analytical concepts and thoughts and statements.

I made the Kierkegaardian Humourist my philosophical stand in my doctoral dissertation and ask how we can live a philosophical life in this Socratic way, and how we can bring this educational (*Bildung*) ideal of the Humourist into adult learning theory and practices and higher education research as such.

So this is probably my first answer to the question: 'What does your work reveal about Philosophical Practice that other related academic fields typically fail to appreciate?'

By taking this philosophical stand I bring into the discussion of Philosophical Practice a very critical view on Philosophical Practice *if* it is only perceived and understood as a way to practice individualized 'self-creation' or described as a new alternative to psychological and psychotherapeutic practice.

This was in fact the reason why I decided to make the overall theme of the 7 International Conference on Philosophical Practice in Copenhagen: Philosophical Practice—A Question of Bildung? This was a conference I organized in 2004.

Philosophical Practice is, in my view, misunderstood and moved from its natural environment, or life form, if it is put into the therapeutic as well as self-developmental (life coaching) approaches and practices. As Martin Buber made clear in his conversations with the American psychologist Carl Rogers there is a fundamental difference between the therapeutic and helping relation on the one side, and the I-Thou-relation on the other side. So if we make Philosophical Practice into a helping and therapeutic endeavor we cannot get into a truly equal community of wonder.

In the same way as we can experience and understand a music concert or a walk in the mountains or a painting course as value in itself and not as a (therapeutic or self-realization) means for something else, in my opinion, we can and should also see Philosophical Practice as a value in itself. Of course Philosophical Practice might have therapeutic *side effects* or help us also with some possible personal problems on a more psychological level, but that is and should not really be the main issue in Philosophical Practice!

The only purpose of the Philosophical Practice is to philosophize in a way that will nurture our deep longing and love for wisdom and the joy and challenge of being in a Socratic dialogue and community of wonder about a subject matter (*die Sache*), which have caught our love and attention. As Gadamer[5] has indicated many times, it is only when we leave our willful and intentional wishes to control and construct our world and ourselves that we will be able to get into a deeper ontological connection and dialogue and relation with the world and the other. Gadamer insisted to call the process and *praxis* of being in a dialogue about a subject matter (*die Sache*) for a *Bildung* process. Here we are not leading the dialogue but the dialogue is leading us. A *Bildung* process (self-edification or liberal education or cultivation) is not to be confused with the psychological-loaded and social constructivistic concepts of self-realization, self-development or self-creation. So, in other words: if the practice of *philo-sophia* is used as a tool for something else Philosophical Practice vanishes.

And if Philosophical Practice is understood and practiced as basically a form of Applied Philosophy it is also a sign of reduction or decay. Philosophical Practice in the Socratic sense points to a deeper existential and ontological level beyond what the theoretical and applied philosopher would be able to see with his or her cognitive oriented reflections and clear philosophical concepts, arguments and methods. He or she is namely only occupied in using philosophical theory *about* life and the subject matter and apply these theories *on* practice and the life of the visitor.

What the philosophical practitioner however is engaged in is the *lived philosophy*—or better 'the living poetics'—of the philosophical companion and what emerges of thoughts, impressions and wonderments during their dialogue and shared questioning. The living poetics and emerging wonder can be seen as an expression of the felt and lived worldview that is tacitly embodied in the life form of the philosophical companion's ordinary life and actions and reflections, and which in the Philosophical Practice is now meet and questioned trough the philosophical practitioner's friendly and playful philosophizing *from* his or her impression of the interlocutor's worldview and the philosophical assumptions which is taken for granted there.

My academic and educational research on Philosophical Practice also reveals that Philosophical Practice is neither just another version of Donald Schön's 'reflective practitioner' who, as we know, has learned to focus on the 'reflection-*in*-action' and 'knowledge-*in*-action'. Nor is it

---

[5] Gadamer, H.-G. (1989). *Truth and Method*. Continuum, London and see also his later writings in *The Gadamer Reader*, ed. By Richard Palmer, Northwestern University Press, Evanston, Illinois. (2007)

to be compared with the situated learning theory and '*practice communities*' of Lave & Wenger.

As I developed my humoristic-philosophical position now with reference to Hannah Arendt and Hans-Georg Gadamer (Hansen, 2008) I underline the important difference between the Humourist '*meaning-receiving-paradigm*' on the one hand and the '*meaning-making-paradigm*' on the other, where the later is at play both in the Sartrean existentialistic psychotherapy and psychology as well as in the social constructivistic learning theory by Schön and Lave & Wenger.

When we think from the position of the 'reflective practitioner' and 'practice community' we are still in the realm of '*practice epistemology*'. Here the professionals are installed in the work situation in basically a *functional* presence and attitude. They are there to solve problems and to function as effective and skilful as possible.

But you can of course also be in a work situation in another way. You could ask more existentially who and where you are in all your skilful and knowledgeable reflections and professional actions. Then you become present in a more existential way *in* the situation or relation, which may open your ear for the call of the situation or relation.

As elaborated on in my later works on Philosophical Practice (Hansen, 2005, 2007a, b, 2008, 2009a, b, 2010) I believe that the existential calling *from* the situation or relation has a lot to do with the ability to think and act with *phronesis*, that is with practical wisdom.

In comparison with the 'practice epistemology' of Schön and Lave & Wenger and their successors I describe my position as a '*praxis ontological* approach' because we here see the activity and actions we do not as just means to something else (an instrumental *practice*) but as a value in itself (an existential *praxis*). And in this *praxis* we must learn to trust in life and be led by, what in the moment is *calling* us to do in the situation or relation. This is the ontological Being dimension where, as Gadamer has shown us, understanding or a dialogue happens *to* us. We are, so to speak, in these moments *taken* by the thinking or dialogue, we are embedded in.

Now, talking in this way about Philosophical Practice as an ontological *praxis* and *event* can unfortunately also too easily get us on another dubious sidetrack away from what is, at least in my opinion, essential when philosophizing in Philosophical Practice.

Just as I see tendencies in the movement of Philosophical Practice to become more therapeutic (when it is seen as an new alternative to psychotherapy), or too academic and cognitive (when it is practiced as an Applied Philosophy) or too instrumental (when it is used to solve problems in business life)—I also see tendencies where Philosophical Practice is transformed into a contemplative and spiritual practice, where it is very difficult to differ from religious practices or New Age meditative practices.

This happens, in my experience, when the philosophical practitioner—though in subtle ways—in tone, attitude and thinking becomes a 'knowing person', that is a person who *knows* which way to go if we want to become wise.

They can for example talk about the importance for the philosophical practitioner to listen to 'The Voices of Life" and more or less understand philosophical practices as a contemplative and spiritual exercise in being able to express these 'Voices of Life'.

But to take this task upon you is—to say it maybe too boldly—the business of the Guru, the Shaman, the holy person or in a way also the poet and artist who also can be said to transcend themselves in order to become a medium for 'The Voices of Life" or what ever they want to name these metaphysical or spiritual voices.

I am of the conviction that a philosopher in the tradition of *philosophia* is *not* a wise person. He or she is only a lover of wisdom, and that to philosophize is not the same as to be a medium for the Voices of Being or Life.

The philosophical practitioner should indeed have the musicality, sensibility and receptiveness to hear these voices, but then to step into character *as* a *philo-sopher* by giving a personal response to these voices or Call of Being. I agree with the French philosopher Gabriel Marcel when he writes in the article 'What can be expected of Philosophy?' (1973): *I think that philosophy, regarded in its essential finality, has to be considered as a personal response to a call.*[6] So, to philosophize is not to be a medium for the Calling of Being, but rather to reflect back and give a personal response to this calling, that is asking who and where am I in experiencing and listening to these overwhelming impressions and voices from life as such? One could also say—which I have elaborated further on in my latest article (Hansen, 2012)—that the Socratic midwifery (*maieutic*) and community of wonder is a precondition and way to deliver the I-response in dialogue with or relation to the Thou.[7]

---

[6] Marcel, G. (1973). *Tragic Wisdom and Beyond*. Northwestern University Press, Evanston, p. 3.

[7] Buber, M. (1923). *Ich und Du*. Leipzig, Insel-Verlag. (English translation by Kaufmann, *I and Thou*, Touchstone edition, 1996).

3. **What, if any, practical and/or social-political obligations follow from understanding philosophy from the point of view of Philosophical Practice?**

As chairman for the Danish Association of Philosophical Practice from 2002-2010 and and as a teacher and counselor for nurses, designers, college professors, social workers, consultants, career counselors, ministers, philosophers and psychologists in philosophical practices, I have always made a strong emphasis on the special attitudes, virtues and ways of being that seem—in practice—to foster a Socratic dialogue and community of wonder.

When I began my teaching and instruction courses in *Philosophical Practice and Practical Knowledge in Professional Education and Work* at my university nearly seven years ago, I started with a stronger focus on the teaching of Philosophical Practice theory and different methods and skills. But soon I discovered that this was not a good way to go, because it made me and the practitioners look too much in the direction of the epistemological and technical dimension of Philosophical Practice. They became more philosophical *technicians* than learning the art of Philosophical Practice, where the philosophical practitioner—like a jazz musician—improvise and play, that is, where you think *from* the moment of wonder in order to transcend the current philosophical knowledge, techniques and community of practice, that you until now has been socialized into when learning the philosophical handcraft.

When asked what practical and/or social-political obligations may follow from understanding philosophy from the point of view of Philosophical Practice I think I have already indicated that. I have talked about the change in the understanding of philosophy—from theoretical and applied philosophy to a kind of Socratic or maieutic philosophizing where we, so to speak, learn to think from *the inside* of a word.

The Philosophical Practitioner shows us how we—whether we are professional philosophers or not—can learn to 'stand-in-the-open' in a fundamental state of wonder if we are: a) lead my a *lyrical impulse* (listening to the call of the lived experience—what has really made an impression on me?) and b) by a *Socratic impulse* where we question the philosophical assumptions and worldview we seem to take for granted in this evocative and lived experience and share that wonder in a dialectical dialogue with other persons in a living conversation.

This brings me to a controversial point of view, namely that being a professional philosopher, that is, having a degree in philosophy from a university, might not be any guaranty or necessary precondition for becoming a good philosophical practitioner!

As Hannah Arendt writes:

"The question, when asked by the professional [philosopher], does not arise of his own experiences while engaging in thinking. It is asked from outside—whether that outside is constituted by his professional interests as a thinker or by common sense in himself that makes him question an activity that is out of order in ordinary living."[8]

What we do in Philosophical Practice is to ask question from inside. Not in a therapeutic or psychological introspective way! On the contrary. We ask from a *phenomenological* 'in-seeing'[9] from within the phenomena of life (*die Sache*). And then—this is the Socratic and *hermeneutic* movement—to ask critical and wondrous questions which can help us articulate a personal response to the call of the lived experience, which had made such an impression on us and which now wants to be expressed through a wondrous voice and living dialogue.

If I as a trainer in Philosophical Practice meet a young philosopher who has just received his master- or PhD-degree in philosophy and an older but experienced nurse who has been working with people for many years and have experienced suffering, hope, consolation, joy, grief, love and other important existential phenomena of life in *real time* situations—I would have a tendency to think that the experienced nurse (with her although tacit *phronesis*) has from the start a greater potentiality to become a good philosophical practitioner than the very theoretical clever and philosophical skilful young newly educated philosopher.

The first has a load of tacit practical wisdom (*phronesis*) that only lacks a philosophical and wondrous language and dialogical form to be redeemed.

The other has a load of theoretical (*episteme*) and methodological (*techne*) knowledge but this knowledge and these skills can so easily get him to only reflect from the outside, as Arendt noticed.

So I believe that the good philosophical practitioner need not neces-

---

[8] Arendt, H. (1978). *Life of the Mind.* Hartcourt, Inc., New York, p. 166.

[9] The concept of phenomenological 'in-seeing' has close affinity to what the German poet Rainer Maria Rilke describes in a letter to Bevenuta in this way: *If I were to tell you my greatest feeling, my universal feeling, the bliss of my earthly existence has been, I would have to confess; it has always, here and there, been in this kind of in-seeing, in the indescribably swift, deep, timeless moments of this divine seeing into the heart of things.* Rilke, R.M. (1987). *Rilke and Bevenuta: An intimate correspondence.* New York: Fromm International,(p. 17) and qouted by the Canadian phenomenologist Max van Manen, Phenomenology of Practice, *Phenomenology & Practice*, Vol. 1 (2007), p. 11.

sarily be a professional philosopher but can indeed also be a nurse, a social worker, a career consultants, etc. *if* they: a) have been through a profound training in practices in community of wonder and Socratic dialogues, and b) have acquired some kind of relevant philosophical insight, knowledge and skills that can help them redeem or deliver their phronetic insights and judgement and also help them in seeing and questioning critically and wondrously the basic assumptions which they and others seem to take for granted in the lived experiences as well as philosophical and logical argumentations, they have. Some kind of philosophical background is of course a precondition for becoming a philosophical practitioner.

But philosophical ideas are not only reserved to philosophical books and text! As I experienced at the Danish *Folkehøjskole* such deep philosophical ideas can also be found in the Great Literature or in the whole culture or way of life at a school. And it can certainly also be found in the living dialogues and questions and wonderments that constantly emerge in daily life, right in the *Agora*, in the midst among common people and in a common language. It is my practical experiences that this typically happens when people are acting out from what I have provisionally listed as the *Seventh Socratic Virtues*. That is: 1) that people asked from an open and longing heart (the Socratic Eros dimension of the Philosophical Practice), 2) learn to let silence be their third interlocutor in their dialogue with another, 3) experience and express an ontological humbleness and vulnerability and reluctance when dealing with the grand words and theories, 4) become playful and humorous in the Kierkegaardian sense that I earlier talked about, 5) have the courage to stand-in-the-open and dare to talk and act from and also question what he or she find is the most important things in life, 6) have self-discipline to live a Philosophical Life, that is, having also a respect for the skillfulness and tradition of the great thinkers and artists and to try and *live* the philosophy and questions that one values mostly and 7) knowing— like Karl Jaspers[10]—that truth only happens in the communication with another (or more) person and the importance of friendship to enjoy, respect and recognize the other. These Socratic virtues: *Love, Silence, Humbleness, Humour, Courage, Self-Discipline* and *Friendship* are my more practical and provisional take on how Philosophical Practice with its community of wonder can be called upon to be.

---

[10] Jaspers, K. (1960). *Way to Wisdom- An introduction to Philosophy.* Yale University Press.

4. What do you see as the most interesting criticism against your own position in Philosophical Practice?

Well, there are of course lots of interesting criticism, which I am not able to give a conclusive response to. One of the assumptions, which I seem to take for granted in my view on Philosophical Practice, is that we should strive to get into a community of wonder. When we are in wonderment, I seem to say, we are where we should be as philosophical companions in Philosophical Practice. This is the highest level — as also Goethe once said — that a human being can ever reach. I believe so too, certainly, but when I am asked to be more precise on what wonder really is, I become silent. Or, I start talking a lot, because the Phenomenology of Wonder is *the* central theme of my thinking, also in my academic work. But still, to be honest, this is a question I do not have a clear answer for.

Is wonder basically an intuition, a feeling, a fundamental mood (a *'Grundstimmung'*) or cognitive puzzlement or maybe an ontological and metaphysical and meta-psychic event similar to how Martin Buber describes love?[11] Or how do we distinguish wonder from intellectual curiosity, interest, critical thinking, exploration, clarification, examination, etc.?

Can we wonder without words? I believe so — I think in fact that wonder comes before the question. But then again: what is it? And, as we know, the idea and concept of wonder has had many different meanings during the history of philosophy from Socrates over Augustine and Aquinas and Descartes and Bacon to Kierkegaard, Fink, Heidegger, Marcel, Wittgenstein and Arendt.

What about the horror or anxiety and *Unheimlichkeit* that might follow being in wonder? Is Arendt taking a too idyllic view on wonder when she talks about *thaumazein* as a fundamental 'admiring wonder'? Or is this *Unheimlichkeit* connected to wonder only a consequence of a too existentialistic and Sartrean approach?

And is and should wonderment really be the overall purpose of Philosophical Practice? Plato tell us that Philosophical Practice should not

---

[11] Feelings accompany the metaphysical and meta-psychic factum of love, but they do not constitute it. () Feelings one 'have'; love happens. Feelings dwell in man; but man dwells in his love. Buber, *I and Thou* (2004, my translation). In the English translation of Martin Buber *Ich und Du* from 1923, *I and Thou* from 2004 (Continuum International Publishing Group), this sentence is translated: *Feelings are 'entertained'; love comes to pass. Feelings dwell in man; but man dwells in his love.* (p. 19).
But in the original German text by Buber he writes: *Gefühle werden gehabt; die Liebe geschieht. Gefühle wohnen im Menschen, aber der Mensch wohnt in seiner Liebe*. Note that similar to Gadamer, but many years earlier, Buber emphasizes love as a *'Geschehen'*, as an ontological event that happens *to* us.

just be a starting impulse in order to get into serious philosophizing and strive for a knowing relation to the world in a more scientific sense (as Aristotle and later Hegel seem to assert). To be in wonder is and should be, Plato claims, the passion, impetus and expression of the philosopher from beginning to end. And yet, I agree with the criticism that if we make wonder the goal for our philosophizing then we too easily turn Philosophical Practice into a subtle kind of wonder-therapy. Wonder should not be the main goal of our Philosophical Practice, but only a positive side affect in our search for wisdom. It should of course be the *content* (what we want to understand better, the subject matter or *Sachen Selbst*) of our dialogue that should be in the centre of our interest, and not whether we are or not are not in a process or a state of wonder.

Experience has taught me that to be too wonder-sensitive as a Socratic facilitator or philosophical counsellor can only bring us into a *process-oriented* awareness, which more or less is similar to the psychological enterprise. But I think that we should only become process-oriented as philosophical practitioners *if* our focus suddenly is disrupted and taken away from the philosophical *content* of our dialogue.

Again this does *not* mean that to be content or subject oriented is to stay only on a cognitive level. In contrast to the professional philosopher (in theoretical or applied philosophy) the philosophical practitioner also have, as I said before, a sense for the lyrical dimension as well as the Socratic dimension, which will help him or her to stay tune to a more open and wondrous (that is ontological) relation to the world, the other or oneself.

5. With respect to present and future inquiry, how can the most important problems concerning Philosophical Practice be identified and explored?

One of my current inquiries into Philosophical Practice as a educational researcher is a three year research project at a Danish Design School where ten design professors participate in a pilot group in order to realize a phenomenological oriented action research project on how to practice a community of wonder in design teaching.

They are very engaged in the thought that wonderment might be a way of being that can qualify the design students ability or readiness to 'stand-in-the-open' and thereby be a way to become more creative. How can we, they ask, not through words or writings but through the use of non-verbal, visual and other kind of design material approaches create a community of wonder between the teacher/designer and the design students? How can we—and can we at all?—strengthen design students musicality for the students own personal artistic voice as well

as their ability to hear the voice of the material (*die Sache*)?
These are also research questions, which brings Philosophical Practice into design research as well as into a possible new development of the way we understand and can practice action research. That is, action research seen as a Philosophical Practice.

Another project, which I am also currently leading, is a two year action research project, where the staff (managers, nurses, psychologists and ministers) at a hospice has asked me to make an inquiry into how the staff can qualify the existential dialogues with their palliative patients and especially their relatives. They want to be better in *not* just showing their recognition and ability to mirror the client in what she or he is saying and thinking through for example active listening methods or other kinds of appreciating inquiry approaches and reflective teams and open dialogues. These approaches focus primary on the process level. What the staff wants to strengthen is their ability to go into a genuine dialogue and reflection *with* their clients on the grand existential questions that the client raises on a *content* level. Only by doing so, will the client really feel that they are met in their authentic questioning. So, the hospice staff asks: How can Philosophical Practice help us *to be* in those dialogues in a more wondrous way and in a way that keep our awareness on the content level?

I have organized and carried out some training sessions in philosophical counseling and used Socratic Dialogue Groups with the staff. I will later follow as an observing researcher and see how they do it by themselves and how they might chose to change and develop further these philosophical practices in order better to meet their clients and to communicate the issues and challenges that are present at this particular hospice.

As you can read in my latest article (Hansen, 2012) another future possibility and challenge for Philosophical Practice can be to entering into Qualitative Research to see how we can design new ways of philosophical practices that can qualify phenomenological and hermeneutical research practices.

So, to conclude, in many ways I am optimistic and hopeful for the future of Philosophical Practice. Not just in the area of educational research but surely also in the qualification of the *Bildung* processes in higher education and at universities, in professional educations (nursing, teaching, career counseling, etc.)—and as a *scholè*, a free space, for our own contemplative and wisdom-seeking questions in our own personal lives.

My only reservation would be that I could be afraid that a growing interest in *using* Philosophical Practice in these educational settings may force Philosophical Practice to become instrumental, that is, become just a mean for something else.

Here I am reminded once again of my experiences when being a young student and later a teacher at a Danish *Folkehøjskole*. From this kind of educational culture we learn, I hope, how paramount it is to hold the space open (as a *scholè*) for genuine wonderment and the joy of contemplation and search for wisdom (*philo-sophia*) in the midst of an utilitarian and too hasty and calculating world.

Bibliography

Hansen, F.T. (2012). One Step Further: The Dance Between Poetic Dwelling and Socratic Wonder in Phenomenological Research. *Indo-Pacific Journal of Phenomenology* (ed. Kate Galvin). July 2012.

Hansen, F.T. (2010). The Phenomenology of Wonder in Higher Education. In Malte Brinkmann (ed.): Erziehung. Phänomenologische Perspektiven. Königshausen & Neumann. Würzburg.

Hansen, F.T. & Amundson, N. (2009a). Residing in silence and wonder: Career counseling from the perspective of 'Being. In International Journal for Educational and Vocational Guidance (IJEVG), Vol. 9, No. 1 (March).

Hansen, F.T. (2009b) Philosophical Praxis as a Community of Wonder in Education and Professional Guidance. In Kenkmann, A. (ed.), Teaching Philosophy. London: Continuum.

Hansen, F.T. (2008) Phronesis and Eros—the existential dimension of Phronesis and clinical supervision of nurses. In Chris Johns and Charlotte Delmar (eds.) The Good, the Wise and the Right Clinical Nursing Practice. Århus University Hospital Press.

Hansen, F.T. (2007a). Philosophical Counselling. A hermeneutical-dialogical approach to Career Counselling. In (P. Plant ed.). Ways. Copenhagen: Danmarks Pædagogiske Universitets forlag.

Hansen, F.T. (2007b). Eros, Authenticity and Bildung as Keywords for Philosophical Practice in Teacher Training. Paideusis—Journal of Canadian Philosophy of Education (ed. H. Bai), December 2007.

Hansen, F.T. (2007c). The Personal Essay as a Philosophical Practice. Can be downloaded for free at www.sesproject.eu.

Hansen, F.T. (2005). The existential dimension in training and vocational guidance—when guidance counselling becomes a Philosophical Practice. In European Journal of Vocational Training, No. 34, April 2005.

Hansen, F.T. (2002). The Use of Philosophical Practice in Lifelong and Self-Directed Learning. In H. Herrestad, A. Holt & H. Svare(eds.) Philosophy in Society Unipub AS, Akademika AS, Oslo.

Hansen, F.T. (2001). Existential Adult Pedagogy and Philosophical Counselling. In AGORA 10. Journal of CEDEFOP—European Centre for Development of Vocational Training, Thessaloniki, Greece.

7. Finn Thorbjørn Hansen

8

Leon de Haas

Philosopher and philosophical practitioner
Netherlands and Germany

INTRODUCTION

Answering the five questions of this anthology, I tell about my history with the practical aspect of philosophy since the 1960's. Within the context of the Marxist and neo-Marxist revival in those years, the 'practical' was, first of all, 'social' and 'political'. For me, Philosophical Practice was the philosopher's emancipatory participation in the community (the 'polis') that he was part of. In the 1980's, the political intentions of the Philosophical Practice got lost; the practice resembled more the therapeutic care for mentally confused or puzzling individuals. By doing so, Philosophical Practice lost its connection to the promises of Modern philosophy. Now, again, the question is how we can develop Philosophical Practice as an emancipatory power in 'the polis'.

'PRAXIS' IN 20TH CENTURY PHILOSOPHY; THE SIXTIES

1. Why were you initially drawn to Philosophical Practice?

In 1969, I started studying at the University of Amsterdam. In the preceding years, the streets of Amsterdam were, like elsewhere in European and American cities, the public stage of new impulses of 'personally engaged' and 'autonomous', non-institutional politics. A typical Amsterdam phenomenon was the Provo's, who joined immediate concrete experiments of 'freedom' (like communes, alternatives to psychiatry, free public bikes, biological food shops) and political actions (like humorous anti-cigarettes-industry ceremonies in the streets, and 'playful' participation in the Amsterdam city government). In that year, 1969, students and critical scientific personnel occupied the management center of the University of Amsterdam. The university was carried away in a process of politicization. Professors lost their 'natural' authority, like science and philosophy lost their intrinsic values of truth. Scientific and philosophical truth became a result of 'democratic' discussion; social relevance became a major criterion for initiating and valuing academic research and education.

In Amsterdam, a group of students in philosophy and social sciences had founded the 'Critical University'.[1] The participants in the Critical University rediscovered what, in those years, was rediscovered in the critical 'freedom' movements all over the world, i.e., Marx and the neo-Marxist philosophies. The Frankfurt School of Critical Theory (like Adorno, Horkheimer, Benjamin, Marcuse) inspired to read Freud and the neo-Freudians (e.g., Reich and Fromm) as well.

The philosophical faculty at the University of Amsterdam was the stage of conflicting schools. There were several demarcation lines. There was the demarcation between the students of the 'a-political' analytical philosophy and the students of 'socially politically engaged' continental philosophies. And there was the demarcation line between the 'political' philosophers (the students of Marxism and Critical Theory) and 'personalism' (followers of Asian gurus, and students of Jasper's existentialism, Jung's psychoanalysis, humanistic psychology, etc.).

I did not exclude any of those schools, but, being a 'boy of the streets of Amsterdam', the fire of 'praxis' had lighted me. To me, it was not possible to do philosophy without being aware of Marx' 11th thesis on Feuerbach: Philosophers have hitherto only interpreted the world in various ways; the point is to change it.

But how could a philosopher possibly change the world as a philosopher? Together with four fellow students, I formed 'The Philosophers Collective'. We were looking for ways to practice philosophy in society. Three of us left the university to participate as political filmmakers in 'Het Amsterdams Stadsjournaal', a political film collective. I missed the philosophical aspect of their decision, and wandered how I could participate in social activities as a philosopher. I found a solution by blending *social action research* in a community development project, and a *critical study of the epistemological and social-cultural aspects* of both the community development and the action research. So, as a member of the action research team, I had two roles, as a participating social researcher, and as a critical philosophical thinker. And I hoped that the unity of the two roles would be fruitful for both the social research and philosophy. What can I say about it now, in 2011? That my intentions were nice and sympathetic, but that my experience as a philosopher was young and immature.

In the 1980's, the impetus of the personal and social emancipation

---

[1] Among them was Pim Fortuijn, who was, some decennia later, to become the notorious populist politician. He became the victim of a political murder in 2002.

movement extinguished. The practice of personal and social emancipation lost its spontaneous and self-organizational drives and space. It got encased by 'repressive tolerance' (Herbert Marcuse) of dominant institutional and economic powers, and by the restoration of 'old politics'. Politics, which had been the enthusiasm of emancipation and liberation of everyday life for a decade, withdrew from the houses and streets, and became the toy of institutionalized politicians again. Likewise, emancipatory change of personal and public life became more than ever the specialism of psychological and sociological change-professionals.

This loss of politics in everyday life—i.e., this loss of self-organized civil governance in the public sphere of the 'polis'—stroked the university, the neighborhoods, the companies, the health institutions, etc. And philosophy lost its sense of 'praxis'. We recognize this loss in Gerd Achenbach's initiative, in 1981, to start a Philosophical Practice. Even though he was critical about the psychological models of psychotherapy, he modeled his Philosophical Practice to the non-political, therapeutic relation between counselor and client.

It was only in 2008, at the 9th International Conference on Philosophical Practice, that the German philosopher and philosophical practitioner Thomas Polednitschek reminded us of the ancient political roots of Philosophical Practice (Polednitschek 2009).

In the meantime, since 1980, I experimented with various forms of Philosophical Practice. I, too, lost the political aspect, but gained more and more experience in both finding and knowing the edges of Modern philosophy, and developing ways of philosophical interventions in social situations. In the eighties, I worked as an organization consultant and as a meditation teacher. As a freelance researcher at the Erasmus University Rotterdam, I found my 'end of (academic) philosophy'. My studies of the works of Georges Bataille, Joseph Beuys and John Cage led me to the edge of philosophy as reasoning and text (De Haas 1988; De Haas 2011d), and forced me to leave 'desk philosophy' behind. 'Praxis' still was the magic word ... but what is *philosophical* praxis?

In the 90ties, I worked as an organization and management consultant, trying to 'embed' my philosopher's perspective and skills in my consultancy job. In the years 2000, through some personal crises, I rediscovered the value of philosophy, thanks to the ongoing study of Wittgenstein's work (De Haas 2008). I knew three things better than ever: philosophy is an *encounter* in 'real life' situations, it is a *dialogue*, and it has *no language of its own*. Besides, the *participating* philosopher acts from and in his engagement in the community that he is part of.

Dialogical encounters in the 'polis'

2. What does your work reveal about Philosophical Practice that other related academic fields typically fail to appreciate?

As an academic philosopher—i.e., I studied philosophy at an European university and I philosophize in the tradition of the ancient Greek schools of philosophy[2]—I know from experience both the challenges and the limitations of this tradition. The perspective spot of this knowledge is given by the above-mentioned social-political context, by the philosophical struggle that is part of my personal life, and by my philosophical business.

Western Philosophical Practice in the academic field lacks the practice of real life encounter and dialogue. Nietzsche bet his own life and discussed the loss (and the denial) of 'real life' in philosophical reasoning, but he himself got stuck in his satirical attacks on Western philosophy and Christian culture, and in his literary dreaming about the *Übermensch* (man who has overcome himself). Marx declared the end of theoretical, interpreting philosophy and the beginning of political philosophy that would change the world, but his declaration stuck in the study rooms of the British Museum, in the totalitarian character of his philosophy[3], and in the practice of fundamentalist politics. Husserl was aware of the otherness of reality in relation to reasoning and developed the attitude and method of *epochè*, but only to be better capable of understanding the conceptually grabbed 'essence' of reality. So, for philosophy becoming a personal and social practice, these innovators in Modern philosophy didn't offer a way out of its rational and theoretical blind alleys.

Hadot's and Foucault's rediscovery of philosophy as an 'art of living' (Hadot 1995; Foucault 1983) helped to revalue ancient Greek and Roman philosophy, but not to develop philosophy as a dialogical encounter.

More hopeful perspectives came from Wittgenstein, Buber and Levinas. Wittgenstein divided his 'real life' off his philosophical investigations; by unraveling the philosophers' thinking knots and pitfalls, he opened (moral) thinking in and from situations of real life (De Haas 2008). Buber did not speak *about* reality and human existence, but his philosophy was a speaking *with* concrete fellow human beings (Buber

---

[2] Besides, I am influenced by Eastern philosophy as well, as I learned it in the practice of sitting Zen meditation and moving T'ai chi meditation. As a part of these studies, I've read Buddhist and Taoist texts.

[3] Levinas' warnings against totalitarian thinking (Levinas 1951) also apply to Marxian thinking; Marx was an ontologist.

1995). Levinas carried on this encountering philosophy (Levinas 1980). I began to understand Philosophical Practice primarily as the always concrete, open and unique encounter of the philosophizing person with his situations, with his fellow human beings, and with himself. Then, from here, the '*supporting interventional*' relation with '*support asking*' people is nothing more and nothing less than a specific occurring of a human encounter with 'philosophical ambition'.

This is crucial in the comparison of Philosophical Practice with so-called 'related' disciplines like psychotherapy, counseling and consultancy. In general, these practices work on account of psychological and anthropological generalizations and reductions. The guest is a *client*, and the client is a *case* of generalized, pre-conceived clinical pictures and personality schemes. There, the clinical conversation is the gathering of information in order to apply the general knowledge. In those practices no encounter happens (they are meetings) and no dialogue is going on (they are conversations). Philosophical practice, as I see and do it, is a unique encounter between two unique, in-reducible persons.

Counseling, as understood and practiced in the spirit of humanistic psychology (like Carl Roger's), is an exception to the generalizing and reductive therapies. The humanistic counselor's attitude is open towards the client; his efforts are aimed at helping the client telling his or her own unique story and understanding himself not through pre-conceived models. As to the art of non-reductive questioning, philosophical practitioners can learn a lot from humanistic counselors. But then, Philosophical Practice steps across the boundaries of counseling. We, philosophical practitioners, are not 'solving problems', and we are not just affirming and supporting the client's own processes of story telling and understanding; we challenge our guest to investigate his thinking thoroughly and critically, and to take his responsibility for the situations he is part of in his life. This responsibility is to be seen both moral and political.

Stephen Toulmin characterized the so-called 'clinical' sciences as situational and non-reductive (Toulmin 2003). However, the bureaucratic and economical pressure to 'prove' the 'truth' of clinical interventions through statistical generalization undermines the open clinical attitude. In the Netherlands, the application of diagnosis-treatment-combinations subverts the openness of the interventional encounters.

Here we also meet second-hand psychologies and philosophies. I mean all those self-declared counselors, coaches and consultants, who know the truth about their clients and use all kinds of means and rituals to heal them. I call them 'second-hand', because they borrow understandings and strategies from philosophy and psychology, to reshape them to indisputable truths in their ideologies of The Self and The Spiritual. They 'forget' to adopt the self-critical and skeptical attitude of serious psychologists and philosophers.

Unfortunately, there are such spiritual moonlighters who call themselves 'philosophical practitioner'. Seen from the self-criticism of Modern philosophy, many a Philosophical Practice fall back on pre-critical metaphysics. The poverty of those practices comes to light, when practitioners take refuge in cognitive therapy or spiritual counseling. Philosophy practiced as cognitive therapy reduces philosophy and the human mind to cognition and rational reasoning, and the spiritual counselor leaves any philosophical criticism and skepticism for a cosmological ontology of The Self.

Philosophical practice, seen as an open, dialogical encounter, keeps free from such generalizations and reductions. For most of the guests in my practice this is exactly the reason to visit a philosopher.

But that is not all. It is not just the relation between philosopher and guest. It is also the relation between the guest and his or her situations of life. In the psychologically defined interventions, the client is indeed defined—to his individual feeling, thinking and behaving, and sometimes to his 'system', being the network of individual relations. As Polednitschek demonstrated, the client is taken as a *homo psychologicus* and *economicus* and not considered a *'homo politicus'*.

In 2008, in Europe, we live in an age of post-bourgeois resignation. Therefore, in my opinion, a Philosophical Practice that wants to resist Western Europe's 'democratic melancholy' (Bruckner), must, as a political philosophy, be the critical theory of a society in which the citizen's 'political I' has been relieved by the de-politicized individual. This de-politicized individual is the homo economicus of our postmodern times, for whom the rationality of business economics is the exclusive criterion of his thinking and acting. And he is the homo psychologicus, whose reflexive individualism makes him the prisoner of his own subjectivity (Polednitschek 2009).

The homo psychologicus is an object of diagnosis and treatment, whereas the *citoyen* is a subject who takes responsibility for his being part of the situations he is living. Polednitschek states, that the philosophical practitioner is not—i.e., should not want to be—a 'counselor' (in German: Berater), but a citoyen who encounters a fellow citoyen.

Polednitschek refers to the political subject of the Enlightenment and the bourgeois and proletarian Revolutions. That is, to the era between the late 18th and the early 20th centuries. The framework of his political philosophy is the 'negative dialectics' of Adorno and Horkheimer (Adorno 1970; Horkheimer 1971). There is some resentment towards the so-called 'Post-Modern' times in his thinking. In my opinion, it is more realistic and fruitful, to understand our time as an era of the development of a global network society.

The political subject that Polednitschek want to revive was related to the political and economic institutions of the kingdoms and democracies of rising and flourishing capitalism. Those abstract institutions—both the falling and the arising—had some substantive grip on the whole of society. Nowadays, they are losing their grips more and more. In the niches and the fallow fields of the globalizing world, concrete networks of human relations are germinating, growing and developing.

In the Enlightenment, the citoyen was a free person in an open society, where freedom was the participation in the institutions, and the institutions defined the openness. Nowadays, the center of his 'polis' is not the institution, but the situations, i.e., situations with open horizons. Through the horizons, situations are linked—situations, which are always concrete situations of concrete persons.

The contemporary citizen's situation is not defined; it has no closed borders, no fixed boundaries. His ordinary life is a network of situations, and by that, of changing connections and interactions. A situation is being here and now, within the horizons here and now. As time is changing, situations are changing in space—and so are the people we are meeting and encountering.

A situation is defined, while the horizons are not. The situation is limited, while the perspectives are infinite. Present-day situations are open; we are living an open society. The horizon is a vague distance from where impulses and powers are influencing us, but where we suspect new possibilities, too. When with 'the polis' we mean our non-institutional community, and with 'politics' the communication and decision-making about the quality and conditions of our living-together, then, the contemporary 'polis' is our own concrete set of situations of the global network society, and 'politics' the practice of thinking and choosing in the currents of our life, in communication with the others with whom we share our situations.

The state and market institutions are abstract processes and powers, interfering into our situations, and often dominating. It is to us, how we experience, value and treat these abstract powers. Why shouldn't we turn round our perspectives from the abstract, institutional point-of-view to our concrete situational network-positions? Is the first decade of the 21st century not particularly the playground of germinating, growing and developing practices and connections of such a global network of situated citizens? And if Philosophical Practice is the practice of concrete dialogical encounters—as I contend in the slipstreams of Wittgenstein, Buber and Levinas -, why shouldn't we consider this practice to be the way we have to think in this becoming 'polis-network' or 'network-polis'? And why should we—be it cynically or agreeing—comment these developments from the outside (as many 'free' philosophers do at the university and in the media), and not participate dialogically in the community that we are part of?

THE PHILOSOPHER AS A LIVING BEING AND AS A 'CITOYEN'

3. What, if any, practical and/or social-political obligations follow from understanding philosophy from the point of view of Philosophical Practice?

The concept of 'practice' in Philosophical Practice is complicated. As I have stipulated above, some currents of Modern philosophy declared its end, and tried to find a way out of its blind alleys. The blind alleys were revealed where the philosophers' reasoning had drifted away from the concrete living bodies and situations, from 'real life' (as noticed by Schopenhauer, Nietzsche, Husserl, Bergson), and where their language had produced its own 'autistic' problems (as criticized by Marx, Nietzsche, Wittgenstein, Levinas). The way out of the self-imprisonment of philosophy was 'practice'. But what is 'practice' in a philosophical sense? For Marx, it was the opposite of interpreting the world, so, changing the human world—socially, economically, politically. For Nietzsche, it was the opposite of reasoning life to death, so, living a life—in a 'distinguished' and 'sovereign' way. For Achenbach, it was the opposite of theorizing in academic rooms, so, consulting clients in consulting rooms next door to the family doctor and the psychotherapist.

Achenbach's concept of Philosophical Practice is restricted. As indicated above, his practice has been developed in the a-political context of the 1980's and 1990's. Where his method and language is that of philosophy (particularly German philosophy), his situational and conversational model is that of the psychoanalytic and psychotherapeutic conversations. Here, the philosopher is acting in the social and economic field of psychotherapists and counselors. His guest is a client with psychological problems. Calling these problems 'existential' does not change the fact that the client is considered a homo psychologicus, i.e., someone with interpreting and healing thoughts about his feelings, thoughts, and behavior. Putting himself and his guest into such an individual hermeneutic situation, he is treating himself as a counselor (Berater) and his guest as a client. Here, philosophizing is primarily and just a hermeneutic conversation and not an encounter in the full sense of this word.

What is a philosophical encounter? Is it a coincidence, that three non-conformist Jewish philosophers in the philosophical traditions of

Athens were able to leave the autistic theorizing and rationalizing of Modern philosophy to find 'praxis'? Martin Buber, Emmanuel Levinas and Ludwig Wittgenstein. To them, the core of philosophy was the real life human encounter[4]. Philosophical text was just there to teach themselves and others about philosophical encounters. Philosophical practice, as we do it nowadays in the economic form of small businesses, is a trial to realize this encountering philosophy in real life social situations with fellow citizens. How can we practice philosophical encounters in the defined and defining contexts of everyday life, community life and business life?

WHAT DOES THIS MEAN FOR PHILOSOPHY?

In this approach, we understand the contemporary 'citoyen' as a human being who considers himself situated in concrete 'real life' networks, and who takes the responsibility for his being part of the situations he is living. When the future of philosophy is practicing real life encounters between 'citoyens', in social and economic situations, what, then, are the challenges?

First, the philosopher is not a therapist, counselor or consultant. He or she is a real Socrates (not Nelson's conversation facilitator (see De Haas 2011a), nor the quasi-Platonic digger of hidden Ideas[5]. On the contrary, he is a citizen who is willing to encounter his fellow human beings and enters into dialogues.

Second, the philosopher is a public challenger. Not like Russell, Sartre, Foucault, Chomsky or Bernard-Henri Lévy, who are prophets, relating to the 'old time' political institutions. The encountering philosopher is not a prophet; on the contrary, he initiates dialogues and takes the responsibility for the situations he is part of.

In my view, Philosophical Practice is the consequence and promise of Modern philosophy, i.e., of those currents of Modern philosophy that are conscious of the pitfalls of theorizing philosophy and are searching for philosophical ways of human encounters. What are 'philosophical ways of human encounters'? Actually, this is a pleonasm. As Buber and Levinas showed, in an encounter—which is not a mere *meeting*—two human beings open to each other and to themselves. They accept the

---

[4] Although Wittgenstein considered 'real life' to be outside of philosophy. He restricted philosophical activity to the critical investigation of the philosophers' dead alleys and thinking knots. See De Haas 2008.

[5] Plato's philosophy resembles more the open philosophy of Levinas than the socalled 'theory of Ideas' as has been thought by Christian users of Plato's writings. Plato's notion of 'eidos' and 'idea' is closer to Buber's encounter and Levinas' countenance than to the ontological 'Proper World' ('Hinterwelt', as Nietzsche called it) of conceptual Ideas.

other human being as an *other* being, not reduced, and not reducible. In a dialogue—which is not a mere *conversation*—they share and explore the endless landscapes that they are and that they inhabit ... without the will to reduce their experiences to concepts and conceptions.

An *encountering* philosopher is someone who musters up the courage to challenge all cognitive and institutional reductions that occupy the situations that he and his guest are focused on in their encounter.

And they do this not just in the text of their dialogue, but particularly in the practice of their lives, in their everyday situations and encounters.

This is the philosopher's challenge, in his own life. And in his *caring* encounters with those who come to visit his place, he teaches his guest to philosophize in this sense, in this perspective.

And his *place* is not just and not primarily his consulting room; it is every situation in the landscape of his life—where another human being is longing for an encounter in his or her struggle for life.

It's a philosopher's challenge to be *present* in those situations in his 'community'—and to initiate that kind of dialogues.

About the Justification of Philosophical Practice

4. What do you see as the most interesting criticism against your own position in Philosophical Practice?

In discussions about my practice, there are two issues: justification and the political.

In the business world where I try to market my practice, clients ask me if I can guarantee the quality of my interventions. They are used to asking for the results of the services they buy from consultants and coaches. I think, they are right; they have to be curious about the results of the services that they pay for. Besides, private customers ask if my services will be paid back by the health insurer. I think it a shortage of Philosophical Practice that we hardly are able to give more than vague hope of 'success' to our guests. So far we have neglected the issue of the justification of our practice. In the new Indian journal of philosophy, Manavayatan, I tried to start this discussion (De Haas 2011c).

Another criticism against my position in Philosophical Practice came from Thomas Polednitschek and was related to the political aspect of it. As I discussed above, I take this criticism very seriously. Again and again I try to understand the political aspects of the encounters with my guests, and I am experimenting with practical consequences of this understanding.

RE-INVENTING PHILOSOPHICAL PRACTICE

5. With respect to present and future inquiry, how can the most important problems concerning Philosophical Practice be identified and explored?

In short, I can summarize the conclusions of this essay in the following questions, which are perspectives for inquiries and dialogues.

Is it—in relation to the Modern history of Western philosophy—still justifiable to practice philosophy as a primarily *rational* and *conceptual* discipline instead of a real and open encounter of human beings?

What does it practically mean for Philosophical Practice to be a situated *encounter* between *in-reducible* human beings?

What does it practically mean for philosophical encounters to be an encounter in *open situations*, in which the people in dialogue are *responsible* members of the social networks that they are part of?

How can we *justify* our practice without reductive objectifications and generalizations, i.e., doing justice to the open, not-reducing and in-reducible character of philosophy and Philosophical Practice?

Asking, researching and discussing these questions, is only possible as an aspect of the everyday practice as philosophizing human beings and practitioners. Doing this, we will be re-inventing Philosophical Practice in the footprints of the great philosophers of our time, and, at the same time, finding contemporary forms for the age-old philosophical traditions.

If '*polis*' stands for the 'significant' community that we are part of; and if '*significant*' means: to make choices about the quality of our everyday lives; and if we consider '*choosing*' to be our own matter in our social relations and situations—then we are talking about the philosopher's political role. I mean, it is the practice of *freedom*. We turn meetings into *encounters*, conversations into *dialogues*. And we brake reducing and reduced conditions open to situations with perspective-full horizons. In whatever social situation, commercial or not. This implies, that we leave behind totalitarian and activist political philosophy (Marx, Sartre, etc.), as well as the *shopkeeper* and *counselor* mentality of Philosophical Practice. On principle, there is no difference between paid and not paid philosophical encounter. It is not a shame that a philosopher wants to earn his money with philosophical encounters. On the other hand, the content of the philosophical service cannot be dependent on the payment; it is always a real and heartfelt human encounter.

Bibliography

Adorno 1970. Theodor W. Adorno, Negative Dialektik. In: Adorno, Gesammelte Schrifte, Band 6. Frankfurt am Main: Suhrkamp Verlag.

Buber 1995. Martin Buber, Ich und Du. Stuttgart: Philip Reclam jun. Original publication in 1923.

De Haas 1988. Leon de Haas, Strategieën van het vlees. Hommage aan John Cage, ondanks Adorno. In: H.A.F. Oosterling & A.W. Prins (ed.), La Chair. Het vlees in filosofie en kunst. Rotterdam: Faculteit der Wijsbegeerte van de Erasmus Universiteit Rotterdam. (English translation of the title: 'Strategies of the flesh. Homage to John Cage, in spite of Adorno'.)

De Haas 2007a. Leon de Haas, De kille dialogen van Oscar Brenifier. In: Filosofie, volume 17, number 3. Budel: Damon. (Dutch; translation of the title: 'The cold dialogues of Oscar Brenifier'.)

De Haas 2007b. Leon de Haas, Wat is filosofische praktijk? Over filosofie, praktijk en markt. In: Filosofie, volume 17, number 6. Budel: Damon. (Dutch; translation of the title: 'What is Philosophical Practice? About philosophy, practice, and market'.)

De Haas 2008. Leon de Haas, Wittgenstein en Levenskunst. In: Filosofie, volume 18, number 4. Budel: Damon 2008. (Dutch; translation of the title: 'Wittgenstein and the art of living'.)

De Haas 2009. Leon J.M. de Haas, De Socratische Coach. Roermond: PlatoPraktijk 2009. (Dutch transation of the title: 'The Socratic Coach'.)

De Haas 2010. Leon de Haas, Praxis en ervaring in de filosofie. Leusden 2010: de 10de Internationale conferentie over filosofische praktijk. In: Tijdschrift Filosofie, Volume 20, Issue 6. Antwerp: Garant 2010. (Dutch; translation of the title: 'Praxis and experience in philosophy. Leusden 2010: the 10th International Conference on Philosophical Practice'.)

De Haas 2011a. Leon de Haas, Encounters and Dialogues. Styles and Levels of Communication in Philosophical Practice. Key note speech at the 3rd International Conference on Humanities Therapy in Chuncheon, South-Korea, at July 7, 2011.Published in: Journal of Humanities Therapy, Vol.2 (December 2011), Chuncheon, Republic of Korea

De Haas 2011b. Leon de Haas, Philosophical counselling as a philosophical dialogue. A situative view, and a discussion of the value of Wittgenstein's philosophical investigations. Lecture before the

Korean Society of Philosophical Practice at July 8, 2011. Published in: "Philosophical Practice and Counseling. Official Journal of the Korean Society of Philosophical Practice, Vol.2, 2011, Chuncheon, Republic of Korea.

De Haas 2011c. Leon de Haas, An Essay on the Justification of Philosophical Practice. In: Manavayatan, Journal on Humanities of Centre for Studies in Humanities, Volume I, Number I (July-December 2011), Assam, India.

De Haas 2011d. Presentie, Ervaring, Aandacht. Aanzetten tot een actuele filosofie van de situatie. Essays 1987-2009. Roermond: PlatoPraktijk. (Dutch; translation of the title: 'Presence, Experience, Attention. Beginnings of a contemporary philosophy of the situation).

Foucault 1983. Foucault, Michel, On the genealogy of ethics: An overview of work in progress. An interview with Paul Rabinow and Hubert Dreyfus at Berkeley in April 1983. In: Paul Rabinow (Ed.), The Foucault Reader. New York: Pantheon Books 1984.

Hadot 1995. Pierre Hadot, Qu'est-ce que la philosophie antique? Paris: Editions Gallimard.

Horkheimer 1971. Max Horkheimer & Theodor W. Adorno, Dialektik der Aufklärung. Philosophische Fragmente. Frankfurt am Main: S. Fischer Verlag GmbH.

Levinas 1951. Emmanuel Levinas, L'ontologie est-elle fondamentale? In: Revue de Métaphysique et de Morale 56, 88-98.

Levinas 1980. Emmanuel Levinas, Totalité et Infini. Leiden: Martinus Nijhoff Publishers.

Polednitschek 2009. Thomas Polednitschek, De politieke Socrates. Filosofie als levensvorm en de politieke filosofie van filosofische praktijk. In: Filosofie, volume 19, number 1. Budel: Damon. (Dutch translation of the originally German lecture at the 9th International Conference on Philosophical Practice, Carloforte, July 2008. English translation of the title: 'The political Socrates. Philosophy as a form of life, and the political philosophy of Philosophical Practice'.

Toulmin 2003. Stephen Toulmin, Return to Reason. Cambridge MA: Harvard University Press.

8. Leon de Haas

9
Henning Herrestad

Senior Reseatcher
Work Research Institute, Oslo

---

1. Why were you initially drawn to Philosophical Practice?

At Norwegian universities all students used to take a preparatory exam in the history of philosophy. I took the exam to gain entry to the faculty of theology, and this study of philosophy opened my eyes. I quit my theology studies in order to study the history of religions and social anthropology before I went on to study philosophy again. But this time my philosophy studies brought me to analytical philosophy where my existential questions were deemed unanswerable and unfit for philosophical investigations. This form of academic philosophy appeared to me as an austere mathematical discipline understood by a few select, a servant to empirical science and engineering. I endured it, but my PhD thesis was largely a formal exercise entitled Formal theories of rights.

While I was studying for my PhD, I volunteered at a crisis telephone hotline. I thought that philosophy, as I first had encountered it in my preparatory studies, might be of relevance to the lives of people who sought telephone counseling. I encountered arguments like a woman cheated on me, therefore all women will cheat on me which I had learned was an invalid inductive inference. In cognitive therapy corrections of such faulty reasoning is one therapeutic measure, but the source is in logic and rhetoric. After my dissertation in 1996 I started reading about Philosophical Practice. I learned how a group in Holland had practiced together for a long while before going public, and I decided to establish a similar group. The group started in Oslo in 1997. In 1998 we established the Norwegian Association of Philosophical Practice (NSFP, see www.nsfp.no), and in 1999 we established the first course for philosophy students who wanted to get the association's license as philosophical practitioners. 50 practitioners have so far been certified by NSFP. In 2001 we hosted the Sixth International Conference on Philosophical Practice at the University of Oslo. In 2011 the course in Philosophical Practice became eligible for university credits and is now run at Buskerud University College with 15 new students.

2. What does your work reveal about Philosophical Practice that other related academic fields typically fail to appreciate?

For a decade now I have been working in the related academic fields of psychiatry and psychotherapy as associate professor in suicidology and mental health research. I have experienced how the *medical approach to human problems* has been subjected to the paradigm of evidence based medicine. This paradigm forces both research and clinical work to adhere to standards where any presented problem requires a diagnosis of what is the underlying problem, and treatment is reduced to administering the interventions found to be statistically most efficient in reducing the symptoms of the given diagnose. To understand this approach we may compare solving human problems to fixing cars. If your car engine stops, you get nowhere by asking it why it won't drive any further. Moralizing is of no avail. Instead you must diagnose what caused the engine to stop.

99 % of such stops are attributed to a small number of commonly occurring causes like running out of gas/petrol or soot on the spark plugs. When the causal explanation is simple, addressing the cause, like filling the tank or changing the spark plugs, fixes each of these problems every time. It might still be that one type of fuel or of spark plugs makes the engine run smoother or longer than another. This can be readily measured, and usually the difference will be reflected in the price of the commodity. If fixing human problems can be compared to fixing cars, we should care only to find the underlying causes of these problems, and like with cars there will be standard measures to fix most of these causes. Just as a car engine can be subdivided into parts like the carburettor or the ignition, filling specific functions, the medical approach teaches that human behaviour is reducible to biological or psychological functions. Treatment means to repair these functions when they are not working properly. E.g. people are said to be suffering from emotional dysregulation[1], self control dysfunction[2], exploratory system dysfunction[3], etc. Dysfunctions may be caused by illnesses, deficiencies or abnormal childhood development. Dysfunctions can be repaired

---

[1] Linehan, M. (1993). *Cognitive−behavioral treatment of borderline personality disorder*. New York: Guilford Press.

[2] Barkley, R. A. (1997). *ADHD and the Nature of Self-Control*. New York: The Guilford Press.

[3] Shear, C.; Monk, T.; Houck, P.; Melhem, N.; Frank, E.; Reynolds, C.; Sillowash, R. (2007). An attachment-based model of complicated grief including the role of avoidance. In *European Archives of Psychiatry and Clinical Neuroscience*, 257 (8): pp 453-461.

through learning new skills, or their symptoms may be reduced through medication.

Philosophical Practice challenges this medical approach to human problems, defending instead *a humanistic approach*. Instead of treating problems diagnosed by an expert, a person seeking Philosophical Practice is engaged in a dialogue about how he sees himself and the world. With human beings it makes perfect sense to ask why he makes a stop and what he thinks is right. In such a dialogue the philosophical practitioner takes a keen interest in the worldview of his guest, as well as offering Socratic questions and alternative views that may put this worldview in perspective. In the end some convictions may be strengthened, some may be changed; the goal is not so much to solve problems as to examine life.

Several proponents of Philosophical Practice have tried to distance themselves from psychotherapy altogether (e.g. at www.nsfp.no one headline expresses that Philosophical Practice is not therapy, a message reiterated in the underlying text). This message has been reiterated numerous times since Gert Achenbach's first publications on Philosophical Practice[4]. But, it is difficult to find any hard criterion to distinguish Philosophical Practice from all kinds of psychotherapy. Several psychotherapies use exploring dialogues similar to Philosophical Practice as their key method (e.g. Rogerian psychotherapy, Existential Psychotherapy, Jaakko Seikkula's Open Dialogue treatment).

In my view the dividing line is not between psychotherapy as such and Philosophical Practice, but between approaches to human problems that follow the medical approach and humanistic approaches. These causal explanations of behaviour contrast to intentional explanations that ask what goals and values a person is pursuing. Following Sartre, I take it that some goals and values are chosen pre-reflexively, so that a person may be unaware of them while acting[5]. Still he may become aware of them through reflection, and he is fundamentally free to change his goals and values or the pathways of pursuing them.

I term this approach to human problems humanistic because it places fundamental emphasis on human freedom and responsibility. Philosophical Practice is not alone in taking a humanistic approach to human problems, but Philosophical Practice can accentuate this humanistic approach as Philosophical Practice lays claim to being a philosophical rather than a psychological practice. However, all such humanistic therapies are losing ground to the medical approach. In several coun-

---

[4] Brown, S. (2010). The Therapeutic Status of Philosophical Counselling, *Practical Philosophy*, vol. 10, nr 1, pp 11-120

[5] Svare, H. (2010). *Livsmestring: Om å finne seg til rette i verden*. Oslo: Pax forlag.

tries health services and health insurance agencies refuse to reimburse treatment that is not supported by research demonstrating its efficiency. Those not following the directions of evidence based medicine are increasingly under suspicion of practising some form of quackery. I will return to this below, as this is what I see as the most interesting external criticism of Philosophical Practice.

3. What, if any, practical and/or social-political obligations follow from understanding philosophy from the point of view of Philosophical Practice?

One practical obligation is to give people the opportunity to participate in philosophical dialogues about the issues they are concerned about.

I also feel an obligation to offer philosophy students a training program teaching them how to become philosophical practitioners, as Philosophical Practice requires practical skills in leading dialogues in addition to their academic studies in philosophy. The training in academic philosophy is largely a training in argumentation; a training in attacking the views of an opponent and defending a theoretical position. We attempt to teach our students how new understanding may be sought in collaboration instead of through verbal warfare. Philosophy students have only been taught skills in writing, while we teach them what to be aware of in an oral dialogue meeting a person face to face. In our training program, mentioned above, the students are required to practice dialogue skills in peer groups and with external volunteers under supervision of experienced philosophical practitioners.

I see a socio-political obligation for Philosophical Practice in warning against the unintended side effects of letting the medical approach to human problems gain total hegemony as the source of human welfare. I believe this medicalization of society is leading us to a society where people will receive treatment but seldom will feel understood.

4. What do you see as the most interesting criticism against your own position in Philosophical Practice?

The most interesting *external* point of criticism is that we don't have any empirical studies demonstrating the utility of Philosophical Practice. This criticism follows as a corollary to the medical approach to human problems. As explained above, the medical approach works on the presumption that there are specific causal mechanisms underlying human problems, mechanisms that may be manipulated in different ways. For instance medication may have an effect on human biology that cures a disease or alleviates symptoms. We don't know all the interacting causal mechanisms well enough to guarantee the same effect of a certain medication on every afflicted person. All that is required is a statistically significant difference in effect on a group of persons treated with the medication to a group treated with placebo. In psychotherapy research the comparison will be with a similar treatment instead of a medical placebo. Randomization of patients to different treatments and double blind procedures are required to avoid researcher bias towards some wanted results. The smaller the difference in outcome is between the effects of the different treatments, the larger groups have to be tested for the difference to be statistically significant. No such measures can be proved to be efficient however, if your problems are one of a kind.

If you take a humanistic approach to human problems, you also take a hermeneutical approach to understanding the person consulting you. You try your best to see the world from his perspective. How does he see his problems? What are his values and goals? What are his underlying presumptions about the world that make his pursuit of his goals so difficult? In trying to understand him, you have to compare his situation to other similar situations, but you keep in mind that still no situations are exactly alike. His outlook may be similar to many others, but in several respects it is unique, as no one has exactly the same experiences and interpretations of them as him. His words have similar meanings to what other people mean by those words, or he would not be able to communicate, but still his words also have special connotations to him that are unique to him. Solutions to his problems that might look easy to you, and that have been pursued by many others, may still be impossible to him. On the other hand, he may find solutions to his problems that have not been perceived by anyone else. His problems are one of a kind, and this rules out the use of statistics to measure the optimal solution or the most efficient response. A humanistic response to human problems cannot be standardized in the way required be evidence based medicine. Instead each person must be understood on his own terms, making each consultation unique. What have been good solutions for other people is only interesting as a reference, not as a prescription.

One of my guests could not decide whether to choose a life with his wife and family or with his lover. Each of these lives had its particular benefits and costs, but they were entirely different. Through our dialogue it became clear how the two different lives represented opposites that were both very valuable to him, and he could not see how he could live happily with only one of these lives. He had tried to calculate the pros and cons of each alternative, but the calculation itself was not enough to convince him of the right choice. Living both of these lives simultaneously, was a difficult balancing act with a great risk of losing both his wife and his lover. He was cornered in a way that hardly has any evidence based cure even if the general outline of his predicament is not that uncommon. The detail of his past history and present situation, made his choices unique to him. No moral maxim or external advice could show him what to do, but laying bare his goals and values made it clearer to him what his choices were about.

The most interesting *internal* point of criticism comes from colleagues who take a more radical approach to Philosophical Practice than I do. They not only counsel their clients, they aim to bring them enlightenment. For instance Ran Lahav, a world renowned philosophical practitioner, argues that Socrates would abhor the idea of making life more comfortable for the people rather than make them discard their false beliefs[6]. You could say that to this internal critic of our form of Philosophical Practice what we do is meaningless because our aims are too mundane. In the metaphor of the cave, Socrates described people as living chained in a cave where they mistake flickering shadows on the wall for reality. Socrates would want philosophers to help people free themselves from their illusions and experience the true reality outside the cave.

Another interpretation of what Socrates would want us to do is presented by the most prolific writer on philosophical counseling in Denmark, Finn Thorbjørn Hansen. Hansen maintains[7] (in my translation) What Socrates attempts to aid the birth of, is, as already stated, not our *doxa* or *episteme* (our clarified discursive and rational opinions and definitions and systems of knowledge), but rather a new form of silence — a silence purified through the art of thinking and dialectics — that brings us to a fundamental wonder. As he writes earlier in the book (p. 67) our preoccupation with The World of Appearance makes us lose the opportunity to experience Being in itself, which is something larger and different from the human universe. Again, the philosophical practitioner is urged to follow in the footsteps of Socrates, this time not to make him discard his false beliefs in order to open up to real knowledge, but to discard the whole chatter about opinions and definitions and knowledge altogether and simply stand back in awed silence about existence itself.

In my view these calls to follow Socrates lead to the conclusion that the Philosophical Practitioner must be a kind of guru, a person leading people from darkness to light, from illusion to reality, from false beliefs to Truth, from the world of appearance to an experience of Being in itself. To me this turns Philosophical Practice into a kind of quasi religion. I believe it to be a kind of vanity to wish to be of such tremen-

---

[6] Lahav, R. (2005). *Reflections on the meaning of philosophical practice*. Web publication at http://www.trans-sophia.net/115845/Reflections (accessed 27.01.2012).

[7] Hansen, F.T. (2008). *At stå i det åbne: Dannelse gennem filosofisk undren og nærvær*. Copenhagen: Hans Reitzels forlag. Page 89.

dous importance to a person seeking counsel, and I believe it to be a kind of hubris to believe that you have such powers as a Philosophical Practitioner. In my view, there are multiple perspectives, there are ethical dilemmas, and there are idiosyncratic world views. In a dialogue over a few hours a philosophical practitioner is invited to share a few glimpses of the world of the guest, and may be used by the guest to set some things straight, to tidy up some messy corners, to help solve some dilemmas; and it is quite an achievement for both the philosophical practitioner and the guest if the guest succeeds in these tasks.

William James writes in his book *Pragmatism*[8]: "The most violent revolution in an individual's beliefs leaves most of his old order standing. Time and space, cause and effect, nature and history, and one's own biography remain untouched. New truth is always a go-between, a smoother-over of transitions. It marries old opinion to new fact so as ever to show a minimum of jolt, a maximum of continuity." I believe, like James, that even when my guest leaves my consultation room energized by a new insight, it is most unlikely an epiphany like St Paul's on his way to Damascus. It is more likely a little jolt that may make him change his course in life by some small degree so that the results will only be visible when time has widened the gap between this course and his original one. A small change of life course is still an important event in a human life. To regard it simply as a rearrangement of prejudices to feel more comfortable, is a rather arrogant view of what people seek in Philosophical Practice.

5. With respect to present and future inquiry, how can the most important problems concerning Philosophical Practice be identified and explored?

I interpret this question as asking how we can identify and explore the most important problems concerning Philosophical Practice today and in the future. My response would be that we need to train philosophical practitioners with the ability to identify and explore these problems. If we are able to create a community of philosophical practitioners that are in dialogue between themselves, I am certain that they will be able to both identify and explore problems that are important both to Philosophical Practice and to the public to whom Philosophical Practice is offered. I cannot see any other way to influence future inquiry.

Another interpretation of this question is to view it as a question about what I believe are the most important problems concerning Philosophical Practice today and in the near future, and how I believe we

---

[8] James, W. (1907/2004). *Pragmatism*. Gutenberg (www.gutenberg.org), public domain online publication. Location 449.

should explore these problems. I find it to be a major challenge to Philosophical Practice today to make our voice heard in a world overflowing with offers of how to cure you, how to make you happy, how to achieve your goals more efficiently etc. Several authors have presented and explained Philosophical Practice in conventional academic prose. Lou Marinoff's book[9] *Plato, Not Prozac!* is probably the foremost example of this literature. What I believe is missing, however, is a book that allows the reader to witness Philosophical Practice dialogues in a way that is interesting to the general reader. I don't think transcripts of actual dialogues would be of much help. What we are missing is a philosophical practitioner with similar literary skills to professor Irvin D. Yalom[10]. A literary account might convey the experience of discovery through dialogue in a way that would make the public able to grasp what participating in Philosophical Practice might be like for them.

Among our attempts to make our voice heard I would like to mention that our 2001 international conference led to the publication of the book Herrestad, H.; Holt, A.; Svare, H. (2002). *Philosophy in Society*. Oslo: Unipub forlag.. In 2004 Helge Svare and I published the first book on Philosophical Practice in Norwegian: Svare, H.; Herrestad, H. (2004). *Filosofi for livet: En bok om filosofisk praksis*. Oslo: Unipub forlag. This book was published in Sweden in 2006.

---

[9] Marinoff, L. (1999). *Plato, Not Prozac!: Applying Eternal Wisdom to Everyday Problems*. New York: Harper Collins publishers.

[10] E.g. see Yalom I.D. (1992) *When Nietzsche Wept: A Novel of Obsession*. New York: Harper Perennial pub.

10

Jos Kessels

Philosopher and Director of Eidoskoop
Amsterdam

INTRODUCTION

In this article which I would like to call *Socratic dialogue—the spectacle of meaning*, I discuss Philosophical Practice on the basis of my own experience with it. I focus on its history and background, some key aspects of it, and some new developments in our ways of working. Most of the five questions will be touched upon, though not in a systematic manner. I didn't want to let them disturb the story that I have to tell.

It is now almost thirty years ago that I first participated in a Socratic dialogue. That was a strange, fascinating experience. For a week we tried in a small group and on the basis of actual experiences to find out what the meaning was of the term 'useless'. Some will regard such an undertaking itself as useless. But I was overwhelmed by the beauty of our mental wanderings, the difficulties to understand each other, my own inability to clearly express what I felt, the shared confusion and the enormous fun we had. That you could actually do philosophy in this manner, without books or authorities, purely by talking together, that was a revelation to me.

The Socratic dialogue has never left me since. I reported about my Socratic experiences in several books and also founded an agency that still conducts and facilitates all kinds of reflection in organizations. Since then the practice of Socratic dialogue in the Netherlands has, through many enthusiasts, taken a number of different forms, from 'diner pensant' to Socratic Café, from individual coaching to weeks of reflection, from careful thought to also, alas, embarrassing charlatanry.

PRACTICE IS DIFFERENT FROM THEORY

The Socratic method has a long tradition and a rich background. I was lucky that I got initiated into it by Gustav Heckmann, Leonard Nelson's successor, and his staff in the German *Philosophisch-Politische Akademie*. There I learned to read Plato in a completely different way than usual in academic philosophy, namely from the perspective of conducting philosophical dialogues yourself. Plato has not left me since, either. I became enchanted by his dialogues, his powerful imagination, the combination of poetic inspiration and sober conceptual analysis. And by his depth, his originality, his superior playfulness. Truly amazing.

What struck me most, in the beginning, was that the practice of Socratic dialogue, as I had experienced it in the *Philosophisch-Politische Akademie*, differed so much from the official theory of how to set up a philosophical dialogue. According to this theory, Plato successively used the methods of refutation, hypothesis and 'collection and division'. Honestly, I have never seen anyone develop a practice of philosophical conversation with these methods yet. What should we conclude from that? I considered it a confirmation of what Plato himself says explicitly, for instance in his Seventh Letter, that he never wrote a a single word about what really matters in the practice of philosophy. Not only did he apparently hesitate to reveal this secret to the uninitiated, he also considered it as fundamentally impossible. For it does not admit of exposition, like other branches of knowledge, he writes; only after much converse about the matter itself and a life lived together, suddenly a light, as it were, is kindled in one soul by a flame that leaps to it from another, and thereafter sustains itself.[1]

Such mysterious pronouncements, not only of Plato himself but also of a number of his pupils, caused all sorts of speculations about an "unwritten doctrine. The master would definitely have had a special method, one that underlies all his dialogues. But he would have deliberately kept it hidden and implicit. It would have been derived from the school of Pythagoras, and been based on his mathematics. He would have referred to it, in a suggestive manner, in several famous images, the myth of the cave in the Politeia, the ladder of love that Diotima describes in the Symposium, the ascent of the soul in the trail of the god that Socrates tells about in the Phaedrus, and others. In his later work he would have developed key aspects of this method in his theory of ideas and his cosmology. But all the time taking care that its essence would remain hidden, accessible only to initiates.

For anyone doing Socratic dialogue, this makes the questions one struggles with in practice only the more tantalizing. What does Plato exactly mean with those images? What do they imply for the design of a philosophical conversation à la Socrates? It is not clear. Nowhere does he talk about how exactly to proceed, nor where the inquiry should lead to. Of course, Socrates demonstrates the practice of philosophical dialogue all the time. But what exactly is it that he demonstrates?

---

[1] Plato, Letters VII, 341 c-d.

What is an idea? What does it look like, when would someone legitimately claim to have found one? And then I'm not even talking about the simpler questions, like how in all the inevitable wanderings of a dialogue one can keep the goal clear and the participants motivated. For every philosophical conversation will quickly go astray without a firm method, no matter how animated it begins—which it often does, because it concerns mostly realistic and fundamental issues. But barely begun, participants generally lose grip on the dialogue pretty soon, not being able to distinguish the trees from the forest anymore, and losing hope that further talk will yield anything of interest at all. The big question in practice is: what can one do to prevent this?

HOURGLASS MODEL. FREE SPACE

If one conducts Socratic dialogues for many years with many different people in many different circumstances, one naturally develops a few useful methodological insights. For me an important one was the hourglass model, an image of the logical structure of a philosophical conversation:

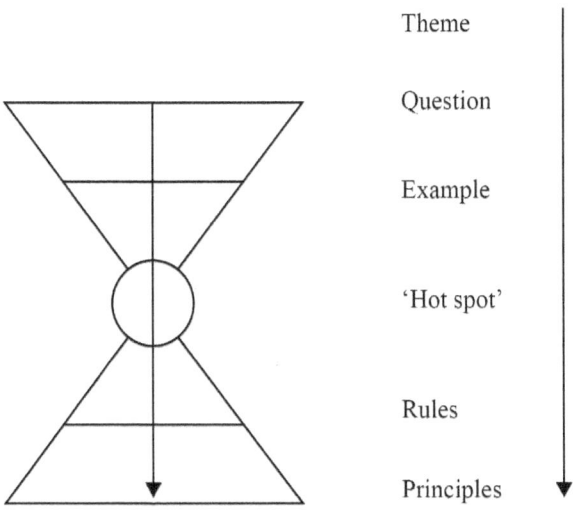

In words, a theme is connected to an example, a personal experience that is relevant to the theme, and to a question to be investigated in the dialogue. The example is focused on one or more 'hot spots', a crucial moment in the experience. That is either an action, or an emotional response or a specific thought. This is what Nelson calls the judgment. The dialogue develops through inquiring into what the underlying assumptions of this particular experience are, the rules, and on what principles, if any, these rules are based. That is called regressive abstraction. The participants in the dialogue put themselves in the shoes of the example-giver and thus inquire into their own (presumed, imagined) experience.

The hourglass model is based on the idea that for a fruitful inquiry a theme should not only be connected to a concrete example, as Nelson and Heckmann taught. It must be constrained to a focuspoint or a 'hot spot', a crucial moment that Nelson calls 'judgment'. The art of philosophical dialogue is to examine the presuppositions of this judgment, by getting others to imagine themselves in that moment. Everyone inquires into what underlies their own (imagined) action, response or thought. Then, after that, one inquires into what these assumptions are based on, i.e. what everyone's principles of thinking and acting are in this case. This approach follows from Nelson's theory of regressive abstraction, the doctrine that a philosophical discussion is a "going back", a regression, to the abstract principles that lie hidden as an "obscure knowledge" in our thoughts and that are the basis of our actions.[2]

Another crucial insight that we developed in The New Trivium (the consultancy firm that I founded in The Netherlands before my present Eidoskoop) was the concept of 'free space'. This is the the idea that a Socratic dialogue can only succeed, only penetrate to the level of principles, when it is not focused on problem solving but only on clarifying vision.[3] This is a subtle but crucial distinction. When participants consider the aim of a conversation to be the solution of a particular problem, they will focus their attention too much on the result, rather than on what that result is based upon, the values or principles that underlie it. To find these you need free space, a state of mind where one is temporarily free from thinking in terms of results or solutions. Free space, *scholè* in Greek (indeed, that is where our term 'school' comes from), is the mentality of the free, the people that do not have to work, that are

---

[2] Leonard Nelson, *Von der Kunst zu philosophieren* (The art of philosophizing), Gesammelte Schriften, BD. I, Felix Meiner Verlag, Hamburg 1870, 219-246.

[3] Cf. Jos Kessels et al, *Free Space, Philosophy in Organisations*. Boom, Amsterdam, 2004.

on vacation. Free space is the presupposition of the liberal arts, the arts that belong to free people and that make you develop into a really free person. Often it is already a big step to release oneself from the servile arts, and achieve the freedom of the liberal arts for a philosophical conversation.

THINKING IS DOING. POETIC REASON

Another useful tool for the practice of dialogue is Socrates' identification of thought and action, the premise that every person always does what they think is best. A cobbler, a skipper and in general any expert knows exactly what's needed for a good result. If the result is not right, that's not a matter of weakness of will (*akrasia*), but of not quite knowing what is at stake, not being skilled enough. This applies to all of us: not doing the right thing can only have one cause, that you do not know well enough what in fact the right thing is. Which makes it necessary to uncover the inaccuracies in one's alleged knowledge and to remedy and improve them by refuting them. For someone who really knows what is right will do the right thing. Action follows understanding.

To many people these two assumptions, of free space and the assimilation of thinking and doing, sound outlandish and unrealistic. Who would get involved in a discussion if it is not directed at a concrete result? And is our actual behaviour not much more determined by emotions and accidental circumstances than by intellectual ideas? I think the greatest strength of Socrates must have been precisely this, that he was able to break through such scepticism, entice people to get involved in a dialogue despite their reserves and investigate the assumptions of their actual, personal doings. This is today not different from twenty-five hundred years ago. Even now one has to seduce people into the practice of philosophy. If one can not do that, one won't get access to the trendsetters of society, the people that may be expected to have "a philosophy", a legitimate vision on what the good life is about.

Another doctrine that appeared important in the practice of philosophy is that of "poetic reason": to achieve some depth in a conversation, to really get an insight into underlying principles of action, participants should be open and have the guts to formulate what really gets them. In most conversations the issue at stake is not only the analysis of a particular topic, but also an inquiry into the personal mastery of the participants, the excellence or virtue needed for 'the good life'. The latter can only be investigated if participants are willing to explore what they really care about. Poetic reason is the level of thinking where these notions dwell, notions that are fundamental to creating your own reality. They are the notions that poets always look for, the creators of reality

10. Jos Kessels

(the word poet comes from the Greek *'poiein'*, i.e. making, creating). In other words, Socrates' pursuit of an idea is not merely an intellectual quest. It is a search for knowledge that includes the whole person, head, heart and belly, i.e. cognitions, affections and actions. It is knowledge that is not only theoretical, nor merely practical or emotional, but all of them together.[4]

THE GLASSBEAD GAME

In my latest book *'De Jacht op een Idee'* (*The hunt for an Idea*)[5] I worked out a further addition to this set of dialogue instruments. There I explained that in his later philosophy Plato seems to have connected the concept of an idea with a famous mathematical structure, the tetractys. This is a figure consisting of the numbers one to four, arranged in a triangle:

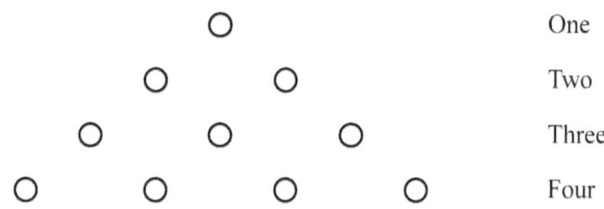

The tetractys was a holy number to the Pythagoreans and stimulated the imagination of many people. It represents not just a mathematical theorem, it is also a metaphysical symbol. Pythagoras (ca. 580-500 BC) believed that the tetractys symbolized the first principles of nature (earth, water, air and fire), the harmony of the cosmos and the structure of music: the ratio of 1:2 in string length provides an octave, 2:3 a fifth and 3:4 a quarter. From these can be formed all other tones of the scale. Since this figure was thought to display the most perfect harmonies, Plato in his Timaeus used it as blueprint of the human soul. The figure is depicted in Raphael's famous fresco The School of Athens and seems to have formed the basis for Hermann Hesse's Nobelprize winning novel The Glass Bead Game. It plays a central role in the speculations that were triggered in the last century, in the Tübingen school of Plato research, about his so called unwritten doctrine. If there is some truth in

---

[4] Cf. Jos Kessels, *Het poëtisch argument, sopcratische gesprekken over het goede leven (Poetic Reason, Socratic dialogues on the good life)*, Boom, Amsterdam, 2006.

[5] Jos Kessels, *De Jacht op een Idee. Visie, strategie, filosofie (The hunt for an Idea, Vision, strategy, philosophy)*, Boom Amsterdam 2009.

these speculations, the figure must have played an important role in the discussions and researches of the Academy, the school that Plato was the founder of. But what role could that have been?

It is, I think, not impossible that it is the role we have given it in our practice: to try to rise from the perception of the empirical world to the contemplation of an idea by the systematic analysis of ten 'beads' or themes, spread over four levels of research: the facts, the person, possible meanings and the 'ideal shape' or *eidos*, as follows:

		10. idea			*form*
	8. big		9. small		*meaning*
5. belly		6. heart		7. head	*person*
1. case	2. hot spot	3. trends	4. question		*facts*

Let us go through the beads one by one. On the lower level of the tetractys there are four beads that identify 'what is', i.e. the facts of a matter, our personal perspective on it or the experience we have with it. Aristotle formulated the doctrine of the four causes for this, presumably because it had been an issue of extensive discussion in Plato's Academy. This doctrine runs roughly as follows. Take something simple from the experience, say some tree, for instance an oak. Now one might wonder: what exactly is that phenomenon? Why is the tree what it is and the way it is? This question can get four types of answers, according to Aristotle. First, it is what it is because it's made of wood, it consists of wood. That is the *material* cause. Then it is what it is because it has become that way, because it started growing from an acorn in the ground. That is the *efficient* or *moving* cause. Besides, it is what it is because it is becoming something, it has a purpose, a built-in direction of development: it aims so to speak to be a fully grown oak tree. That is the *final* cause. And finally, it looks what it looks like because it just is an oak. That is the *formal* cause, the essence or basic principle of the oak.

Although western science and philosophy abrogated teleology long ago, in the practice of socratic dialogue it still makes sense to map an experience or a case history in a similar way, on the basis of these four causes. An experience consists of some particular 'matter': the facts, circumstances, persons of the story. Together they have become a case because of some 'efficient cause', a difficulty, conflict or other 'hot spot', by which over time an issue arose, something that deserves to be investigated. Further, a casestory is always part of a field of forces, a framework of trends, that shows some target direction, or goal or intent ('what will happen if you don't do anything?'). This is the final cause. And the case raises a question or issue: what now? What is the correct interpretation, the real meaning, the hidden essence of the situation? One better finds an answer to that question, in order to deal with it. This is the formal cause, presenting itself initially as a questionmark, inciting a query after the 'key' to the situation. I think it is conceivable that this doctrine of four causes, together with the other beads of the tetractys, played a role in the Academy as a heuristic tool for reflection or research.

Whereas the lower level of the Glass Bead Game concerns the experience, the world of external phenomena, the second level is about the person(s) involved and their internal phenomena. The feelings and sentiments they have about the matter are the main 'colorants' of opinion or doxa. Plato assumes a tripartite division of the soul into 'belly', 'heart' and 'head'. They function as three centers of motivation that together determine how we perceive reality. The belly is the desirous part, focused on what is pleasant. The heart is the spirited part, where 'thymos' resides, the fire of indignation, the ambition to contribute and to gain recognition for this, the need for respect and influence. The head is the reasonable part, focused on understanding, seeing how it really is, not being led astray by illusions. If one of these centers gets too much under pressure, our perception gets distorted by, respectively, fear, anger or sadness. When on the other hand they function properly and undisturbed, we preceive reality with self-confidence, calmness and joy. In a dialogue, it is usually not easy to bring these feelings in the open and examine them properly. Yet to find a common idea about some matter, the emotional level needs to be clarified and sometimes purged of contortions. It is the examination of the right attitude, the right kind of emotion or reaction in a specific situation, or, in terms of the theory of virtue, what temperance, courage or prudence are adequate or asked for. These virtues are the basis of the leadership virtue par excellence, justice, the ability to bring balance to a situation. Socrates'constant assumption is that we need these excellences, in all circumstances, to be a 'phronimos', a wise person.

The third level of the tetractys is mostly referred to as the 'big and small' or the 'indefinite dyad'. It is the level of dialectic, of balancing arguments and comparing perspectives. Whatever the 'colorant', feeling or attitude towards some matter, be it fear or ambition, enthusiasm or indignation, it's validity depends on one's outlook or viewpoint, on the criteria that one uses for their assessment. Each viewpoint changes as one changes the relative weight or importance of the set of arguments supporting it. Why should one assign a compelling interest to argument A, and a less compelling one to B? Or what's there to be feared in the situation and to what extent? Examining such questions may lead to different scenario's, different ideas of what is at stake and how to deal with it. This is the business of dialectic, of opposing thought forms. Here the facts of the situation and the feelings of the person are associated with values and meanings, in an attempt to—at the top level of the tetractys—find a definition, an idea, an accurate understanding of the matter and an indication of the right principle of action. This third level is also the level of sharpening concepts: what exactly do we mean by the concepts that we are using? Obviously, investigating this level is not a purely objective, scientific inquiry. The hunt for an idea is never purely objective, only concerned with some issue in itself. It is always also subjective, about what the issue is for you personally, and for the other participants in the dialogue.

The top of the tetractys represents the principle of one, the good or the idea, in Plato's philosophy. It corresponds to the principle of leadership, justice, applying the right balance. This is the fourth and highest of the cardinal virtues and the virtue par excellence of the leader. That's what the whole investigation, every hunt for an idea, is ultimately directed at. It is what Plato called the *eidos* or form or idea, an image of what you yourself, the parties involved and the situation as a whole looks like when everyone and everything is in shape and works perfectly, when justice is done to the situation and everyone plays their own proper role role. That is what we are after in a socratic dialogue.

PROPERTIES OF AN IDEA

It will be clear that, compared to such an analysis, what we call an idea in everyday language is usually only a fragment of an idea: a thought without context or without a question to be answered, consisting of abstract concepts without recourse to personal feelings, empirical data or alternative meanings. In the Glass Bead Game an idea is well-formed only if the beadstructure is complete, explicit and consistent. The purpose of philosophical dialogue is to uncover this mental structure.

Let us go a little deeper into the criteria for determining whether some thought may be considered an idea. It is important in order to understand a new development of the Socratic practice that we are working with. The first and main characteristic of an idea is that it has a unifying effect. An idea creates unity where before there was only a plurality, of ideas, thoughts, opposites. This unity is not only a cognitive matter. An idea makes you feel that you want to be part of it, support it, or stronger, that you belong to it. That an idea has this effect, is because it gives one the impression to be true or truthful, that it strikes home or articulates the heart of the matter. Moreover, an idea makes one surpass one's conventional, daily self, taking the person to a higher level, of being 'in shape'. Besides, an idea is attractive, it has an original, captivating form, despite its severity. It gives 'wings to the soul', in Plato's poetic language.

A second characteristic is that an idea gives a definitie limit (*peras*) to a field of possible meanings and thoughts (*apeiron*), in such a way that both extremes—the too much and too little, the indefinite dyad—become clear, including the center position, the main target of Aristotelian ethics. This center position is not a compromise, a bit of this and a bit of that, mixing opposites into an insipid taste. It is itself an extreme, a qualified choice, one that gives the intuition of a moral compass, the sensation that in this matter this is precisely the right choice. That's what makes up the center position, it gives one the feeling of having found the right thing in an extended field of possibilities.

A third characteristic is that an idea transforms the 'opinions' or feelings of belly, heart and head (roughly fear, anger, sadness) into the virtues of classical virtue theory: temperance, courage and prudence. The Glass Bead Game and the final idea make clear what temperance is needed, what courage and what particular prudence. Only with them it becomes possible to bring about a new balance in the situation as a whole. That is, as we saw above, the virtue of the leader, justice, the ability to bring about balance by giving each his due.

A fourth characteristic is that an idea, by its internal structure, and because one has played the full Glass Bead Game, provides not only a balanced answer to the initial question, but also reconciles one, as a person, with the facts as they are: 'This is what the situation is and it is okay.' 'Such is how the world is made up and I can be at peace with it.' The idea makes one, despite the difficulty of the situation, experience harmony, both in the world around and within oneself. For those not actually involved in a matter, this effect of course is not felt. For them, the Glass Bead Game remains a shadowy operation, without much engagement, and the idea that comes out of it at most dull guesswork. But for those who feel connected with the inquiry an idea can have a strong emotional impact.

All these characteristics are based on the assumption that Socratic inquiry is a thorough self-examination. An idea is not some knowledge outside oneself, but a state of being, a propositional attitude, an ordering of the soul. Based on observation and facts (the four lower beads) one examines one's own opinions, including the three parts of the soul (the three beads of the second level) and subjects them to an accurate reflection, the purifying dialectic of the great-and-small. Only then can one truly come to understand and catch a glimpse of 'the Idea' (with a capital), that reduces the multiplicity to unity and shows what the issue looks like if everything is in shape.

THE PHILOSOPHER AND THE POET

I will give here a sketch of an idea, displaying the structure of the Glass Bead Game—without going into the process of developing it in the dialogue that led to it, nor what the role was of the methodological issues I described above. The idea proceeded from a discussion about structural change in a bureaucratic organization:

Topic: internal versus external focus

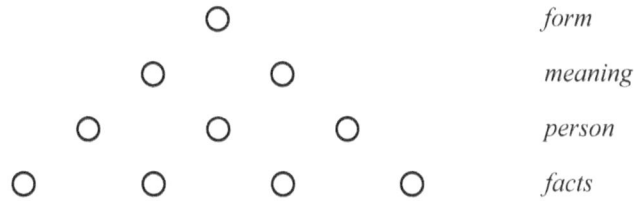

FACTS

- Under pressure from internal interests and views on work quality deadlines are not met. I get complaints about that.
- For a monopolist, the external environment and customer needs are not dominant. Internal approval is important. We have a non-intervention culture.
- The neglect of interests of citizens will in the (near) future no longer be accepted.
- How can we ensure that people organize their work so that outside interests are met?

PERSON

- A change of culture to external domination is a tough process, affects the interests of the staff, takes time and leads to unpopularity of the management (i.e. me).
- I must face that this cultural change, however necessary, will not be easily achieved and not at the pace we have in mind. I will have to bear unpopularity by addressing people and giving them feedback.

- The ideal of external domination requires great responsibility and a culture of feedback: more birds with one stone.

MEANING

- At one extreme: 100% internal interests remain dominant, the public just had to adjust to it.
- At the other extreme: 100% outside interests are dominant, the staff has just to adapt to it.

FORM

- .....

It takes a lot of thinking to formulate such a small text. Much can be said about each one of the different beads. But the main question is of course: what should be set down under Form? What could be the answer to the central question, the final conclusion, the view of what is right? At first, in my initial attempts at forming Glass Bead Games, I always left this last bead open. Even without a closure I read the text as a kind of poem. And its very effect as a picture puzzle was increased by the lack of a conclusion. But eventually of course one cannot escape it, something needs to be articulated at the top of the Glass Bead Game. What could that be? What can represent the idea that according to Plato gives one insight in 'the good' and forges a unity of all the particular beads, all the fragments in oneself?

To be able to see what the final bead could be, it is important to keep a few things in mind. First of all, the premise of Socrates (and Plato, Kant, Nelson in his wake) is that the knowledge one is looking for in a philosophical conversation already is present in oneself, albeit as an "obscure knowledge". The point is to recall this knowledge (anamnesis). That's what the conversation is always focused upon, the memory of an original, but obscure knowledge. Second, Plato makes clear, for example in his myth of the cave, that for anyone sitting in the darkness of the cave, the words of one who has seen the sunlight outside are not intelligible. They are beyond comprehension, they sound like gibberish to him, or even abracadabra. At best, if he is not immediately opposed to them, he considers them as an oracle, a message from another world. At the time of Socrates and Plato especially the Delphi Oracle played that role. Plato himself gave brisk examples of such oracle language, for example in his Parmenides.

Based on these considerations, I started at some point to ask people to finish off their reasoning by writing an oracle, some text that articulates in a picturesque, poetic way their own 'truth intuition' (cf. about truth intuition Nelson's "The Impossibility of Epistemology", Nelson 1994). Poetry is capable with it's original language, surprising images and unexpected angles to show a reality that eludes the ordinary everyday consciousness. An analysis like the one above, focused on external domination, is then closed with a text like this:

> My house has a door.
> Directly on the street.
> I open the door.
> Passers-by are happy to come in.
> My fellow residents welcome them home.
> No one is cold.

Can such words, of one of the participants in the discussion, act as the final idea? Can they, enigmatic as they are, provide a satisfactory answer to the central question? In practice, this appears to work very well. And it is consistent with the Platonic theory. According to Plato, the idea itself can not be articulated. It may 'suddenly emerge in the soul', after 'prolonged, dedicated dealings with the subject', but 'it cannot be put into words' itself. Yet it must, if it is to fulfil it's guiding role in practice, it should receive some comprehensive, manageable formulation. One can use a picturesque, poetic text as the one above for that, or a more pragmatical, strategic sentence like this:

> The new structure of the organization contributes to heighten the external focus.

Both texts played a role in the actual conversation. Which of the two, the oracle or the strategy sentence, most approaches the idea? Let us consult the aforementioned characteristics of an idea. Which formulation has the greatest binding force? Which one defines and restricts the scope of possible meanings, in such a way that it tastes of excellence, of pursuing a true and worthy ideal? Which words have the greatest precision, cognitive and affective, or the strongest appeal? I myself think: it is the poetic text, the oracle. That one comes closest to the core, to the essence that itself remains unstable. It also makes clear why it is useful before formulating a strategy, in management language, to look into the idea that underlies it, in poetic language. That is where the inspiration is, the motivating idea. And it is exactly what Socrates always does, in Plato's view. At crucial moments, Socrates resorts to poetic images: a comparison of the cave, the sun, the line, the myth of Er, the winged soul, etc. At the end of the Meno, Socrates says explicitly that the knowledge they have been looking for cannot be taught, it must be the result of some 'divine dispensation' that comes about 'without understanding in those who receive it'[6]. It is not knowledge in the usual sense, but knowledge of another order, which requires a language different from our regular, everyday speech.

Here, too, lies the explanation why Plato expels the poets from his ideal state. Poets are dangerous. They enchant the mind. The attractiveness of their images, their seductiveness, make one consider as true what they say, before one has taken the trouble to carry out the full analysis that the Glass Bead Game requires. Yet that is precisely the characteristic of an idea, that is not only attractive, but also true. That it can be explained, substantiated. That it is affiliated with experience, with how one actually lives, with head, heart and hands. And that one can give an account. That is what Socrates always did, ask for an account. All the poets that he interrogated appeared not to be able to give that sufficiently.

But is giving an account, an explanation impossible? Can a poetic text be connected to an argument that does give an account? That's exactly what one expects from leaders or politicians. They must have a certain charm, in order to believe them, a form of originality or charisma, personal appeal. But they must also be able to debate and explain the how and why of what they want. They have to be capable of both things, appeal to the imagination and to analytical thinking. Also many philosophers are an example of that combination, Plato himself in the first place. In many places he supplements an argument with images, metaphors, stories, allegories. Only he takes good care that the two are complementary, supportive and reinforcing. Is not this the way to bring the Glass Bead Game to a closure?

PLAYING WITH MEANING

In this way conducting conversations and reconstructing ideas leads to interesting and exciting sessions. Some participants hesitate to write an oracle at first, others feel challenged and amused. I am amazed at the impact of the texts. Usually the recipients of the oracle consider the words not as a casual, non-committal thought, but—even in spite of overt skepticism or distance—as a meaningful signal that in the context of the preceding analysis has something substantial to say about their view of themselves and the issue they have investigated. Apparently that's how the Glass Bead Game works. Somehow or other one tries to give the oracle a place in the system of meaning that one has articulated.

In my book, *The hunt for an idea*, I described in detail how the game

---

[6] Plato, *Meno* 99 e.

is applied in a large organization, a hospital. In that case, a group of governors (i.e. Board of Directors and Management Team) sets out for a vision and a strategy using the Glass Bead Game. At the end of the track the assigment was to think up a text so authoritative and inspiring, that it would support and focus the joint efforts of the whole organization for several years. There, too, the rational analysis of the Glass Bead Game had to be attached to some visionary or poetic text, one that could lift you above one's usual, trampled thoughts. It was quite a job to achieve that. But ultimately we succeeded, in a way that was surprising for every participant.

Since then, the Glass Bead Game never left me, like the Socratic dialogue and Plato's theory of Ideas. They are closely related. All three are a game with meaning, with ideas, values, opinions. They take the form of sentences and arguments. One plays with them, in order to achieve a coherent picture of an issue. The aim is always to find an idea, a thought or a concept or an image at some higher level, that expresses the essence of a topic and shows the right direction for action. That combines emotion and intellect. That connects the language of the poet, the politician and the philosopher. That sets truth, goodness and beauty all three at stake. It has always been the intention of the theory of ideas and Socrates' conversations that they would be a living reality, instead of the pale, academic abstraction that they became later and now have been for centuries. With the Glass Bead Game, searching for the right idea becomes a game again, both lighthearted and profound, practical and philosophical, and equally accessible to laymen and philosophers.

Bibliography

Brisson, Luc (1998), *Plato, the Myth Maker.* University of Chicago Press.

Elias, Julius A. (1984), *Plato's Defence of Poetry.* MacMillan Press, London.

Friedländer, Paul (1958), *Plato, An Introduction.* Princeton University Press.

Gadamer, Hans-Georg (1934/1980), *Dialogue and Dialectic. Eight Hermeneutical Studies on Plato.* Yale University Press.

Hyland, Drew A. (2008), *Plato and the Question of Beauty.* Indiana University Press, Bloomington.

Jaeger, Werner (1943), *Paideia. The Ideals of Greek Culture.* Oxford University Press.

Janaway, Christopher (1995), *Images of Excellence. Plato's Critique of the Arts*. Clarendon Press, Oxford.

Kessels, Jos
   (1997), *Socrates op de markt. Filosofie in bedrijf*. Boom, Amsterdam (translated in German: *Die Macht der Argumente*. Belz Verlag, 2001)
   (2006) *Het poëtisch argument. Socratische gesprekken over het goede leven*. Boom, Amsterdam.
   (2009) *De jacht op een idee. Visie, strategie, filosofie*. Boom, Amsterdam.
   (2012) Spelen met ideeën. *De kunst van het filosofisch gesprek*. Boom, Amsterdam.

Kessels, Jos, Erik Boers, Pieter Mostert (2004), *Free Space. Philosophy in organisations*. Boom, Amsterdam
   (2008), *Free space Field guide to conversations*. Boom, Amsterdam

Miller, Mitchell (2004), *The Philosopher in Plato's Statesman*. Parmenides Publishing, Las Vegas.

Mitchell, Joshua (2006), *Plato's Fable. On the Mortal Condition in Shadowy Times*. Princeton University Press.

Murdoch, Iris (1950/1997), *Re-reading Plato*. In: Peter Conradi (ed), *Iris Murdoch, Existentialists and Mystics,* Part VII. Penguin Books, Harmondsworth, England.

Nelson, Leonard (1994), *De socratische methode. Inleiding en redactie Jos Kessels*. Boom, Amsterdam.

Plato (360 BCE, 1928), *The Seventh Letter*, translated by John Harward. http://classics.mit.edu/Plato/seventhletter.html

Reeve, C.D.C. (1988), *Philosopher-Kings. The Argument of Plato's Republic*. Princeton University Press.

Rosen, Stanley (1980), *The Limits of Analysis*. Basic Books, New York.

Sayre, Kenneth M. (2005), *Plato's Late Ontology. A Riddle Resolved*. Parmenides Publishing.

Schäfer, Christian (Hrsg) (2007), *Platon-Lexikon. Begriffswörterbuch zu Platon und der platonischen Tradition*. Wissenschaftliche Buchgesellschaft, Darmstadt.

Tanner, Sonja (2010), *In Praise of Plato's Poetic Imagination*. Lexington Books, Plymouth.

Vaihinger, Hans (1923), *Die Philosophie des Als Ob. System des theoretischen, praktischen und religiösen Fiktionen der Menschheit aud Grund eines idealistischen Positivismus*. Felix Meiner Verlag, Leipzig.

I am grateful to Edu Feltmann for his lucid and playful comments on an earlier version of this article.

10. Jos Kessels

11

Dieter Krohn

Erster Vorsitzender der Gesellschaft für Sokratisches Philosophieren/Chair of the Society of Socratic Facilitators

---

How and why I was drawn into Philosophical Practice

In the early 60s I started to be interested in philosophical questions. As a working-class child I did not have access to shelves full of philosophy books in our crowded flat or philosophical discussions at the dinner table. But I was lucky. A public library was opened near my home, understanding librarians helped me to find and choose the appropriate books. I read one introduction after the other into philosophy and developed a tentative position of my own. My best friend, who stemmed from the educated classes and is now a professor of mathematics and an expert facilitator of mathematical Socratic Dialogues, encouraged me to accompany him to evening classes on the history of philosophy. I developed the habit of enjoying long nightly discussions in dark basement party rooms drinking red wine and smoking a pipe (only on these occasions, although I hated it) and thought I was a philosopher. (Some people might still think doing this is Philosophical Practice!) I overindulged in existentialism: knew truth does not exist and that it is futile to search for it.

With this attitude I began my career in higher education. Philosophy was one of the subjects offered and I had no doubt about choosing it. Nevertheless, I went to a session at which this subject was introduced to all first-year students and the lecture and seminar programme was described. The professor, who had come to the college on his bike and, to my mind, looked much too normal and conventional to be a philosopher, talked about one of his seminars at greater length. He called it Socratic Dialogue. He explained that a group, under his facilitation, would slowly and systematically search for truth in a philosophical matter. I was shocked. How could a philosophy professor be so naïve? He surely could not really believe in truth! The students were encouraged to ask questions and I could not restrain myself from asking him whether he really believed that this would work, as everybody knew there is no truth. Gustav Heckmann, the professor who had given the talk, just answered: Come and see. So I went to my first Socratic Dialogue, facilitated by Gustav Heckmann, in the summer term of 1965. This is how and why I was drawn into Philosophical Practice, if you want to call Socratic Dialogue a form of Philosophical Practice.

When I was about to graduate, Gustav Heckmann had decided to try and find, as he said, about five people he wanted to teach how to facilitate Socratic Dialogues. He offered to accompany them when they prepared for the facilitation on the content level, i.e when they worked on the philosophical question they intended to choose for their dialogue, and he was willing to help them as their mentor when they facilitated their first Socratic Dialogue, which lasted a whole week. Gustav Heckmann invited me to work with him on the topic I had chosen for three days in his secluded weekend house near Hannover. And this we did, from morning till night, during the meals, between the meals, and on walks through the woods. He was convinced that it was the best preparation for a facilitator to think through the topic or question and discuss it thoroughly with somebody else. After that, in 1969, I facilitated my first Socratic Dialogue lasting a whole week on the topic of Truth and Tolerance.

Over the years more and more people participated in the Socratic seminars organized by the Philosophisch-Politische Akademie (PPA; Philosophical-Political Academy, a non-profit organization), which was founded by Leonard Nelson (philosopher at the University of Göttingen) and his followers in 1922, and more and more facilitators were needed and trained. In 1994 the Gesellschaft für Sokratisches Philosophieren (GSP, Society of Socratic Facilitators) was founded as an independent advisory and discussion forum. For the time being the GSP has more than forty members from different European countries (Austria, Belarus, Bulgaria, Czech Republic, Germany, Great Britain, Italy, the Netherlands, and Turkey). Only people who have been trained as Socratic facilitators can apply for membership. Whenever they facilitate in our seminars, they do it on a voluntary basis. They are not paid for it but are given the chance to take part in another Socratic Dialogue free of charge to use it as a kind of further training, very often in cooperation with the facilitator of that Dialogue. Some of our members work with Socratic Dialogue in their respective professional fields outside our seminars for an appropriate fee, which is excellent, I think.

11. Dieter Krohn 151

SOME MYTHS ABOUT SOCRATIC DIALOGUE —
OR: BELIEFS CHANGE THE PRACTICE

In publications on Socratic Dialogue some myths seem to have evolved that may lead to over-simplification of the theory and a stereotyping practice. Gustav Heckmann's considerations are reduced to a simplified form of his pedagogical measures. I would like to comment and, hopefully, shed light on some of the points and, in doing so, address, at least implicitly, some of the five questions of this anthology. More is to be found in: Dieter Krohn/Barbara Neißer/Nora Walter (eds.), "*Sokratisches Philosophieren*" *(Series on Socratic Philosophizing)*, Volumes 1-12, 1994ff, dipa, Frankfurt/LIT, Münster).

THE NELSON-HECKMANN TRADITION

To talk about Socratic Dialogue in the Nelson-Heckmann Tradition is to blur the differences between Nelson's and Heckmann's approach. Heckmann was enormously impressed when he in 1922, as a student, heard Nelson's lecture The Socratic Method[1] He had started a career as a physicist, had written his doctoral dissertation under the supervision of Max Born, the future Nobel Prize winner, had worked together with Pascual Jordan, was in close and friendly contact to Werner Heisenberg and Friedrich Hund, famous nuclear physicists, who studied and worked in Göttingen in those days. And then he decided to follow Leonard Nelson, to join his political movement, which meant to leave the church, to become a vegetarian, to give nearly all the money he earned to the movement, to be engaged in political activities. And the strongest motive for all that was to learn to facilitate Socratic Dialogues.

In his 1922 lecture Nelson criticized Socrates' methods as shown in some of the Platonic Dialogues as unacceptable and to be in contrast to the true Socratic approach. On the other hand, he explained why he, nevertheless, named his method of philosophizing in groups Socratic: "Socrates was the first to combine [the] confidence in the ability of the human mind to recognize philosophical truth [with] the conviction that this truth is not arrived at through occasional bright ideas or mechanical teaching but that only planned, unremitting, and consistent thinking leads us from darkness into its light. Therein lies Socrates' greatness

---

[1] First published in 1929, reprinted in Leonard Nelson, *Gesammelte Schriften in neun Bänden*, Bd. I, Meiner Verlag: Hamburg 1970, pp. 269-316; and in Dieter Birnbacher/Dieter Krohn (eds.), *Das sokratische Gespräch*, Reclam: Stuttgart 2002, pp. 21-72; in English also in: Leonard Nelson, *Socratic Method and Critical Philosophy*, Yale University Press: New Haven 1949, pp. 1-40; and in: Rene Saran/Barbara Neißer (eds.), *Enquiring Minds*, Trentham Books: Stoke on Trent 2004, pp. 126-162.

as a philosopher. His greatness as a pedagogue is based on another innovation: he made his pupils do their own thinking and introduced the interchange of ideas as a safeguard against self-deception."[2] Behind the flowery style of this passage we detect the two essentials Heckmann has always adhered to: the belief in the ability of the human mind to find answers to philosophical questions and the conviction that the dialogue of autonomous thinkers is the best method to reach those answers. The practice of Socratic Dialogue he learned primarily from Minna Specht, the head of Nelson's boarding school near Kassel in the state of Hesse, and his colleague in the small school for emigrant children in Denmark.

The most important difference between Nelson and Heckmann lies in their expectations regarding the outcome of a Socratic Dialogue. For Nelson, Socratic Dialogue was the best way to learn how to philosophize, to arrive at results through systematically thinking together. As Nelson was convinced to know the true answers to the philosophical questions dealt with in the dialogue the Socratic facilitator had to patiently wait till the students found those answers. He could help them by steering the process, which does not mean that he manipulated their thoughts, but that, e.g., he drew their attention to a particular statement that had been uttered without gaining adequate attention. Nelson's concept of truth was no longer tenable for Gustav Heckmann after he came back from the emigration in Britain in 1946.

For me, and in this I follow Heckmann in principle, Socratic Dialogue has reached its end when there is no longer any doubt about the result the group has found. Everybody, including the facilitator, has to express doubt, if they have reason to doubt. And even if the reason for that doubt cannot be clearly formulated at first the group needs to try to clarify the matter and look for ways to address their doubt. To my mind, the truth that we can formulate in a Socratic Dialogue, as in all other fields where we search for truth, lies in a statement about which we no longer have any doubts. The criterion for the truth that can be reached by a group through thinking together is: There is no doubt about it. That, of course, means: There is no doubt about it *now*. We must be aware of the provisional nature of such discovered truth. Doubt may arise in the future on the basis of new experience or be brought into the group by a person who offers new arguments.

META-DIALOGUE

Statements of our beliefs which are repeated again and again tend to become unshakable. This is the case with some of the attributes frequently

---

[2] Quotation taken from the English translation in: Rene Saran/Barbara Neißer (eds.), *Enquiring Minds*, Trentham Books: Stoke on Trent 2004, pp. 140f.

associated with Socratic Dialogue. One of them is the meta-dialogue. Very often you find the assertion in publications on Socratic Dialogue that the meta-dialogue is a necessary part of it. Without any doubt, there can be matters related to the Socratic Dialogue proper, i.e. the dialogue on the philosophical question, which have to be addressed but are not directly part of the Dialogue itself. Maybe participants are irritated by one of the participant' behaviour; they want to complain about the facilitation as being too rigid or to lax; they want to ask methodological questions; they want to suggest what to deal with next. All such concerns do not belong to the content dialogue. Strategic questions about, for example, what to address next or what to park for a while can in most cases be sorted out during the Socratic Dialogue proper. Other concerns need more time and dealing with them should be separated from the Socratic Dialogue proper and the discussions not chaired by the facilitator. But whether a meta-dialogue is needed depends on the situation and the actual needs of group members. The space in which group and facilitator talk about such matters relating to the Socratic Dialogue proper has always existed and has been realised in different ways. It was given the specific name meta-dialogue in the early 70s when specific times were set aside during six-day-dialogues. This was the time when rebellious students kept constantly asking why. The invention of the meta-dialogue was a sensible response to the fact that participants liked frequently to interrupt the content dialogue asking, for instance, for justification of facilitator interventions. I was present when Gustav Heckmann and Erna Blencke (one of Nelson's students as well and head of the resistance movement of the Nelsonians against the Nazis, before she had to flee to France and, later, to the USA) thought about how to deal with this new situation and how to separate discussions *about* the dialogue from the *content* dialogue. A name was invented and a new time schedule for Socratic seminars was organized to accommodate the needs of the rebellious participants. Thus the content dialogue was freed from constant interruption. But with a name, a nice name without any doubt, people got the impression that the meta-dialogue is a necessary part of a Socratic Dialogue, which, of course, it is not. The meta-dialogue was invented as a very wise institution, and space should be made for it if participants and/or facilitator want it. But if everybody is willing, without brushing anything under the carpet, to continue with the content dialogue, why not do so?

STRATEGIC DIALOGUE

The same is true for what came to be called the strategic dialogue. To discuss which question to address next or which of two or more possible ways to go is an element that has always been related to the dialogue, but it was not set apart as a dialogue of its own. Since this term was invented, it has given rise to more and more calls for strategic dialogues during Socratic Dialogues. In the beginning of the Nelson-Heckmann-tradition strategic decisions—they were then called Wegentscheidungen (decisions on which way to take)—were taken on the way, as the dialogue progressed. Under Gustav Heckmann's facilitation they were agreed upon, mostly during the content dialogue and following a suggestion from the facilitator. Once the meta-dialogue had been introduced, the decision how to proceed was often taken at the end of the meta-dialogue. Considering the transparency of the process and the autonomous thinker, it is, of course, desirable that all the participants in a Socratic Dialogue understand the procedure and agree on the steps taken. But more and more often I observe that true followers of the belief that Socratic Dialogue necessarily consists of three parts (Socratic Dialogue proper—meta-dialogue—strategic dialogue) tend constantly to ask for strategic dialogues which unnecessarily interrupts the flow of a Socratic Dialogue and—sometimes—adds a tactical element that can destroy the character of serious philosophical inquiry.

BACK TO THE MARKET-PLACE

The appeal that Socratic Dialogue should go back to the market-place, from a pale academic abstraction to a living reality, might be based on a misunderstanding. Does this appeal mean we should dialogue about really relevant and important issues? Or that really relevant and important people talk about their issues? We no longer have the noisy market-place where we could stop people we want to engage in conversations. Our market-place today may be the comfortable board room or a venue well-equipped with all the technical devices that help to document the process. It may as well be a staff room in a school, a prison, a private home. Resistance groups in Nazi Germany formed by Nelsonians met to discuss in a Socratic manner their reasons why to resist. They, of course, did not meet in the market-place but in private homes, not noisily sounding out what they had found but silently having strengthened their conviction that the values underlying their deeds were valid. Grete Hermann facilitated those Dialogues. She had been Nelson's academic assistant, co-editor of his works, a mathematician whose findings are still praised among mathematicians; and a physicist who discussed nuclear physics with Werner Heisenberg and Carl-Friedrich von Weizsäcker among others. The artificial contrast between the market-place and pale academia conceals what is really at stake: that Socratic Dialogues ought to deal with questions or problems that are relevant to the participants; and that they think honestly, seriously and thoroughly about those questions or problems. Participants ought to be challenged not to accept quick and easy answers. Wherever this happens we experience Socrates' market-place again and a Dialogue that can change people's lives.

RULES AND MODELS

Gustav Heckmann was very reluctant to write about Socratic Dialogue at all. He was of the opinion that people could not understand Socratic Dialogue without having experienced it many times. Intensive and frequent experience as a participant was a very important precondition of starting to be trained as a facilitator. When his wife Charlotte, who knew that ideas had a better chance to survive when printed, had convinced him to write a book on Socratic Dialogue, he decided to write about concrete Dialogues he had facilitated, to describe them and to reflect on them. He explained what he thought to be characteristic of Socratic Dialogues in contrast to other forms of dialogue and he gave some advice on how to act as a facilitator.[3] He knew that a concrete Socratic Dialogue can take very different paths and that it is wrong to make a doctrine out of a specific procedure even if this procedure might be sensible in many cases.

A set of rules or a model of a Socratic Dialogue like Jos Kessels' hour-glass model can be helpful for a novice facilitator if he or she applies them sensibly, which is not easy for beginners. But in too many cases they are harmful. Those who start facilitation very often misinterpret a set of rules or a model as operating instructions or a recipe from a cook book. In trying to follow the operating instructions meticulously their Socratic Dialogues become monotonous and anaemic. They mistake Socratic Dialogue for a technique, which it is not.

I believe to be in accordance with Gustav Heckmann when stating the following features to be essential for a Socratic Dialogue; and facilitators who orientate themselves to these essentials will better know what to do in their role:

The question (or the topic) of the Dialogue needs to be philosophical (or mathematical). The analysis of an inner experience is a kind of preform of a proper Socratic Dialogue.

The thinking process has to be based on concrete experience and remain in contact with concrete experience: Answers to philosophical questions dealt with in a Socratic Dialogue are gained only when in all

---

[3] Gustav Heckmann, *Das sokratische Gespräch—Erfahrungen in philosophischen Hochschulseminaren*, Schroedel Verlag: Hannover 1980; new edition with an introduction by Dieter Krohn: dipa-Verlag: Frankfurt/Main 1993.

phases the link between any statement made and personal experience is explicit. This means that a Socratic Dialogue is a process which concerns the whole person.

Full understanding between participants has to be reached: This involves much more than verbal agreement. Everyone has to be clear about the meaning of what has just been said by testing it against their own concrete experience. The limitations of individual personal experience which stand in the way of full understanding should be made conscious and thereby transcended.

Adherence to a subsidiary question until it is answered: In order to achieve this the group is required to bring great commitment to their work and to gain self-confidence in the power of reason. This means, on the one hand, not to give up when the work is difficult but, on the other, to have the necessary calmness to accept for a time a different course in the dialogue in order then to return to the subsidiary question.

Striving for consensus: This requires an honest examination of the thoughts of others and being honest in one's own statements. When such honesty and openness towards one's own and other participants' feelings and thinking are present, then the striving for consensus will emerge, not necessarily the consensus itself.

These indispensable features of Socratic Dialogue tell us much about the tasks and the behaviour of those who participate in such dialogues. The most important point in all this is the autonomy in thinking: answers to philosophical questions are gained only by those who engage in the process of knowing in their own mind, not through instruction. External influences through the facilitator should not do more than stimulate independent and common thinking in the group.

Bibliography

Detlef Horster/Dieter Krohn (Hg.), *Vernunft—Ethik—Politik: Festschrift für Gustav Heckmann*, SOAK: Hannover 1983.

Dieter Krohn, Gustav Heckmann, in: Detlef Horster/Dieter Krohn (Hg.), *Vernunft—Ethik—Politik*, SOAK: Hannover 1983, S. 9-32.

Dieter Krohn/Jürgen Heinen-Tenrich/Detlef Horster (Hg.), *Das Sokratische Gespräch—Ein Symposion*, Junius: Hamburg 1989.

Gustav Heckmann/Dieter Krohn, Über Sokratisches Gespräch und Sokratische Arbeitswochen, in: *Zeitschrift für Didaktik der Philosophie*, 10 (1988) H. 1, S. 38-43.

Dieter Krohn, Gustav Heckmann zum 95. Geburtstag, in: *Zeitschrift für Didaktik der Philosophie*, 15 (1993) H. 3, S. 200-202.

11. Dieter Krohn

Dieter Krohn, Vorwort zu: Gustav Heckmann, *Das sokratische Gespräch*, dipa: Frankfurt 1993, S. 7-10.

Dieter Krohn/Nora Walter, Sokratische Gespräche der Philosophisch-Politischen Akademie seit 1966—eine Dokumentation, in: Silvia Knappe/Dieter Krohn/Nora Walter (Hg.), *Vernunftbegriff und Menschenbild bei Leonard Nelson*, dipa-Verlag: Frankfurt a.M. 1996, S. 135-148.

Dieter Krohn, Theorie und Praxis des Sokratischen Gesprächs, in: Karl Reinhard Lohmann/Thomas Schmidt (Hg.), *Akademische Philosophie zwischen Anspruch und Erwartung*, Suhrkamp: Frankfurt a.M. 1998, S. 119-132 (Under the title Theory and Practice of Socratic Dialogue also in: Rene Saran/Barbara Neißer (eds.), *Enquiring Minds—Socratic Dialogue in Education*, Trentham Books: Stoke on Trent 2004, pp. 15-24.

Dieter Krohn, Das Sokratische Gespräch in philosophischer und pädagogischer Praxis—Zur Einleitung, in: Dieter Krohn/Barbara Neißer/Nora Walter (Hg.), *Das Sokratische Gespräch—Möglichkeiten in philosophischer und pädagogischer Praxis*, dipa-Verlag: Frankfurt a.M. 1999, S. 7-13.

Dieter Birnbacher/Dieter Krohn (Hg.), *Das sokratische Gespräch*, Reclam: Stuttgart 2002 (The introduction by Dieter Birnbacher und Dieter Krohn under the title of Socratic Dialogue and self-directed learning also in: Rene Saran/Barbara Neißer (eds.), *Enquiring Minds-Socratic Dialogue in Education*, Trentham Books: Stoke on Trent 2004, pp. 9-14.

Silvia Knappe/Dieter Krohn/Nora Walter (Hg.) [ab Bd. III: Dieter Krohn/Barbara Neißer/Nora Walter (Hg.)], *Sokratisches Philosophieren*, dipa-Verlag: Frankfurt a.M. 1994-2000; ab 2002 im LIT Verlag: Münster.

12

Ran Lahav

Philosophical Practitioner
Johnson State College in Vermont, and Siena Heights University in Michigan, U.S.A.

---

1. Why were you initially drawn to Philosophical Practice?

I remember sitting in a class on Freud at the Hebrew University in Jerusalem—at the time I was doing my BA studies in philosophy and psychology. We learned that Freud explained personal predicaments in terms of early childhood experiences. I thought to myself: How strange that if I feel a sense of meaninglessness, Freud would tell me that my early relations with my mother are at fault! Doesn't the question of the meaning of life deserve to be taken seriously, not as a symptom, but as a real philosophical question? I remember myself looking out the window and fantasizing about the idea of a philosophical therapist.

It must have been 1977, a few years before Gerd Achenbach started the Philosophical Practice movement. In my philosophy studies I was fascinated by the big questions of life. But at the same time I was also greatly disappointed, because the lectures were too abstract, too theoretical, too remote from everyday life. The philosophy texts we read had promising titles, but the promise remained unfulfilled: they had little to do with human beings flesh and blood.

This mixture of fascination and disappointment stayed with me for many years. The fascination kept me going through my PhD studies at the University of Michigan. But throughout those years I was also deeply dissatisfied and even bored. I longed for a philosophy that would touch real life, that would shed light on people's yearnings and concerns, that would help me deal with life more deeply and meaningfully.

After finishing my doctorate in philosophy (and Masters in psychology), I found myself teaching at the philosophy department of a university in Dallas, Texas. I worked energetically—lecturing, writing, discussing abstract issues with colleagues, but deep inside me academic philosophy left me cold. What kept me going was the hope to find some sort of philosophy that would touch real life.

And then, in 1991, while still teaching in Dallas, I heard about philosophical counseling, or Philosophical Practice. My reaction was: Of course, why not?

Soon afterwards I got in touch with virtually every philosophical counselor I could find. At that time there were two small groups in Germany and Holland, as well as a handful of individuals in South Africa, USA, and Israel. I soon realized that Philosophical Practice was still at a nascent stage, still experimenting, still struggling to find itself. I encountered a few interesting ideas, but also many other ideas that were immature, even simplistic. Nevertheless, I felt that the field had a potential. I realized, however, that if Philosophical Practice was to develop, it was necessary to attract more philosophers—especially from the academic world—and create an international dialogue. This was a huge task, given that the field was virtually unknown. Still, I decided to take it upon myself.

Looking back at the years 1992-1994, I don't know how I found in me the energies to work so hard, together with fellow practitioners, on advancing the field. I experimented with Philosophical Practice with individuals and groups, I published articles in academic journals, I gave seminars and lectures wherever I could. In 1992, when I spent a year on a scholarship at the Hebrew University in Jerusalem, I was interviewed on the radio and television several times. Then I started collecting articles from philosophical counselors around the world and composed an anthology, *Essays on Philosophical Counseling,* the first book in English on the topic (University Press of America, 1995).

As luck would have it, one of my radio interviews was heard by the head of the counseling department of the school of education of Haifa University in Israel. He called me and invited me to teach the topic at his department. I was excited. This was to be the first university course in the world on philosophical counseling! I gladly agreed to start teaching in 1993. For the next 15 years I would come to Israel one semester a year to teach this course at his department, and occasionally at the philosophy department as well.

Soon after starting to teach this course, I envisioned the idea of an international conference on philosophical counseling(or practice). Looking for an institution to host the event, I approached several universities in the USA (I was still teaching one semester a year in Texas), but they all turned me down for financial reasons. At last I was helped by one of the contributors to my anthology, Lou Marinoff, who at the time was an assistant professor at the University of British Columbia in Canada. Together we met his boss and managed to convince him to host the event. The conference took place in 1994, and it was the first in a series of international conferences on Philosophical Practice, which still continues today in various countries around the globe.

When the conference ended, I knew it was time to end my public and organizational activity. After three years of working incessantly to help create an international dialogue, it was time for me to rest. Thanks to the efforts of several activists and enthusiasts, there was now a small network of practitioners around the world, and an ongoing international dialogue among practitioners in several countries.

Since then I have been working in the field in a more personal way, writing, leading groups of philosophical self-reflection, giving philosophical counseling to individuals, and most importantly developing my vision of Philosophical Practice. I was certainly not the only enthusiast in those early days, but I am glad to have been instrumental in establishing the field.

2. What does your work reveal about Philosophical Practice that other related academic fields typically fail to appreciate?

In the early 1990's, when I joined the field of Philosophical Practice, there was much debate within the small community of practitioners about the question: How are we, philosophical practitioners, different from psychology (psychotherapy, psychological counseling)?

I think that people were preoccupied with this question because Philosophical Practice was indeed quite similar to psychotherapy. Unfortunately, the first pioneers of Philosophical Practice adopted from psychotherapy the framework of one-hour talking sessions with an individual. In other words, Philosophical Practice took the shape of philosophical counseling. Just like the psychologist, the philosophical counselor met the counselee in her office, spoke with him for an hour or so about his life, took her fees, and made an appointment for next meeting. Furthermore, very often philosophical counseling aimed at solving the client's personal problem: marriage difficulties, dissatisfaction at work, etc., just like the goal of many psychotherapies.

I find it unfortunate that Philosophical Practice took this direction of predicament-counseling or problem-solving. This tendency continues to bias our field to this very day. I find it unfortunate that in our first decades we have not directed ourselves primarily to where philosophy really belongs: the search for wisdom and meaning. We could have appealed to the many seekers who seek meaning and growth in their lives, instead of to those who want to solve their marriage problems or their low self-esteem and then return to their normal life. After all, countless people seek to deepen their lives, and they do so through religious sects, New Age workshops, yoga and meditation, enrichment classes. Why not philosophical reflection?

Today we are more aware of other forms of Philosophical Practice which are not geared towards solving personal problems: self-reflection workshops, philosophical companionships, wisdom-oriented counseling (which I sometimes call philo-sophical counseling), etc. But I think that these alternative forms of Philosophical Practice have not received sufficient attention, and as a result they are still underdeveloped. I myself started my work in the field primarily as a philosophical counselor, and after a few years realized that this was a misguided direction. For the past fifteen years I have been exploring the idea of Philosophical Practice as a search for wisdom, and to do so I prefer working in groups rather than in individual counseling.

In any case, since Philosophical Practice is strongly oriented towards the counseling format, the question arises: How does Philosophical Practice differ from psychology and psychotherapy? What does Philosophical Practice do that psychotherapy fails to do?

For the past century, psychology has gained a monopoly over people's well-being. If you have a personal problem, if you feel unsatisfied, if something is not working in your life, you go to see a psychologist. Thus the psychologist has become today's priest of well-being. This trend has been strengthened by society's institutions: there are laws that allow only psychology-trained professionals to deal with personal problems, insurance companies pay you to go see a psychologist to deal with your anxieties, the military and many other organizations employ psychologists, and so on.

What, then, does a philosophical practitioner have to offer which the many types of psychologists operating today cannot offer?

My answer is: ideas, and the power of ideas. Psychology (including psychotherapy) deals with the psyche—that's why it is called psychology. It deals with processes and mechanisms that presumably underlie the individual's emotions, thoughts, behavior. It deals, in other words, with the sequence of mental and behavioral states (anxieties, desires, memories, experiences, thoughts, behavioral tendencies, etc.) that presumably lead to one another, influence each other, and produce the person's visible behaviors. Although there are hundreds of different approaches to psychological therapy, to the extent to which they are forms of psychology, they all understand the person in terms of such processes. And if they wish to intervene, they do so by attempting to influence these processes. Indeed, the training of a psychologist focuses on mental mechanisms and processes: how various mental states develop, how they lead to one another, what influences them, how they shape behavior, etc.

I am not opposed to this kind of psychological thinking, only to the monopoly it enjoys in our society. What psychology fails to appreciate is the important role of ideas in our lives, their power to inspire us and enrich us (or conversely distort our life and limit it). To see this power, consider people whose life has been transformed as a result of a new idea: those inspired by a religious vision, those moved by a social ideal which made them leave everything and devote themselves to the poor, those shaken by an existential realization about the meaning of their lives. To be sure, some of these influential ideas are destructive—for example, racist ideologies—but they too are evidence for the tremendous power ideas have, for better or for worse.

Consider also smaller and more common influences which ideas have on our lives: How our values influence the way we choose, how our conception of the family impacts our behavior towards our spouse and children, how our understanding of what is important in life effects our attitudes and preferences, how our understanding of friendship and love influences our relations towards others.

In everyday life we constantly encounter basic life-issues: What is meaningful in life? What is real love? What does it mean to be authentic? What is moral or immoral to do? and so on. Our way of understanding these issues helps shape our life. Of course, very often we do not articulate in words our understanding of these basic life-issues. We respond to these issues through our choices, emotional reactions, attitudes, without being fully aware that we are giving answers to important philosophical questions. And yet, although we are not fully aware of our answers, we are constantly expressing our understanding of these basic life-issues, usually implicitly, through our attitudes and behaviors. In this sense, we are all philosophers.

It is the role of philosophy to expose those hidden understandings and deal with them philosophically. This was in fact a view shared by many ancient schools of philosophy. The Stoics, the Epicureans, the Cynics, and others sought to direct their practitioners towards the good life with the help of philosophical reflection on ideas.

In short, ideas have a tremendous power to influence us, and they have a tremendous potential to enrich and deepen our life. Philosophical practice, at least as I practice it, is based on this realization, and it therefore takes ideas seriously. It regards ideas not as mere symptoms of something else, not as a byproduct of emotional process, but as something valuable that needs to be taken seriously—nourished, developed and enriched. This means that as philosophical practitioners we treat ideas as ideas, and we carefully examine their meaning, their implications, their hidden assumptions. In other words, in order to help life grow we discuss life-issues, which means that we philosophize.

This is something which psychology fails to do. If I complain to my psychologist that my life is empty, she would not discuss with me different conceptions of the meaning of life, but would probably regard my predicament as a product of some emotional process. Even if she did attempt to discuss with me the meaning of life, she would be untrained for this kind of discussion.

Interestingly, some forms of psychotherapy, notably cognitive psychotherapies, acknowledge the power of thoughts. However, being psychologists they regard ideas as a psychological process to influence, rather than as serious attempts to understand life. Prominent cognitive psychologists, such as Albert Ellis or Aaron Beck, use ideas in order to influence their patients in the direction which they deem desirable, rather than seriously discussing them as possible responses to basic life-issues. Transcripts of their sessions show very clearly how they seek to simplify their patient's ideas and make them more positive, functional, optimistic.

In contrast, Philosophical Practice as I see it seeks to enrich the individual's understanding of life, not to simplify life or make it more convenient and trouble-free. Its goal is not to normalize people, not to make them satisfied within their little world, but to open for them new horizons, deeper ways of understanding and encountering life. This process may be confusing and frightening—it is not always easy to question the normal ground upon which you stand. But the goal of Philosophical Practice is not satisfaction, but wisdom.

3. What, if any, practical and/or social-political obligations follow from understanding philosophy from the point of view of Philosophical Practice?

Philosophical practice, I believe, is a search for wisdom, and as such it should be seen as a way of life, not merely a profession. True philosophical practitioners are individuals who seek to impregnate their personal life with wisdom, and in this way to live more deeply and fully. Thanks to philosophical self-reflection they are aware of the limitation of their normal way of being, and they seek to overcome their boundaries, to open themselves to greater horizons, and live a bigger life.

Here Plato's allegory of the cave is illuminating. Plato compared us, human beings, to people sitting in a cave and seeing only shadows dancing on the walls. Since we have never seen anything else, we believe that this is what life is. The role of philosophy, Plato tells us, is to turn people away from the wall, to make them realize that they have been seeing mere shadows, and to show them the way out of the cave to the real life out there, and to the sun that gives out the light of wisdom.

I take this allegory very seriously. For me, the role of Philosophical Practice is to lead us out of our little caves to greater horizons of life and reality. This means that Philosophical Practice is a personal journey. It is not a profession, nor is it an occupation you do in your spare time. Unlike being a banker or a mechanic or a psychologist, being a philosophical practitioner is a full-time occupation. It is not something you do for two or five or eight hours, and then return home to rest. It pervades your entire life. Because wisdom is not something you do between three and four in the afternoon; it is not a matter of what you do, but of who you are.

For this reason, the practical implication of Philosophical Practice is this: If you are a philosophical practitioner, then you live as a seeker. As a philosophical practitioner you practice philosophy—in other words, you search for wisdom—in your everyday life.

Unfortunately, from the very beginning philosophical practitioners were eager to give services to others before working on their own life. They were quick to adopt the format of psychology, instead of realizing that philosophy is a very different thing. Philosophy is a personal journey, not primarily a profession. You may help others only if you are already a true seeker. As Plato says in his Allegory of the Cave, after the philosopher has stepped out of the cave, he returns inside to help others step outside too. But he can do so only because he has already been outside.

This is not the way Philosophical Practice is generally viewed today. The ideas of consumerism, professionalism, and capitalism have invaded the field. How strange—the philosopher who was supposed to be the critic of society has become a provider of services.

Maybe there is nothing wrong with practitioners who wish to make philosophy a profession, a commodity to sell, a professional service. But if so, then let us distinguish between two very different practices: Philosophy as a profession that sells philosophical products to others, and philosophy as a personal journey towards wisdom and growth.

4. What do you see as the most interesting criticism against your own position in Philosophical Practice?

I am often being told that my ideal of making philosophy a way of life is impractical, because philosophers need to make money. What's wrong with philosophers selling their services to those who want to enjoy them? What's wrong with a philosophy that solves marriage problems, or career difficulties? What's wrong with helping people be satisfied with their little lives?

My response is that a philosophy that is a service-provider is no longer a genuine philosophy. Philosophy is philo-sophia, a search for wisdom. And a philosophy whose primary goal is satisfying clients and making them feel good will inevitably find itself sacrificing its depth in exchange for practical results. A practice which tries to solve a client's problem and make her feel good would be more concerned about the client's mood than about the depth of the conversation. Such a practice would regard ideas as tools for making the client feel good, and become cognitive psychotherapy, and no longer a form of philosophy.

But a related criticism of my work seems to me more interesting. I am sometimes told that my approach is too spiritual. Instead of focusing on logical reasoning, as philosophers presumably should do, I try to awaken the individual's inner powers to understand and feel. Instead of engaging the individual's logical thinking, I seek to engage his deeper self. To be sure, I also use logical analysis and traditional philosophical texts, but I try to go beyond a straightforward understanding of them. I often use techniques such as meditation, text-contemplation, and similar exercises designed to awaken our deeper self.

This, I think, is a fair characterization of my approach. My philosophical work does indeed combine philosophical and spiritual elements. This is why I sometimes call it Trans-Sophia: philosophy and beyond. I believe that our capacity to think logically is only a small part of our capacity to understand. As many thinkers throughout history have pointed out—Plato, Plotinus, Marcus Aurelius, Rousseau, Emerson, Nietzsche, Bergson, Buber, and many others—we have resources in us that are deeper than our usual ways of thinking. And in order to tap into them, we need to awaken them, which means that we need more than logical thinking. In fact, we need an inner transformation.

Thus, for me Philosophical Practice aims at a personal transformation. And in this respect it is in line with most of the important philosophers in Western history who have also talked about inner transformation. For some reason, the philosophy you find in universities is not very interested in these transformational ideas. It prefers abstract theories. But you cannot deny that almost every important philosopher in Western history envisioned a personal transformation that can be effected by, or at least be understood by, philosophical thinking. In this sense, my approach to Philosophical Practice is traditional.

In recent years I have explored some of these historical transformational philosophers. Although most of them died a long time ago, they can still teach us about our own life. Some fruits of my exploration are displayed on my website www.PhiloLife.net, which I set up with the help of my colleague and friend Carmen Zavala, a philosophical practitioner from Lima, Peru.

5. With respect to present and future inquiry, how can the most important problems concerning Philosophical Practice be identified and explored?

For me, the most important question in our field that needs to be investigated is: What does it mean to live philosophically? How can philosophy help us live our everyday life with greater wisdom and depth? To put it differently, how can philosophy help us transform ourselves so that we can go beyond our limited and superficial everyday self?

This question is not unfamiliar in Philosophical Practice circles, but I believe that it has not been investigated sufficiently, and has not yet been given a satisfying answer. Part of the problem is that such a question must be investigated in practice, not just theoretically. Life has its own dynamics. In order to explore this question we must experiment with life, not just talk or write about it.

The most promising way to explore this, I think, is through a philosophical companionship: a group of committed philosophical practitioners who would seriously take upon themselves to investigate how to be true philosophers—how to live philosophically. Most of the practitioners I know, however, are not ready for this demanding task. They have other projects in their lives, or are too busy with their work and family. Free time is a rare commodity nowadays. In fact, I made several attempts to establish such a companionship, but they were only partly successful.

I hope that philosophical practitioners will take upon themselves this challenge. It seems to me that only if we envision Philosophical Practice as a way of life and explore it as such, can we save Philosophical Practice from the marginal state in which it is found today. As a profession, Philosophical Practice has failed: very few practitioners have sufficient work, and the field has never gained popularity in any country around the world.

But the fact that practitioners and others still show interest in it suggests, I think, that philosophy still holds its promise. Indeed, if you feel that your life is lacking and want to deepen it, and yet you don't want to resort to questionable New Age sects and religious dogmas, then where else can you turn but to an open, non-dogmatic, free investigation, in other words philosophy? I believe that if we stop treating philosophical as a profession and turn it into a way of life, then it could become a significant contribution to seekers around the world.

Bibliography

Lahav, R., *Essays on Philosophical Counseling*, Lanham: University Press of America, 1995.(An edited anthology with second editor Maria

Tillmanns).

Lahav, R., *Comprendere la Vita: La consuelza filosofica come ricerza della sagezza* (In Italian: Understanding Life: Philosophical Counseling as a Search for Wisdom), Milan: Apogeo, 2005.

Lahav, R., *Oltre la Filisofia: alla ricerca della sagezza* (In Italian: Beyond Philosophy: the investigation of wisdom), Milan: Apogeo, 2010.

Lahav, R., A Conceptual Framework for Philosophical Counseling, in: Lahav and Tillmanns (eds.), *Essays on Philosophical Counseling*, Lanham: University Press of America, 1995.

Lahav, R., What is Philosophical in Philosophical Counseling?, *Journal of Applied Philosophy*, 13: 1996.

Lahav, R., Philosophical Counselling and Taoism: Wisdom and Lived Philosophical Understanding, *Journal of Chinese Philosophy*, 23: 1996.

Lahav, R., Philosophical Counselling and Existential Therapy: On the possibility of a dialogue between the fields, *Journal of the Society for Existential Analysis*, 9: 1997.

Lahav, R., Philosophical Counseling as a Quest for Wisdom, *Practical Philosophy*, 1: 2001.

Lahav, R., The Efficacy of Philosophical Counseling: A First Outcome Study, *Practical Philosophy*, 4: 2001.

Lahav, R., Transcending the Unconscious: Philosophical counseling sessions with Arthur Schopenhauer, (written with Eli Eilon), in: Peter Raabe (ed.), *Philosophical Counselling and the Unconscious*, Trivum 2005.

Lahav, R., Philosophical Practice as Contemplative Philosophy, *Practical Philosophy*, 8: 2006.

Lahav, R., Beyond Our Perimeter, *Practical Philosophy*, 9: 2008.

Lahav, R., What Philosophical Counseling Can Learn from Buber? (in Italian: Cosa puo impararela consulenza filosofica da Buber?) in: Ed. Luca Bertolino, *Martin Buber: Colpa e Sensi di Colpa*, Milano: Apogeo Press, 2008.

Lahav, R., Self-Talk in Marcus Aurelius Meditations, *Philosophical Practice*, 4: 2009. Previously published as Auto-Conversación de Marco Aurelio en las Meditaciones, *Sophia* 5: 2009 (Ecuador).

Lahav, R., Il potere delle idee nella pratica filosofica, [The Power of Ideas in Philosophical Practice] in: Ed. Cloe Taddei Ferretti and Luca

Lahav, R., Nave, *Pensiero, Meditazione, Ragionamento: La filosofia in esercizio*, Milano: Mimesis Editore, 2010, pp. 37-46.

www.PhilLife.net

www.Trans-Sophia.net

13

Anders Lindseth

Philosophical Practitioner and Professor
Centre for Practical Knowledge at the University of Nordland, Norway

---

1. Why were you initially drawn to Philosophical Practice?

I remember when I first heard of Philosophical Practice. It was the early 80s at the Inter-University Centre in Dubrovnik. There I met Arnold Lorenzen from Hamburg, who excitedly told me that in Germany, in Bergisch Gladbach near Cologne, Gerd B. Achenbach had opened up a Philosophical Practice in 1981. Now, several philosophers were considering to follow his example. Lorenzen had interviewed Achenbach and had asked him about his motives to open up his Practice, the world's first Philosophical Practice. In his answer, Achenbach[1] mentioned three factors: First, philosophy had withdrawn into an academic ghetto where it had lost the direct relationship to the real problems experienced by human beings. Secondly, in our time psychology had the task to help people with their problems, a task which was formerly assigned to pastoral care. And now psychology suffered the same fate as pastoral care by seeking to provide general solutions for individual problems. So for questions people struggle with, there should be (more or less) ready-made answers, general solutions—which psychology tries to justify by empirical research, whereas pastoral care tries to base its answers on the doctrine of faith. In both cases, it can easily happen that the person seeking assistance is not encountered in his or her personal history. Here—and that was Achenbach's third point—there is the traditional task of philosophy to reflect upon human experience and to try to find words that can put the experience into perspective and that can reconcile its inherent contradictions. In Philosophical Practice, the philosopher encounters various human beings with their specific questions and problems; so this practice may help philosophy to find a way out

---

[1] Achenbach, G. B. (1984) *Philosophische Praxis*. (Mit Beiträgen von M. Fischer, T. H. Macho, O. Marquard und E. Martens.) Köln: Verlag für Philosophie Jürgen Dinter. (Schriftenreihe zur Philosophischen Praxis, Band I.), pp. 5-12.

of its academic ghetto and back into a public political sphere and into a communication community—where philosophy is no longer a topic for experts, but a concern for all experienced and thoughtful human beings who want to find orientation on the way of life.

After my encounter with Lorenzen in Dubrovnik, I contacted Achenbach and began a training in his Philosophical Practice in Germany. Married and having become father of twins in the meantime, my family and I moved back to Norway in 1989, to the world's northernmost university in Tromsø, and I opened up Norway's first Philosophical Practice in this town.

I was immediately attracted by the idea that philosophers can and should talk with human beings about topics which are not only of general importance but are experienced as urgent by the human beings themselves. What was appealing to me was not only the enjoyable opportunity to help human beings but above all the idea that philosophy itself had to find its way back to the real questions of human beings. My concern was philosophizing in dialogues with human beings looking for orientation in life—which does not exclude the inner dialogue, the reflective exploration of one's own experiences. This dialogical philosophizing is the main issue of Philosophical Practice for me (cf. Lindseth, 2005).

Being asked why I was *initially* drawn to Philosophical Practice, it is suggested to me to think about my intellectual autobiography. Why has the idea of Philosophical Practice convinced me from the very beginning? Of course, I cannot say this with certainty. Who could tell exactly why he or she is attracted by certain ideas? When I think about the impulses my family has given me as a child, of course certain experiences come to my mind. My grandfather on my mother's side was a quiet and kind working class man who loved to read novels and travel reports. My uncle on my mother's side had probably inherited from his father the warmth and openness which I appreciated so much in my childhood and adolescence. Thanks to a scholarship, he had received some higher education and was quite open for philosophical talks, although at home philosophy was never considered a discipline which could be studied. However, I do recall how my interests in philosophy, mathematics, literature and religion were awakened in grammar school. As part of the history of literature, philosophical issues were taken up, and I still remember how I wrote a short essay on determinism, which was praised by the teacher for its clear presentation.[2] In the fall of 1967 I left my

---
[2] If we are determined by the laws of nature in our human actions, I discussed in my essay, do we still have freedom in life? I probably felt early on that this question suggests an artificial opposition between nature and freedom.

home town Bodø in northern Norway, and began studying at the University of Oslo. Teachers and others had asked me if I wanted to study medicine or maybe theoretical physics, but I was determined to become a philosopher! At that time there was a lively Spinoza research at the philosophical institute, initiated by professor Arne Næss. Thus, the study of Spinoza's *Ethics*[3] became my way into philosophy. I had read and understood little, but every once in a while insights came flashing up that made me happy. I still remember how the distinction between active and passive emotions in Spinoza's teachings on emotions (in the third part of his *Ethics*) became clear to me and helped me to a better understanding of its three modes of cognition (*imaginatio*, *ratio*, *intuitio*). We are subject to the passive emotions — they keep us under their spell, so to speak — while I perform active emotions myself and in freedom. At this time I had started to meditate, and my new-found insight into the nature of emotions was certainly supported by my meditation experiences. In the ACEM School of Meditation founded in Norway, where I am teaching, meditation is seen as an action that we can perform freely or unfreely. While meditating, we are constantly captured or influenced by emotionally charged ideas, by passive emotions, what challenges us to find a freer meditation performance. This performance is not merely feeling, is not a static condition, but rather an activity that is experienced as liberating and as relaxing on a physical level. To talk about feelings is an abstraction if we neglect the activity in which they manifest themselves. So we are subject to the passive emotions in everyday knowledge of the world, in the *imaginatio*, which Spinoza describes in the second part of his *Ethics*, his theory of knowledge.[4] Reason wants to liberate itself from this bondage of the feelings, and there are two ways of such a liberation, two forms of reason. The highly esteemed rational reason, the *ratio*, is an unemotional calculation, a strictly logical thinking, staying away from feelings if possible, whereas the intuitive knowledge, the *intuito*, dares to reconnect thinking with emotion, which enables it to see the universal in the individual. In order to realize what the phenomena of the world and of life are in their essence, we must be guided by a quiet feeling, by an active emotion. The *ratio* does not enable us to see actively, it can only — logically and tamed — work with what has been seen already, with what the *imaginatio* has provided us with.

My first steps into philosophy had led me to a question, to which life

---

[3] Spinoza, B. (1951) *The Ethics* (Original title: *Ethica—Ordine Geometrico demonstrata*). In: *The Chief Works of Benedict de Spinoza*, Vol. II, pp. 43-271. (Translated from the Latin with an introduction by R. H. M. Elwes.) New York: Dover Publications. (Original work first published 1677.)

[4] Ibid., Proposition 40, note 2.

itself had already guided me: How can we find freedom in the unfree? We might be pulled back and forth in life by likes and dislikes, by desires and anxieties, but in our experience of the world and of life, we can still find a foundation which allows peaceful orientation. Plato, Aristotle and the other philosophers of antiquity and the Middle Ages have referred to the virtues and to the experience of a primary foundation, which was called God. However, the social and economic development, especially the Thirty Year War in the Seventeenth Century and later on the industrial revolution, brought the Occident a shock as well as a new optimism that led to a reorientation. The fundamental orientation was redetermined. The meaning of reason and morality was thought through anew. Descartes had emphasized methodological reflection, Spinoza intuition, John Locke and David Hume wanted to return to natural knowledge, Immanuel Kant saw practical reason as a foundation of life. I do not want to list the names of all the major philosophers of modern times which have impressed and influenced me, but I would like to mention that the emphasis on dialogue in the philosophical hermeneutics of Hans-Georg Gadamer and the emphasis on the relationship to the Other in the phenomenological ethics of K.E. Løgstrup have become particularly important for me.

What are the reasons why Philosophical Practice is so important for me? On the one hand, I see the conception of philosophy that I have, and on the other hand, I see an experience of our current life situation. We believe too much in rational reason. We turn public life too much into a machinery of production, under which we suffer increasingly. We bet on the wrong horse, so to speak, we rely on the *ratio*, not on the *intuitio*. Of course, technology and production are of enormous importance in the modern world. We can not avoid the *ratio*. The disaster is that we no longer really understand that we need to recognize the universal in the individual. If the deviation of the individual from the universal does not strike us enough, we do not wonder, for example: Does this father meet the expectations we have of a father? Does this priest, teacher, student etc meet our idea of a priest, a teacher, a student? Such questions can only be answered in individual cases, and to think of answers necessarily leads to the normative: What (and who) is a good father? What (and who) is a good priest, teacher, student, etc.? Mostly we do not really try to ask ourselves out of our life experiences: Am I a good father, am I a good mother, a good teacher, a good doctor or a good Philosophical Practitioner? We do not really ask ourselves: Is my life a good life? This makes us disoriented. We do not really know what's important in life. Because of this lack of intuition, the *ratio* is weakened, too; it is so much based upon consistency in reasoning and acting that we do not longer question critically enough whether the goals are reasonable.

Such critical questioning must be done by every single person, and we can only do so in the dialogue. For such dialogues, we need philosophers. That does not necessarily mean that professional philosophers are needed, but rather human beings who are able to question critically and see the universal in the individual.

2. What does your work reveal about Philosophical Practice that other related academic fields typically fail to appreciate?

The common scientific thinking of our time—typically—estimates the necessity of the individual's life orientation incorrectly. Usually, general solutions are offered for all problems and tasks of life. So when the individual is trying to find orientation, it is expected that empirical research results can be applied. However, to apply empirical scientific theories to one's own life is not the same as to orient oneself in life. I'd like to point this out with the help of an example.

Some years ago, I was invited to give a lecture at the Psychiatric Hospital in Bodø at a seminar on eating disorders. After the lecture, a psychiatrist objected: Your presentation has been interesting, but actually you have not talked about eating disorders. You have only dealt with problems that we all as human beings can have with eating. Would you want to talk about eating disorders, you would first have to define the notion of eating disorder, you would then have to refer to collected data about such disorders and see which theories or models useful for the treatment of disordered eating behaviour could be developed based on these data. This psychiatrist's objection was very welcome to me, because it gave me an opportunity to deepen a point which I had mentioned at the beginning of my presentation. I had said that I could choose two different, almost opposite approaches when speaking about the topic of eating disorders. I could either talk about something that we approach from the outside, that we only realize through disturbing observations of disordered behaviour. Or I could assume that we all can approach an understanding of the phenomenon of the eating disorder because we all eat, and therefore know the desire related to it, which is charged and often difficult to deal with. Since I was asked to give a *philosophical* lecture as introduction to a seminar on eating disorders, it was clear to me I had to choose the second approach. By doing so, I wanted to show not only an alternative to the scientific approach but rather show in how far this scientific approach is problematic, because it implies that eating disorders can not be understood properly, not well enough out of the experience of the affected people themselves. Because only researchers who have studied the disturbed eating behaviour scientifically have the desired skills to deal with eating disorders.

People who suffer from bulimia or anorexia can not cope with their problems, therefore they are not able to understand them properly. And also the people around them usually do not know how to deal with these problems. In this situation we have the hope and the belief that research can help. It is assumed that scientific theory is superior to the experience-based view of those affected. However, this assumption is problematic. It is not problematic because eating disorders were not too difficult to understand. It is also not problematic because empirical research can not find something proper. What is problematic is that even the most correct scientific explanation of the disturbing eating disorders do not help those who suffer to orient themselves in life and to get ahead, if the theory can not be understood by the persons themselves, out of their own lived experience. If theory shall help, then a bridge to experience is needed. An experienced therapist can help building this bridge, but only if he or she can understand from their own experience what the theory is about. The last few years I have had several guests in my Philosophical Practice that had such problems we can call eating disorders. However, it would not occur to me to try an immediate scientific explanation of their problems. First I listen to what they say; I let their stories affect me. For instance, one woman told me: My mother always says that I am wonderful, but she never listens to what I say. Another says: As long as I can remember, my mother was always sad in my childhood, but when her favourite programme was broadcast in the radio, a weekly musical request program, she seemed a little bit happy. Then I always stopped playing with the other kids and went home to be with her. Such remarks touch me. They show me an effort to gain importance, to have meaning and to get recognition. However, what terms such as importance, meaning and recognition actually mean has to be understood by the person him- or herself. In the dialogue, I can mention them, but if I feel that they are of no use for my guest, I have to find different terms suggested to me in the course of our conversation. So I would not insist that my guest's eating behaviour has to be understood as a disturbed self-assertion just because this is a proven scientific hypothesis. If, however, my guest him- or herself understands that these problems can be seen in such a way, then the view that eating disorders are a disturbed self-assertion is no longer a hypothesis for this person but rather an insight (cf. Lindseth 2010, pp. 95ff). It is no longer a hypothesis requiring even more thorough research but rather an insight that is always looking for more adequate words and narrations so that it can find a satisfying and liberating expression. The liberating effect of such an insight is shown by the slow transformation of passive into active emotions. This liberating effect has to show itself gradually in the life and actions of the guest. If this insight is starting to unfold its effect, then—in the dialogue of the Philosophical Practice—we might have a closer look together at the scientific theories of eating disorders and see what there is to it. However, we will then quite naturally go beyond the empirical explanations and ask ourselves what eating and what importance, meaning and self-assertion mean to us. These are existential, philosophical questions that occur to us as soon as we seek orientation in life. We can only answer them if we are able to recognize the universal in the individual, in every case, not because we know and are intellectually able to repeat a general explanation. The general statement attempts to be final, even though we (disappointingly) have to admit that empirical-scientific explanations are always hypothetical and tentative. Realizing the universal within the individual is linked to the (not at all disappointing) insight that even though we might never find a final explanation, we still can find a fundamental certainty in life orientation.

3. What, if any, practical and/or social-political obligations follow from understanding philosophy from the point of view of Philosophical Practice?

The obligation of the Philosophical Practitioner in dialogues with people seeking orientation is to contribute to the clarification of issues that affect human life. This clarification must result from the guests' questions and experiences, not only from ready-made answers, neither from given philosophical views nor from empirical-scientific research results. The task of such clarification presupposes that the Philosophical Practitioner is able to see the universal in his guests' narrations and can thus help the guests to gain a better understanding of what matters in life. Such vision of the universal in the individual requires *Bildung*. Therefore, it is the task of the Philosophical Practitioner to contribute to *Bildung*, to general education and to critical thinking as well as to the personal *Bildung* of the guests of the Philosophical Practice (cf. Lindseth, 2005, pp. 67-79; 2011). On the socio-political level, this means working against the dominance of the calculating and rule-oriented reason (*ratio*, which is represented today so vehemently) over the intuitional reason (*intuitio*).

4. What do you see as the most interesting criticism against your own position in Philosophical Practice?

Three objections have been raised against my position of Philosophical Practice:

  1. It is hostile to methods;

2. It implies that Philosophical Practice has to be a form of therapy, not of philosophy; and

3. It is too individual, just therapeutic, and not politically and socially critical enough.

In his essay *"Beyond Method, Anders Lindseth style: The Quest to open up Philosophical Space in the Consulting Room"*, Morten Fastvold[5] has claimed that my position of Philosophical Practice distances itself from methods of such practice. However, my approach within Philosophical Practice is certainly accompanied by methodological considerations, which I demonstrate in my essay On the Method of Philosophical Practice as Dialogical Counseling. Here I write in the abstract:

"On the way of life we—sooner or later—end up in situations where we do not quite know how or where we can and should go on. In order to find orientation in life, Philosophical Practice as dialogical counseling can be particularly helpful or necessary. The procedures of such practices are not fixed, such as the methods of modern technology and modern management, but they must remain open for the particular issue that comes to expression and is at stake in the dialogue. In this essay I attempt to describe the method of Philosophical Practice as dialogical counseling in three consecutive steps (although they do not have to strictly follow each other in the dialogue):

1. As Philosophical Practitioner, I refrain from immediately subordinating my guests' expression to my previous knowledge (*epoché*). I have to dare to let his expression make an impression on me in an unprotected way. By doing so, a *space* of attention opens up in the dialogue in which the guest's expression may unfold its voice, so that the guest is listened to and can even listen anew to himself.

2. The dialogical space of attention creates a *place* to which the following dialogues return and which they can examine further. The impressions—which develop their own images within the dialogue—have to be guided back to this space (*eidetic* reduction). Thus, Philosophical Practice can give orientation in life by exploring this place.

3. At this place in the guest's life which is created in the dialogue, there is always a certain *issue* at stake. It is also this issue that the impressions of the dialogue have to be guided back to (*transcendental* reduction). It appears as an *inevitable life topic*, which

---

[5] Fastvold, M. (2005) *"Beyond Method, Anders Lindseth Style: The Quest to open up Philosophical Space in the Consulting Room"*. In: *Philosophical Practice*, *1*(3), 171-183.

presents a challenge precisely because we so often try to avoid it in life. When we experience crises, this avoidance does not really work anymore so that an openness for the connections of life arises which can lead to more wisdom and to increased life mastery" (Lindseth, 2010, pp. 67f).

I do not want to deepen any further my answer to the first objection. The second objection, and related to it, the third objection, are more interesting to me.

Ever since I opened up my Philosophical Practice in Tromsø in 1989, I have stressed again and again: What I offer is not therapy but philosophy. My reason for this is quite easy to understand, I think: Therapy is treatment, and I offer no treatment. As a philosopher I am not under the pressure to treat any problems in the lives of my guests. What I offer is the willingness to consider together with my guests what their narratives are really about. Several times I have said: The fact that someone wants to talk and think about his life does not mean that he is in need of treatment: It may simply mean that the person takes his life seriously and has realized the simple fact that life is not always easy to live.

However, one can not completely dismiss the objection that my Philosophical Practice is in fact therapy. I myself often say that although my practice is no treatment, it still produces therapeutic effects. Are these effects—that my guests feel better and cope better with life's problems—merely the side effect of a philosophizing that focuses primarily on something else, on intellectual clarification and insight? I actually do not want to claim that. This not only sounds hard to believe but even contradicts my own conviction about what Philosophical Practice essentially is. For reconciliation with the most painful aspects of one's own life might be the most essential and inevitable life issue of Philosophical Practice. Such reconciliation is about transforming passive emotions into active ones. Passive emotions can be wonderful, but then they turn into fear and trembling. For instance, in one moment we are carried by the bliss of being in love, whereas in the next we fall out of this bliss and fear not to be loved anymore. Then it is a challenge to transform the passive emotion of being in love into the active emotion of a mature, patient and generous love. Such transformation does not avoid the pain that life brings with it. All attempts to avoid life's pain lead to a life in the irreconcilable. Thus, I see the way out of the irreconcilable as the core of Philosophical Practice (and as the core of philosophizing). Such a way out, that can be performed only through the pain of life, can of course be called *therapy*. In so far I can readily admit that the deepest concern of Philosophical Practice is therapy. But still I maintain that I am not a therapist, that I do not treat. I even think that modern society, which we sometimes call therapeutic society, fundamentally misunderstands what therapy actually is. For therapy which constitutes the heart of philosophizing is not primarily a making-bearable of life but rather an obligation to realize what really matters in life. This also responds to the third objection, because Philosophical Practice is not primarily a method of calming down and relieving individual suffering and problems of life, at the expense of political engagement, but rather and above all it is a dialogue that wants to enable the individual guest of the Philosophical Practice to actively participate in his or her own life. And with active I do not mean unrestrained and undisturbed but rather conscious and critical. What matters is participation in social life. So it is important that the guest of the Philosophical Practice can understand him- or herself as a citizen, influencing the direction of social developments. Therefore we can say with complete justification that the purpose of Philosophical Practice is deeply political.

5. With respect to present and future inquiry, how can the most important problems concerning Philosophical Practice be identified and explored?

For me, the main problem of Philosophical Practice is the philosopher himself, or more precisely, whether the person who calls himself a Philosophical Practitioner is really capable of philosophizing. Philosophizing in dialogues with people looking for orientation—that is what is at stake in Philosophical Practice, and the crucial question is: Is the Philosophical Practitioner capable of such philosophizing? It is not only about dealing with problems and providing relief, it is not only about having good discussions or to wonder about life, rather, it is above all about not avoiding the inevitable but to encounter the life issues consciously and actively and to participate in them. It is about seeing the universal in the individual case of the guest of the Philosophical Practice. To see this also means being able to realize that someone lives in the irreconcilable. To be able to perceive this and to possibly even resist an irreconcilable behaviour without rejecting the guest is required for the difficult, tedious and often long-lasting reconciliation work that can not always succeed in the Philosophical Practice. For me, such reconciliation work is the heart of philosophizing. To understand what it means to accomplish this is the great challenge and responsibility of Philosophical Practice.

Bibliography

Anders Lindseth: On the Possibility of Establishing a Meta-Scientific Foundation for Psychoanalysis. In *Annals of Theoretical Psychology*,

1986, *4*, pp. 59-98.

Anders Lindseth: Reality, Psychoanalysis, and Hermeneutical Science. (Reply to commentators.) In: *Annals of Theoretical Psychology*, 1986, 4, pp. 133-156.

Anders Lindseth: Meditasjonens etikk. In: *Dyade*, 1991, *23*(2), pp. 26-43.

Anders Lindseth: Hva kan Løgstrups etikk lære oss om moralbegrunnelsens oppgave? In: D. T. Andersson, F. R. Johannessen & A. Lindseth (eds.), *Skabelse og Etik. Motiver i K. E. Løgstrups filosofi*, pp. 199-225. Hadsten: Forlaget Mimer, 1994.

Anders Lindseth: What The Other Says—And What (S)He Talks About: Some Foundations of a Theory of Philosophical Practice. (Lecture at the 5th international conference on Philosophical Practce, Oxford, July 27-29, 1999.) In: T. Curnow (ed.), *Thinking Through Dialogue. Essays on Philosophy in Practice*, pp. 134-136. Surrey: Practical Philosophy Press, 2001.

Anders Lindseth: Løgstrups etikk i et omsorgsperspektiv. In: J. Wolf & M. Gjerris (eds.), *Spor i sandet. Bidrag til forståelse af K. E. Løgstrups forfatterskab*, pp. 63-79. (Replikk pp. 87-92.) København: Forlaget ANIS, 2002.

Anders Lindseth: Philosophical Practice: What is at Stake? In: H. Herrestad, A. Holt & H. Svare (eds.), *Philosophy in Society. Papers presented to The Sixth International Conference on Philosophy in Practice, Oslo, Norway 2001*, pp. 17-22. Oslo: Unipub Forlag, 2002.

Anders Lindseth: Samtalens plass i et menneskeliv. Anders Lindseth i samtale med Helge Svare. In: *Samtiden*, 2002, no. 3, pp. 114-123.

Anders Lindseth: A phenomenological hermeneutical method for researching lived experience. By A. Lindseth & A. Norberg. *Scand J Caring Sci*, 2004, *18*, pp. 145-153.

Anders Lindseth: *Zur Sache der Philosophischen Praxis. Philosophieren in Gesprächen mit ratsuchenden Menschen.* Freiburg/ München: Verlag Karl Alber, 2005.

Anders Lindseth: Spüren und Versöhnen als Aufgaben einer hermeneutischen Ethik. In: U. Gahlings, D. Croome & R. J. Kozljanic (eds.), *Praxis der Philosophie—Gernot Böhme zum 70. Geburtstag* (III. Jahrbuch für Lebensphilosophie 2007), pp. 127-141. München: Albunea Verlag, 2007.

Anders Lindseth: Wirken Philosophischer Praxis. In: *Jahrbuch der Internationalen Gesellschaft für Philosophische Praxis (IGPP)*, 2008,

3, pp. 10-24.

Anders Lindseth: Ort und Gespräch. In: *Aufgang. Jahrbuch für Denken, Dichten, Musik*, 2008, 5, pp. 110-116.

Anders Lindseth: Ethik des Dialogs. In: *Zeitschrift für systemische Therapie und Beratung*, 2008, 26, pp. 14-22.

Anders Lindseth: Lehrjahre Philosophischer Praxis—und die Frage nach der Lebenskönnerschaft. In: T. Gutknecht, T. Polednitschek & T. Stölzel (eds.), *Philosophische Lehrjahre. Beiträge zum kritischen Selbstverständnis Philosophischer Praxis*, pp. 39-56. Berlin: LIT-Verlag, 2009. [Schriften der Internationalen Gesellschaft für Philosophische Praxis (IGPP), Band 1.]

Anders Lindseth: Von der Methode der Philosophischen Praxis als dialogischer Beratung. In: D. Staude (red.), *Methoden Philosophischer Praxis. Ein Handbuch*, pp. 67-100. Bielefeld: transcript Verlag, 2010.

Anders Lindseth: Personlig dannelse. In: B. Hagtvet & G. Ognjenovic (eds.), *Dannelse. Tenkning, modning, refleksjon. Nordiske perspektiver på allmenndannelsens nødvendighet i høyere utdanning og forskning*, pp. 183-194. Oslo: Dreyers forlag, 2011.

Anders Lindseth: Når vi blir syge på livets vej—en udfordring for filosofisk praksis. In: Jeanette Ladegaard Knox & Merete Sørensen (eds.), *Filosofisk praksis i sundhedsarbejde*, pp. 139-167. Danmark: Frydenlund, 2011.

14

Lou Marinoff

Professor and Chair of Philosophy

Department of Philosophy, The City College of New York

---

1. Why were you initially drawn to Philosophical Practice?
"Why"? That sounds like a metaphysical question. I will offer you a speculative response toward the end. Meanwhile, I am happy to tell you *how* I was initially drawn to it.

To begin with, I am a practical sort of person, who likes to focus more on the utility rather than the theory of various pursuits. For example, I prefer playing and performing sports to coaching or studying sports science. Similarly, I prefer playing and performing music to studying composition or musicology. As an undergraduate student, I chose mathematical physics over pure mathematics, because physics utilizes mathematical languages to solve problems and to derive laws that pertain to extra-mental reality, as opposed to utilizing such languages to prove abstract theorems (however important or fascinating). Of course I have always enjoyed contemplation, but typically of a practical kind. I like to think about things, people, and processes, rather than dwelling on axiomatic logics, or on hypothetical or counterfactual questions. To the extent that they can be resolved, I do enjoy getting to the bottom of logical or empirical paradoxes.

By stages I was drawn to practical philosophy as a teen-ager, and specifically to the Asian traditions of Hinduism, Buddhism, and Taoism. Each of these traditions is profoundly esoteric in its own way, yet all of them directly address the human condition, seeking to make sense of consciousness, community, and cosmos. In Western philosophy, I identify most strongly with British empiricism, neo-Platonism, and Stoicism. Why? Because the early modern empiricism of Bacon and Hobbes, and the Enlightenment empiricism of Hume and Locke, contributed mightily to natural philosophy, from which sprang modern science and political liberty alike (see e.g. Ferris 2010). Neo-Platonist revivals, from the Italian Renaissance to New England Idealism, gave rise to immortal art and expansive insight into the art of living. And Stoicism (along with Taoism and Buddhism) is among the most robust cognitive operating systems ever devised for warding off the "slings and arrows of outrageous fortune,"[1] and attaining imperturbable serenity.

But being a practical sort of person is still a far cry from engaging in Philosophical Practice (for oneself), or indeed in becoming a philosophical practitioner (for others). From my teenage years though early adulthood, I was content to practice philosophy, intermittently and eclectically, primarily for self-development, with no intention of ever utilizing it as a means of assisting others. I crossed that Rubicon and became a practitioner only in 1991 when, at the age of forty, I took up the position of Moderator of the Canadian Business and Professional Ethics Network (CBPENET), at the University of British Columbia's Centre for Applied Ethics. The Centre had a group of in-house applied ethicists, with various specialities (e.g. Biomedical Ethics, Business Ethics, Engineering Ethics, Environmental Ethics, etc). Part of our work involved interviews with local and national media—radio, TV, print—on a variety of newsworthy issues. Mostly the media sought "sound-bytes"; sometimes more in-depth analyses. We applied ethicists more or less took turns granting such interviews, and thought nothing more would come of them. We were hugely mistaken.

It was not long before members of the public began to phone the Centre, asking to speak to a philosopher, seeking help to resolve their moral dilemmas or professional ethical issues. That's how I got my first client, a high-school principal embroiled in a professional ethical quandary. Some people actually walked-in to the Centre, wanting to see a philosopher in person. That's how I got my second client, a graduate student with a moral dilemma. Our secretary become quite adept at what would properly be called "intake"—matching clients with particular specialists where possible, or simply asking "Who wants to field this one?" in more generic cases.

It soon dawned on me that, notwithstanding Canada's relatively generous array of medical, social, and educational benefits, some citizens needed an additional service from time to time, a service that was nowhere defined or officially offered, but which nonetheless addressed burning issues in a particular domain, namely the philosophical. And the name of this service provider? For lack of a better term, one might call him or her a "philosophical counsellor."

So, in consultation with my colleagues at the Centre, I began to develop protocols for handling such cases, which clearly fell into a grey area as far as the University was concerned. These self-selecting clients who explicitly sought philosophical guidance, advice, clarification, or

---

[1] Quote from the celebrated soliloquy in Shakespeare's *Hamlet*, Act 3, Scene 1.

counseling were uniformly rational and functional, and were clearly helped by the process of deliberating with a professional philosopher. It would have been inappropriate to refer them to psychological or other counsellors, as the problems they presented were distinctly philosophical; while at the same time the mandate of the Centre for Applied Ethics (a research unit under the aegis of graduate studies) did not explicitly include provisions for offering individual counsel. We spoke primarily to issues, and not to persons. Yet there emerged a consensus at the Centre, to the effect that we could certainly justify "ethics counseling" as part of the public service component of our mandate. After all, offering analyses via public media about passive euthanasia in general (for example), and offering analyses via private consultation to a client whose elderly mother may be a particular candidate for passive euthanasia (for example), lie on the same continuum. So we justified seeing clients—pro bono, of course—as part of our public service.

Two important observations follow from this account. First, philosophical counseling (at least for us philosophers at the Centre) began as an outgrowth of applied ethics. While applied ethicists are trained to address broad-spectrum issues (e.g. environmental ethics), we can also address individuals facing cognately specific issues in their own lives (e.g. a student who wishes actively to protest the logging of old growth forests, but who asks: Which actions are justifiable?) After all, social issues *are* issues precisely because sufficient numbers of people grapple daily with them. A philosopher who can speak to social issues can also speak to persons grappling with those issues. And the second observation is this: It was members of the public themselves who cast us philosophers in this alternative role, that of personal consultants. In this light, at least for me, philosophical counseling began as a grassroots initiative. Citizens stepped forward requesting our services; we developed ways to honour their requests.

My next steps—from a local practitioner operating in a provincial vacuum toward a global practitioner helping pioneer a world-wide movement—were taken in collaboration with Ran Lahav. In 1992, Ran emailed a philosophy e-list, asking for referees for contributed papers to a seminal anthology that he was co-editing with Maria Tillmanns: *Essays on Philosophical Counseling* (Lahav & Tillmanns, 1995). I responded to Ran, saying that I would be happy to act as a referee, and also offering to contribute a paper based on my counseling experiences at the Centre. That paper found its way into the anthology, along with works by German pioneer Gerd Achenbach, Dutch pioneers Ida Jongsma and Dries Boele, and American pioneer Elliot Cohen, among others.

In 1993, Ran visited me in Vancouver, and proposed that we co-organize the First International Conference on Philosophical Counseling, to take place at the University of British Columbia in the summer of 1994. Ran and I were ideal partners for such a joint venture. He knew, personally, the leading lights of philosophical counseling in Holland, Germany, Israel, Canada, and the US (among other countries), and could thus construct the programme. I had the wherewithal to raise seed money, and to provide a hospitable venue for the conference at UBC. The First International was a watershed event. It attracted fifty-five practitioners from around a dozen countries, and we all realized that we constituted a genuine *movement* in philosophy, a movement with the potential to gain considerable momentum—which of course it has since that pleasantly memorable summer.

Having been drawn this far into Philosophical Practice—by public happenstance and private design—I brought many aspirations for the movement with me to New York when I relocated to City College, in that autumn of 1994. But these were the initial circumstances that drew me in.

So I have recounted the "hows," not the "whys." As promised, here's one possible "why." Philosophical Practice is an ancient idea, manifest in many different times, places, and ways across the ages. Here and now, its time has come again. But an idea whose time has come, or has come again, needs more than timing to be actualized in this world. It also needs embodied beings to play the roles of actualisers. Such beings themselves require certain attributes in order to succeed. These include a vision, a mission, an ability to attract able collaborators, a temerity to challenge regnant dogmas, a hide thick enough to withstand vociferous critics, and a willingness to persist in the face of (and ultimately to surmount) many obstacles. I had but a bare minimum of some of these attributes (save temerity and persistence, which I possess in abundance), but somehow managed to get started. I felt impelled to do it, as though it were a duty.

2. What does your work reveal about Philosophical Practice that other related academic fields typically fail to appreciate?

It is far too early to proclaim that any field has typically *failed* to appreciate revelations of Philosophical Practice, at least to date. After all, we barely constitute a field ourselves. So it is very generous of you to imply that Philosophical Practice is itself a field, if only in the associative sense that "other related academic fields" have possibly failed to appreciate our merits. Wikipedia, for example, defines an *academic discipline*, or *field of study*, as "a branch of knowledge that is taught and researched at the college or university level. Disciplines are defined (in part), and recognized by the academic journals in which research is published, and the learned societies and academic departments or faculties to which their practitioners belong."[2]

While Philosophical Practice is certainly a movement, one that continues to gain strength and momentum world-wide, it still falls short of being an "academic field," for at least one compellingly obvious reason: Philosophical Practice is not yet taught, studied or researched at anything like a critical mass of universities. Nor, at this writing, is there yet an accredited graduate program—M.A. or Ph.D.—that grants degrees in any branch of Philosophical Practice. Philosophical practitioners themselves are distributed across a broad spectrum; some function within academic contexts, others completely outside academe. While the latter group, which includes some of the world's leading practitioners, are to be commended for successfully pioneering Philosophical Practice outside the academy, it nonetheless remains a fact of life that the formation of every recognized and credible profession that works with people—be it education, law, medicine, psychology, social work, among others—takes place within a formal academic field. If Philosophical Practice is to enjoy the status of a field, it must become similarly established within the universities. At this writing, my colleagues and I at City College are taking steps to implement an M.A. Program in Applied Philosophy, including a branch in Philosophical Practice, which would be the first of its kind in the USA, and which could serve as a template for the proliferation of such programs. So much, then, for the aspirations of Philosophical Practice to become a legitimate academic field.

As regards failure by related academic fields to appreciate our work, I would rather term it "delayed recognition." The related field that is most delayed in this regard is philosophy itself, and for quite comprehensible reasons. For the past several decades, Anglo-American philosophy has been dominated by the analytic school; European philosophy, by the continental school. Both of these dominant schools, however mutually divergent if not incompatible, are nonetheless theoretical in their orientations. This is well and good, as far as theory goes. But almost every field of study in the academy has two branches: theoretical, and practical. Once can pursue pure or applied mathematics; theoretical or experimental sciences; literary theory or creative writing; musicology or instrumental performance. In philosophy, applied ethics is a noteworthy complement to analytic theory. Moreover, various forms of political and social activism among feminists, environmentalists, and animal rightists, provide further complements to theory-based philosophical and ideological (among other academic) approaches in these areas.

---

[2] http://en.wikipedia.org/wiki/List_of_academic_disciplines

That said, the majority of academic philosophers are still theoretically-oriented; that is to say, their formation is that of scholars and teachers of philosophy, and not of practitioners. This purely theoretical formation habitually misrepresents philosophy as an activity that takes place exclusively in insulated minds, or in disputations between otherwise insulated minds, and nowhere else. For us practitioners, philosophy is an activity that can indeed take place in the mind of a theoretical philosopher, but can also take place in dialogue between and among philosophers and clients, people and communities, groups and organizations, in the whole wide world.

For example, a theoretical philosopher can teach a variety of canonical accounts of what it might mean for something or someone to be "good" or "right" or "just," and can assess the strengths and expose the weaknesses of virtually any hypothetical ethical position. By contrast, a philosophical practitioner can assist a client in attaining goodness or rightness or justice in the particular circumstances of his or her life. It is often the case that a client rehearses or reinvents significant fragments of some well-established ethical framework, of which the client had been incognizant until being oriented by the philosophical counsellor.

And for example, a theoretical philosopher can teach a course on Plato's renditions of Socratic dialogues, stimulating philosophical inquiry among students. Yet these students remain spectators of the philosophical dialogue itself. By contrast, a philosophical practitioner can facilitate a Socratic dialogue with participants from any or all walks of life, stimulating philosophical inquiry along with *an experience of doing philosophy*—as contrasted with merely being spectators of philosophy.

And the efficacy of the Nelsonian Socratic method is truly impressive, as anyone who facilitates or participates in a Socratic dialogue can attest (e.g. see Gronke 2010). For example, a group of "ordinary" people—including an educator, a journalist, a graduate student, a manager—with no formal qualifications in philosophy, answered the question "What is hope?" in a far more balanced and nuanced manner than did either optimistic Hobbes or pessimistic Schopenhauer, who had each articulated a definition following solitary contemplation. Hobbes (1992, Ch. 6) defined hope as "Appetite with opinion of attaining"; Schopenhauer (2009, p. 49), as "Confusion of the desire for a thing with its probability." After long and careful deliberation, based (as prescribed by the method) on examples drawn from actual life experience, our group defined hope as "Maintaining an expectation for a preferred outcome, consistent with one's current life experience" (Marinoff 1999, pp. 262-8). While merely quoting the result of two days work hardly conveys the richness of the experience itself, Socratic dialogue's reliable methodology gives participants an opportunity *to be* philosophers, and offers facilitators unlimited potential for marketing this activity to myriad groups. Thousands of philosophers could be gainfully employed as facilitators of Socratic dialogue, working with constituencies within and beyond the groves of academe. But this possibility had been vastly under-appreciated, to date, by philosophers and the general public alike.

Theoretical philosophy and practical philosophy both entail several functions, including reading, writing, and reflection in solitude, as well as dialogue with others, including peers, students, and—additionally in our case—clients. The student body of theoretical philosophers is normally circumscribed by requirements of the institutions that admit them. The students pay fees to attend courses whose subjects matter are largely determined by the teachers. The client body of philosophical practitioners is not circumscribed by any institution—we engage with individuals, groups, and organizations of every kind, as long as they are willing and able to work philosophically. Our clients pay fees to participate in dialogues whose subjects matter are largely determined by the clients themselves.

In sum, theoretical philosophy has been the slowest among related academic fields (e.g. coaching, education, medicine, religious studies, pastoral counseling, psychiatry, psychology, social work, theology) to recognize the merits of and opportunities afforded by Philosophical Practice. Some of our best young minds are attracted to philosophy, which confronts them with a rigorous and demanding path for completing graduate degrees in the field. At the same time, their career prospects (as theoretical philosophers) are severely restricted and scandalously scarce. It is both ironic and tragic that so many fine young minds are rendered unemployable by virtue of having worked so long and hard to complete PhDs in their field. But now the larger culture in general, and many aspiring young philosophers in particular, are beginning to awaken to the benefits of and opportunities afforded by Philosophical Practice. Ultimately, it is up to philosophers themselves to appreciate that Philosophical Practice has a lot to offer, to clients and practitioners alike.

3. What, if any, practical and/or social-political obligations follow from understanding philosophy from the point of view of Philosophical Practice?

To be clear, I would first deny the existence of anything remotely resembling a uniform "point of view" in the nascent field of Philosophical Practice, except for the meta-view that practitioners obviously believe that philosophy has utility in extra-mental reality. When Henri Poincaré reputedly toasted "Here's to pure mathematics—may it never be useful for anything," a good many pure mathematicians probably raised their glasses. But this placed no constraint upon the subsequent and prolific development of applied mathematics. I suspect that a good many philosophers are willing to paraphrase Poincaré, substituting "theoretical philosophy" for "pure mathematics." Whereas our toast is "Here's to Philosophical Practice—may it always be useful for something." While most philosophical practitioners would raise their glasses to this, no two of us share anything like identical philosophical positions, either on the theoretical or the practical side of the street. And while theoretical philosophers may become bitterly and non-cooperatively divided over theoretical issues, philosophical practitioners who hold radically different views across the spectrum of theoretical subjects, and also about practice itself, can nonetheless come together and dialogue (with only a few stellar exceptions), precisely because we all share the same meta-view that philosophy is always useful for something.

A host of obligations flows naturally from this point of meta-view, but each given set of practical or socio-political obligations is bound to be a corollary of some particular view espoused by a given practitioner. Some may develop applications in specialized areas, as for example Vaughana Feary (1998) has done among two different US populations: prison inmates, and cancer survivors. Others may seek to defend the field against ill-conceived legislative initiatives that would allow psychology to monopolize words like "counseling," as Sam Brown (2010) has ably defended it in the UK. (Thanks in no small way to Sam's persuasive essay, the UK legislation in question was withdrawn.) Some may undertake IRB-approved[3] research on philosophical counseling within their universities, as Kathy Russell and Andrew Fitz-Gibbon

---

[3] IRB stands for "Institutional Review Board," a body constituted and governed by US Federal regulatory laws and Department of Health and Human Services guidelines. Every institution that conducts research on human beings, whether iatrogenic or not, must have said research pre-approved by its in-house IRB. This measure protects research subjects against potential risks, and protects researchers against frivolous lawsuits. Significantly, when City College's IRB approved my research protocol for philosophical counseling in 1998, it adjudged that philosophical counseling poses no greater risk to subjects than that entailed by normal daily life. IRB risk-assessments recognize no "zero-risk" scenarios; they realize that getting out of bed in the morning, commuting to work, or going shopping, all entail some degree of minimal risk: that of normal daily life. The location of philosophical counseling in this category, as has been done by IRBs at City College, SUNY Cortland, and Eastern Michigan University, provides a strong rebuttal to unsubstantiated and irresponsible accusations, levied by some mental health professionals and even university administrators, to the effect that clients of philosophical counselors are likely to commit suicide (see Marinoff 2004).

(2009) have done at SUNY Cortland, and Kate Mehuron (2009) has done at Eastern Michigan University. Others may collaborate with clinical medicine, as APPA has done with the Spinalis Foundation and Rehabstation in Stockholm, to integrate philosophical counseling into a menu of services for newly-injured spinal patients and newly-diagnosed MS patients (Levi 2010). Some may facilitate informal philosophical dialogues on a variety of topics, as octogenarian Peggy O'Neill does in her elder care facility in Pennsylvania; while others may do so in their local libraries, bookstores, cafes, or community centres. And some practitioners will inevitably designate themselves as critics of other practitioners, for a host of possible reasons.

The obligations that I willingly and often joyfully assume are professional, administrative, and political in character. Professionally, I continue to develop my own practice, to as full an extent as possible. That entails not only working with individuals, groups and organizations, but also writing for, speaking with, and educating various constituencies, world-wide, about Philosophical Practice. Administratively, I donate considerable time to APPA (the American Philosophical Practitioners Association): not only as president of the association, but also as editor of its Journal. Moreover, as mentioned, I am working to establish an M.A. Program in Applied Philosophy at City College, and that is no small administrative challenge. Politically, I aspire to further the recognition of Philosophical Practice as a legitimate and beneficial profession.

4. What do you see as the most interesting criticism against your own position in Philosophical Practice?

To re-iterate my position: I am impelled by a sense of duty to professionalize Philosophical Practice, to draw philosophy and philosophers out of the ivory tower, to help create opportunity for them to render services to a broad spectrum of humanity. Virtually all my activities as a practitioner and pioneer, for the past twenty years, have been consecrated to developing this position, and to fulfilling my mission and realizing my vision to help evolve the movement into a profession.

The most absurd criticisms, predictably, have been advanced by philosophers themselves. Some pure theoreticians seem quite unable (or unwilling) to grasp that philosophy can be applied to anything. Some of them exhibit resentment or hostility toward applied philosophy, in some cases because they attempt to exert proprietorship over philosophy itself: They seek to own it, to control it, and to dictate what is and what is not philosophical. Some of them take pride in having confined philosophy uniquely to the ivory tower, in perpetual captivity and isolation from reality and humanity. They regard their part of philosophy (pure theory) as its whole.

As to co-professionals, far fewer licensed psychologists and psychiatrists these days still allege that we are practicing psychology or medicine without a license, or conclude (without a shred of evidence, for none exists) that clients can be harmed by speaking with philosophers. These and kindred charges have been refuted in our literature, and are more than balanced, on the other side of the ledger, by referrals *from* physicians and psychiatrists, who realize that some of their patients' problems turn out to be philosophical indeed. We are also garnering strong support from many psychologists, who realize full-well that philosophy and psychology share common ground.

In my view, the most interesting criticisms to date have been advanced by psychiatrists: specifically, by Prof. Dr. Ronald Pies (Tufts) and Prof. Emeritus Dr. Irvin Yalom (Stanford). Critiques by psychiatrists have proved remarkable for a number of reasons. First, psychiatrists are also MDs, whose general outlook is scientific and therefore also (on a good day) objective. Second, given the organ they treat (the brain), many psychiatrists sustain vital interests in the mind-brain problem, and are thus predisposed to philosophical inquiry. Third, unlike some psychologists (who seem ever-ready to wage turf wars against any profession that appears to rival their authority), physicians and psychiatrists do not view philosophers as competitors; rather, as potential collaborators. Fourth, there is a natural alliance between philosophy and medicine (rather than an uneasy co-existence, as often obtains between philosophy and psychology, and between medicine and psychology). For these among other reasons, certain criticisms of philosophical counseling advanced by psychiatrists have been not only interesting but also fruitful.

For example, some years ago Dr. Pies published a critical piece in the newsletter of the American Psychiatric Association, voicing a number of concerns about philosophical counseling—some ill-conceived, others well-founded (Pies 1998). My reply to him was published in a book on philosophy and psychiatry, co-edited by a philosopher (Thomas Schramme) and a psychiatrist (Johannes Thome)—which engendered further correspondence between us (Marinoff 2004). It turns out that Dr. Pies sustains practical interests in Stoicism and Buddhism, which he utilizes (when appropriate) with his patients, in addition to or even instead of psychotherapy and drugs. He subsequently published a book on the benefits of these philosophical systems to people suffering from unhappiness, and cited case studies from my practice as well as his own (Pies 2008, Weaver 2008). So what began as a conflict of ideas (fomented partly by misleading and sensationalist American media coverage of philosophical counseling) ended as a fruitful collaboration between philosophy and psychiatry.

For another example, consider at Dr. Irvin Yalom: a prominent existential psychiatrist, professor emeritus of psychiatry at Stanford, and celebrated author of many books, including three historical novels that specifically entail forms of Philosophical Practice: *When Nietzsche Wept*, *The Schopenhauer Cure*, and *The Spinoza Problem* (Yalom 1993, 2006, 2012 respectively). Yalom's fiction is multifaceted, not simply posthumous psychoanalyses (à la Erikson) of noteworthy historical figures. Yalom is an "old-school" psychotherapist and group therapist, strongly committed to insight and interpretation (which philosophers call "hermeneutics"), and to exercising the curative power of dialogue (what we call "maieutics" and dialectics). Yalom is also a critic of the DSM (1994) and its paint-by-numbers diagnoses, of big pharma's colonization of psychiatry, and of purely molecular psychiatry itself (in so far as it eschews talk-therapy). He is also candidly critical of the professional troubles that psychiatrists can court if their own egos are not sufficiently shrunk (e.g. Yalom 1997).

In case it is not already evident from the foregoing, Yalom is a self-described iconoclast (2012). He identifies not only with his institutionally-embedded psychotherapeutic traditions, but also with the totally dis-embedded lives led by certain outstanding philosophers—for example, Nietzsche, Schopenhauer, and Spinoza.

When Nietzsche Wept was published before Philosophical Practice emerged publicly in the US; and if Yalom had not previously heard about it privately, then he did an admirable job of re-inventing it. *When Nietzsche Wept* presents an incurable case—or rather, two incurable cases, which imaginatively embroil Frederick Nietzsche in an ironic deception. Nietzsche is deceived by Lou Salomé into believing that the eminent Dr. Breuer (Freud's mentor) seeks philosophical counseling from him, whereas in fact Salomé is endeavouring to obtain psychological help for Nietzsche, but knows he is too proud (or too far gone) to seek or accept it himself. So Breuer poses as Nietzsche's client, the better to win his trust and to clandestinely offer him talk-therapy. Freud too gets drawn into this net. To no philosopher's surprise, Nietzsche is portrayed (and ultimately diagnosed?) as intellectually brilliant but incurably mad, and irremediably incapable of leading a "normal" and apparently boring life (such as Breuer's); whereas at the same time Breuer is exposed as pathetically bourgeois but incurably sane, and irremediably desirous of leading an "abnormal" creative life (such as Nietzsche's).

When Nietzsche Wept is ultimately a kind of stand-off between Yalom's two most cherished personae: a pioneering physician, and a towering philosopher. Nietzsche proves too tough a nut for Breuer to crack; while Breuer is too soft a heart for Nietzsche to harden. Yalom succeeds in illustrating that some "philosophical personality disorders" lie beyond the pale of medical treatment; while some artistic aspirations of physicians lie beyond the pale of philosophical remedy. At the end of the day, and the end of the novel, the physician and the philosopher inhabit worlds apart and go their separate ways—except in Yalom's fertile mind, in which their failed attempts to render mutual assistance continued to reverberate.

During the ensuing decade of the 1990s, Yalom's interest in the psychology of philosophy waxed stronger, while at the same time he witnessed the emergence of philosophical counseling and some of the associated (and inevitably distorted) media attention it attracted. In his foreword to *The Schopenhauer Cure*, Yalom cites many of the relevant books on philosophical counseling that were available at the time. He digested them, along with works by and about Schopenhauer, in order to craft his critical albeit fictional response to philosophical counseling. Yalom is also a devoted punster, in love with *double-entendre*. Thus his title "The Schopenhauer Cure" turns out to have two meanings. The first is embodied by his main character, Philip, a highly intelligent but angry and misogynistic young man, who adopts Schopenhauer's philosophy and persona in an ultimately futile attempt to "cure" what ails him. The second meaning evolves more gradually, as Philip is eventually "cured" of his "Schopenhauerian personality disorder" by the novel's other protagonist, a psychotherapist (and avatar of Yalom) named Julius.

Yalom's critique is crystal-clear: Not all philosophers are salutary role-models, neither in their worldviews nor in their lifestyles. If someone has an axe to grind or a bone to pick, then identifying with a philosopher who ground a similar axe or picked a similar bone is not necessarily or at all a therapeutic course. It may in fact backfire, by further inflaming underlying and unresolved emotional problems, while at the same time hardening external defences and internal resistance alike, making it more difficult for the sufferer to seek and accept the help he needs. Yalom is certainly justified in advancing this criticism. Most philosophers know other philosophers who suffer from unresolved psychological issues, and who respond very much like Schopenhauer, only not as brilliantly: Inflamed by narcissism and tormented by non-recognition, they utilize their capacious intellects to launch venomous attacks on their targets of choice (including colleagues), or tragicomically to tilt at their windmills of fancy. But as Yalom purports to illustrate in *The Schopenhauer Cure*, some of these "philosophical personality disorders" are curable by psychotherapy.

In both novels, Yalom artfully states the obvious: Great philosophers are sometimes chronically unhappy people, who lead unenviable lives. Some evidently cannot find happiness without psychological help; while others prove immune to psychology, psychiatry, philosophy, and religion alike, and so cannot be helped at all. Moreover, such philosophers cannot provide effective guidance to other troubled people, and may only exacerbate their problems. If one were to apply Yalom's criticisms straightforwardly to Philosophical Practice, one would recommend that aspiring philosophical practitioners take care not to neglect their own issues. If it is reasonable to demand that aspiring psychoanalysts get psychoanalyzed, and that aspiring psychotherapists get psychotherapy, then it is also reasonable to demand that aspiring philosophical counsellors get counselled philosophically.

Yalom's third novel, *The Spinoza Problem*, is a different kettle of fish, and is in my view his most brilliant fiction to date. In brief, it illustrates a case in which—for once!—a great philosopher's madness turns out to be socially constructed. Yalom clearly admires Spinoza greatly, and searches deeply into his life in an effort to ascertain what inner forces this excommunicated philosopher was able to mobilize in order to withstand and transcend the impossible and unenviable circumstances in which his insatiable thirst for truth, and his society's entrenched dogmas, had landed him. As Yalom realizes, Spinoza was lucidly sane; the community around him, deluded by inconsistent superstitions yet bent on communal self-preservation. An unrepentant anathema to their delusions, Spinoza had to be ostracized.

The counterpoint of Yalom's *double-entendre* is nowhere starker than in *The Spinoza Problem*. The title refers on the one hand to the problem Spinoza posed to his community: How can an incurably *rational* philosopher be given safe haven in a society governed by unchallengeable dogma? And the title refers on the other hand to the nightmare of Nazism, and how even Goethe's reverence for Spinoza cannot dissuade the Goethe-loving Nazi, Alfred Roseburg, from hating Jews. Thus Yalom has discovered and worked a sublime irony, namely the impenetrable and unfathomable isolation of Spinoza: reviled and excommunicated for life by his own Jewish community, only to be posthumously reviled as a Jew, by genocidal murderers of millions of Jewish people.

Moreover, Yalom's depiction of Spinoza's character is that of a saint, incapable of harbouring even an iota of ill-will against any his contemporaries: from the betrayers who pose as his clients (the better to discern his thoughts and denounce him for heresy), to the rabbi who excommunicates him, to the girl who jilts him. In Spinoza Yalom has unearthed a philosopher possessed of profound clarity of compassionate mind and unwavering strength of benevolent will, truly fit to counsel humankind. Yalom's appreciation of Spinoza seems to imply that if only many more people were as sane as that great philosopher, then the world would need fewer psychiatrists, and World Wars, alike.

At the same time, Yalom plausibly illustrates how the pathological prejudice of anti-Semitism and the toxic ideology of Nazism took root in the twisted mind of Alfred Rosenberg, Hitler's leading ideologue. In the process, Yalom shows how Rosenberg's pathology proves resistant to both Freudian analysis and Spinozan ethics alike, even though administered by a skilled German psychiatrist and Spinozaphile whose patient Rosenberg had consented to become. Thus Yalom probes the boundaries of psychiatry and philosophy both, with a view to understanding the kinds of souls that neither can cure.

While Yalom's novels are imaginative, entertaining, and heart-rending, his criticisms are philosophically significant because they contribute to elucidating what Popper (2009) called a "demarcation problem": How can we reliably distinguish between and among philosophical, psychological, psychiatric, and spiritual dimensions of human discontent and suffering? In what ways are these dimensions distinct? In what ways do they overlap?

Yalom's critiques have also presented opportunities. They led to our meeting in San Francisco in 2007, to the beginnings of a dialogue on these foregoing questions, to my publication of an article in response to Yalom's (2006) critique of philosophical counseling (Marinoff 2009), and to the publication of a compendium review of his works (Hole 2011). Nowadays I have a better understanding of Yalom's position, as he does of mine. That he recently referred a client to me is indicative of the trust that he now places in philosophical counseling. Thus his criticisms have been fruitful indeed. I only wish our movement had more critics, and allies, of the calibre Drs. Irvin Yalom and Ronald Pies!

5. With respect to present and future inquiry, how can the most important problems concerning Philosophical Practice be identified and explored?

The future always reveals itself, and usually soon enough. Just as I could never have foreseen, in the 1960s, 1970s or 1980s, that I'd become a philosophical practitioner during the ensuing decades, so I cannot possibly predict what future shapes the emergent field will take. At present, however, I can readily identify a few priorities, two of which relate more to action than to inquiry.

The first priority is to establish a graduate program in Philosophical Practice. This will attract and graduate serious and credible practitioners, who will be able to develop the field for subsequent generations. It will also solve the problem of marginalization—too many practitioners at present are regarded (whether justly or unjustly) as marginal players on the fringes of the academic and social fabrics. Once an accredited graduate program is successfully up and running, at any institution, it will get cloned at others.

Then the second priority can be furthered: namely, the political process of recognition of our profession by US states. Governments do not create professions; they recognize the ones that merit recognition. Four necessary criteria for recognition are: a national certifying body, a code of ethics, a corpus of scholarly and professional publications, and accredited graduate programs in the field. The American Philosophical Practitioners Association (APPA) has satisfied the first three of these, but cannot satisfy the fourth, for which we need a university. Once that fourth criterion will have been satisfied, it will change the landscape of our movement in a very important way.

As far as inquiry is concerned, many avenues of research can be suggested. Herein I will propose just a few.

But first, a preliminary observation is in order. It is empirically obvious that political process and national ethos differ greatly from polity to polity, and so too differ the ways in which philosophy is perceived. Whenever one crosses a political border (and as a frequent traveller, I do so regularly) one immediately senses being in a different cultural climate. What many people do not realize is that each and every political entity on earth compels its citizens to inhabit a kind of semipermeable and translucent cultural "bubble." Under the most brutal regimes, this bubble becomes all but impermeable and opaque. But in any case, news of the world is always filtered in through each national bubble, and interpreted according to prevailing ethos. Every single national bubble conditions its citizens to think, and so to see themselves and the world, in certain politico-specific ways. It is very difficult for people who remain in one country only—be it any polity whatsoever—under the aegis of one particular bubble, not to be brainwashed along certain axes. Even in the freest countries, citizens' perspectives are still skewed and conditioned by overarching influences and undergirding norms that prevail within their particular bubble. The only people who can recognize these bubbles for what they are, and remain largely immune to their effects, are those who travel to and operate within a host of nations, across continents. Those who sustain this global perspective can appreciate that while human problems are fundamentally the same everywhere, they are subject to wildly differing interpretations and solutions, some of which exacerbate while others ameliorate the human condition, according to differing political systems and national ethos.

One practical consequence of the differing self- and world-views inculcated by each polity is the particular way in which its citizens contextualize cultural artefacts, art-forms, pastimes, and professions. The implications for Philosophical Practice are inevitable. Within each national bubble, philosophy and religion tend to play pre-conceived (though also mutable and evolvable) roles, once again conditioned by prevailing ethos.

It follows that one very interesting avenue of research on Philosophical Practice, or perhaps within it, is to understand how and why it takes such different shapes in different countries. In Germany, philosophical counsellors and facilitators of Socratic dialogue comprise two distinct schools and national associations, separated by historical and socio-political wedges. In neighbouring Holland, under the aegis of a single national association, practitioners work across a spectrum of counseling, facilitation, and consulting services. In France, pioneering practitioners such as Oscar Brenifier and the late Marc Sautet (founder of the cafephilo phenomenon) cut all ties with the academy in order to further the development of their practices. In South Korea, academic philosophers (who are also founders of their national association for Philosophical Practice) have been contracted by the Defence branch of the government to provide counseling services to front-line troops (Rhee 2011). These telling contrasts in the ways in which philosophy is (or is not) practiced arise precisely from differing political (and therefore cultural) climates that are fostered in the respective national bubbles.

Looking through the other end of the glass, we see that the clients of Philosophical Practice are also differently pre-disposed, again according to the bubble they inhabit. In Holland, Socratic dialogue is practiced in many segments of society, including within government agencies themselves. Since Dutch culture both champions plurality of opinion yet greatly values consensus, Socratic dialogue (imported in its current Nelsonian form from Germany) has tremendous purchase in the Netherlands. In the US, popular culture is more oriented toward polarized conflict: two views clashing, and two heads bashing, across some unbridgeable divide, with both sides castigating each other's differences. In Argentina, where psychoanalysis took root and flourished in a combative cultural soil rich in *machismo* and egoism, philosophical counseling has also blossomed. Why? Because it offers a credible and effective alternative, in many cases, to reified psychological diagnoses or interminable psychoanalysis. In addition, since philosophical counseling is an educational service, its clients tend to feel uplifted rather than stigmatized. In the US, whose citizens are psychologized from cradle to grave, preyed upon voraciously by a gargantuan industry of diagnosis and drugging, rendered physically incapacitated by epidemic consumption of junk food, cognitively impaired by massive overdoses of trash television, and deprived of philosophy during the formative years of what passes for their primary and secondary educations, the popular culture could not be better *un*prepared to consume Philosophical Practice. The American bubble predisposes its citizens overwhelmingly to contextualize philosophical counseling as a new form of psychotherapy. Nothing could be more absurd, since historically it's just the other way around: Psychotherapy is a new form of philosophical counseling.

From these and cognate considerations, it is clear that both the intellectual history and the comparative sociology of Philosophical Practice afford promising fields of research for future scholars.

Another interesting cross-cultural question that arises, and that must be answered empirically, is the following: What results obtain—either comparable or non-comparable—from conducting Socratic dialogues on the same question (e.g. "What is liberty?" or "What is responsibility?" or What is integrity?) in different cultures? If significant cross-cultural differences ensued, would these be explicable in terms of the distorting effects on worldviews exerted by different national bubbles? Or would such putative differences serve to falsify Plato's epistemology (as regards the claim to universality of innate wisdom) and ontology (concerning his posited pure forms)? Then again, if comparable results were to obtain cross-culturally, to what extent could this be seen as an empirical confirmation of Platonic theory?

By no means does this exhaust the richness of Plato as a basis for research in Philosophical Practice. Another thing I would like to see is an anthology of essays refuting the central claims of the *Protagoras* and the *Gorgias* alike, which assert in various ways that virtues cannot be taught. We philosophical practitioners have ample experience in this domain, both inculcating and instilling virtues in our clients, and as such do not merit the pejorative appellation of "sophistry" that has from time-to-time been hurled at us.

As we saw in Yalom, a perennially fertile field of inquiry, based in the philosophy of science, centres on the Popperian problem of demarcation: in the context of philosophical counseling, demarcation between philosophy, psychiatry, and psychology (e.g. Marinoff 2011). Empirically, in Philosophical Practice, we find some cases in which the demarcation is clear: There are both distinctively philosophical, and distinctively psychological, avenues via which some kinds of cases can be approached. Questions then arise as to what advantages or disadvantages, benefits or detriments, ensue from the client-side given distinctly different possible approaches. These kinds of cases illustrate most strongly that philosophical counseling can be a credible alternative, and sometimes a preferable one, to psychotherapy.

Then again, other kinds of cases fall into greyer areas, in which the demarcation itself is blurred. In these kinds of cases, philosophers may find themselves employing quasi-psychological approaches, while psychologists may find themselves employing quasi-philosophical ones. This seems to signal a fertile area of inter-disciplinary research, such that philosophers and psychologists could come together and compare case-based approaches. On this view, instead of assuming the role of competitors in professional turf-wars, we can become collaborators in exploring apparently common ground, with a view to teasing out more nuanced criteria of demarcation, should they be lurking beneath the surface. Philosophy is the parent discipline of psychology—a prodigious offspring—and their bifurcation in recent decades has been mutually impoverishing. Now we can foresee opportunities, on the horizon, for collaboration and mutual enrichment.

Bibliography

Brown, Sam (2010). "The Meaning of 'Counsellor'," *Philosophical Practice: Journal of the APPA*, 5.1, 549-566. *Diagnostic and Statistical Manual of Mental Disorders* (DSM-IV, 1994) Arlington, VA: American Psychiatric Association.

Feary, Vaughana (1998). "The Role of Philosophical Counseling in Rehabilitating Criminal Offenders, *Inquiry: Critical Thinking Across the Disciplines,* 17.3, 85-99.

Ferris, Timothy (2010). *The Science of Liberty*. New York: HarperCollins.

Fitz-Gibbon, Andrew and Russell, Kathy (2009). "Case Studies from Research at SUNY Cortland," *Philosophical Practice: Journal of the APPA*, 4.3, 502-18.

Gronke, Horst (guest editor, 2010). Special Issue on Socratic Dialogue, *Philosophical Practice: Journal of the APPA*, 5.3.

Hobbes, Thomas (1992). *Leviathan*, edited by Richard Tuck. Cambridge: Cambridge University Press.

Hole, George (2011). "Compendium Review: The Yalom Curriculum for Philosophical Counselling," *Philosophical Practice: Journal of the APPA*, 6.2, 811-15.

Lahav, Ran and Tillmanns, Maria (eds. 1995). *Essays on Philosophical Counselling*. Lanham, MD: America University Press.

Levi, Richard (2010). "Philosophical Practice in Rehabilitation Medicine," *Philosophical Practice: Journal of the APPA*, 5.2, 607-14.

Marinoff, Lou (2004). *Thus Spake Settembrini: A Meta-Dialogue on Philosophy and Psychiatry*. In *Philosophy and Psychiatry,* Schramme, Thomas and Thome, Johannes (eds). Berlin: De Gruyter. pp. 27-49

Marinoff, Lou (2009). Synchronicities, Serpents, and Something-Elseness, in *Philosophical Practice: Journal of the APPA*, 4.3, 519-34.

Marinoff, Lou (2011). "Transforming Poison into Medicine: The Role of Dualism in Psychiatry", in *World Journal of Biological Psychiatry*, 12(S1), 66-69.

Mehuron, Kate (2009). "Case Studies from Research at Eastern Michigan University", in *Philosophical Practice: Journal of the APPA*, 4.3, 492-501.

Pies, Ronald (May 15, 1998). "Philosopher Therapists", in Letter to the Editor. In *Psychiatric News*. American Psychiatric Association.

Pies, Ronald (2008). *Everything Has Two Handles: A Stoic's Guide to the Art of Living*. Lanham, MD: Hamilton Books.

Popper, Karl (2009). *Stanford Encyclopaedia of Philosophy*, http://plato.stanford.edu/entries/popper/#ProDem

Rhee, Young (2011). "Philosophical Practice and Humanities Therapy in Korea", in *Philosophical Practice: Journal of the APPA*, 6.1, 734-43.

Schopenhauer, Arthur (2009). *The Horrors and Absurdities of Religion*. London: Penguin.

Weaver, Britni (2008). Review of *Everything Has Two Handles*, by Ronald Pies, in *Philosophical Practice: Journal of the APPA*, 3.3, 365-6.

Yalom, Irvin (1993). *When Nietzsche Wept*. New York: HarperCollins.

Yalom, Irvin (1997). *Lying on the Couch*. New York: HarperCollins.

Yalom, Irvin (2006). *The Schopenhauer Cure*. New York: HarperCollins.

Yalom, Irvin (in the press, 2012). *The Spinoza Problem*. New York: HarperCollins.

Books by Lou Marinoff

Plato, Not Prozac (1999). New York: HarperCollins.

Philosophical Practice (2001). New York: Academic Press.

Therapy for the Sane (aka *The Big Questions*) (2003). New York & London: Bloomsbury.

The Middle Way (2007). New York: Sterling.

Tetsugaku Runessansu no Taiwa (*Dialogue on Philosophical*

Renaissance), with Daisaku Ikeda (2011). Tokyo: Ushio.

El Poder del Tao (*The Power of Tao*) (2011). Barcelona: Ediciones B.

15

Peter Raabe

Professor of Philosophy and philosophical counselor
University of the Fraser Valley, Abbotsford, British Columbia, Canada

---

1. Why were you initially drawn to Philosophical Practice?

I was born into and raised in a fundamentalist, evangelical Christian family. This would not have been a problem in itself were it not for the fact that, through its publications and teachings, our religious organization promoted the idea that higher education was a waste of time. After all, why would anyone need worldly knowledge when this world was soon going to be destroyed at Armageddon? We were taught from a very young age that the only worthwhile learning came from reading the Bible, and the only sensible occupation was preaching the word of God. This left many of my generation sadly unprepared for life in the real world. This church, and others like it, has a suicide rate among young people much higher than the national average. It also took a mental and, dare I say it, spiritual toll on its members. We were taught that we were God's special chosen ones and yet we were all sinful; loved but punished harshly for minor infractions; practicing Christian virtues but helping only the needy in our own congregations. These beliefs create a schizophrenic view of life and of oneself. To avoid this most church members I know simply applauded the teachings and ignored all the contradictions in practice. In fact, while the church claimed it encouraged thinking for oneself, it actually discouraged asking questions. The kind of metaphysical questions I began to ask in my early teens were considered wrong questions stemming from a sinful attitude.

I consider myself one of the lucky ones. Contrary to church teachings and the wishes of my parents, I had a worldly friend who went to university. Jim and I spent many late nights discussing what I now understand to have been deep philosophical issues. My naive defence of my church's teachings slowly unravelled under his patient questioning, and eventually I stopped going to religious meetings. But after graduating from high school, due to my lack of interest in education, I was only qualified to work for minimum wage menial labour jobs. For years I resented my church, and also my parents, for convincing me that the Bible had all the answers to life's problems. I eventually married my worldly wife Anne, and with her encouragement and support decided to take some courses at a local college. It was my first critical thinking course in philosophy with a friendly instructor named Mark Battersby that started me off on the path that led me to eventually writing my Ph.D. thesis on philosophical counseling and becoming a practitioner.

There was a time in my life when I considered becoming a psychoanalyst. I liked the idea of helping other people think things through. But I found out that psychoanalysis had much more to do with medicine than with thinking. This eventually led me to philosophy. I was actually drawn into philosophical counseling by others. After completing my Masters degree in philosophy I volunteered to teach reasoning/critical thinking skills to men in a residential centre for recovering alcoholics and drug abusers. I knew that once these men went back to their families and friends they would be facing the same life pressures with the same limited personal resources that had made them addicted to alcohol and drugs in the first place. Teaching them reasoning/critical thinking skills was helping them to improve their lives through better judgments; I was giving them tools that would help them avoid relapse. The men often asked to talk privately with me to help them resolve various personal problems and issues. When I told a university colleague of mine that I was using philosophy to help these people she told me that what I was doing is called philosophical counseling and that there had recently been the first international conference devoted to this new field. I was very excited to learn that there were others using philosophy to help people, and that this practice actually had a name.

Many of the men at the recovery centre told me what we were doing with philosophy was much more useful to them than what they had been, or were, getting from standard therapy. This led me to examine what is involved in the more conventional forms of therapy. I discovered that many aspects of conventional psychotherapy and counseling, especially so-called talk therapies, are actually philosophy under different names. The deeper I researched psychotherapy and counseling the more I realized that most of the best, and best known, therapists and counsellors in history were very well read in philosophy. I also found that many contemporary psychotherapists and counsellors with whom I came into contact had very little knowledge of philosophy. They had learned therapeutic methodology but not the philosophy at the heart of those methods. I often tell my students the story of the counsellor who told me she was a practitioner of existential therapy, but was unable to tell me what existentialism is. I came to the conclusion that to be a good therapist or counsellor the practitioner should focus less on the science of psychology and medicine and much more on the practice of philosophy.

After I completed my doctoral thesis on philosophical counseling, which was published as my first book—*Philosophical Counselling: Theory and Practice*—I had the opportunity to teach philosophical counseling in a university classroom. But I soon found out that offering philosophical counseling to philosophy students was a mistake. Most philosophy students enjoy theoretical disputation with other philosophy students; they're not interested in working face-to-face with people from the community who are suffering from real life problems. So I shifted my focus away from philosophy students, and now offer a course of philosophy for counsellors which draws students in from all the disciplines that contain an element of counseling such as psychology, social work, nursing, and teaching. My experience with Philosophical Practice is exclusively in the area of philosophical counseling. Therefore I will address the following questions from this perspective.

2. What does your work reveal about Philosophical Practice that other related academic fields typically fail to appreciate?

There is so much about philosophical counseling that other related academic fields fail to appreciate that I hardly know where to begin.

The way biological psychiatry has been defining mental illness for the past twenty years—as disease of the brain—has misrepresented the experience of most people suffering from mental anguish and distress. Biological psychiatrists and some psychotherapists have claimed that what they do is in line with the so-called medical model of patient treatment. But this is simply false.

THE SO-CALLED MEDICAL MODEL

Philosophical counseling makes little sense in light of a medical or biological model of the mind and a medical model of mental illness, and the psychobabble used to defend them. Advances in the research on the functioning of the brain have not led to any significant discoveries of organic causes for any of the many so-called mental disorders whether they are in adults or in children. The medical model involves medical tests used to identify distinct physiological dysfunction or biological causes, leading to a diagnosis that is consistent across cultures, and finally to a consistent treatment protocol. But with mental illness a diagnosis is given without any medical testing for dysfunction or causes because there are no medical tests which indicate mental illness. Then a treatment protocol is followed which may be completely different not only from one culture to the next but from one psychiatrist or psychotherapist to the next. The so-called 'instruments' used to find mental illness are questionnaires which require the therapist's subjective interpretation and evaluation of the patient's responses. This is not at all like an objective medical test. Mental illness is clearly not treated according to the medical model regardless of what clinicians try to get their patients to believe.

Furthermore, one of the strangest problems that exists, unexplained, within the definition of mental illness as organic brain disease is that there are significant differences from one culture to the next. This does not occur with organic diseases. For example, personality and eating disorders are not universal. They are found only in Western societies. And the diagnosed symptoms of depression and anxiety are highly varied from one culture to another. The recently 'discovered' mental illness of sexual addiction seems to be located exclusively within the North American culture. The biological brain is universal, but mental illnesses are not. Some mental illnesses are unique to particular cultures; some cultures do not recognise the diagnosis of a particular mental illness as legitimate. Biological psychiatry ignores these cultural differences and isolates behaviours and experiences from their context when claiming mental illness is brain disorder. In 1997 a formal dialogue between seven New York psychiatrists and nine consumer-practitioners criticized the medical model and the current quasi-biological diagnostic system as disempowering and detrimental when used to the exclusion of other explanatory frameworks.[1]

THE INVENTION OF MENTAL ILLNESSES

The term mental illness implies that philosophical counseling cannot be an effective treatment. But the splitting of psychological problems into illness categories is a social, not a scientific, endeavour. When common professional consent declines or a particular diagnosis becomes the target of too much public opposition, that mental illness is declassified by the board of professionals which produces the classificatory and diagnostic manuals. It thereby simply vanishes into thin air. Multiple personality disorder, homosexuality, and masturbation, all at one time considered serious mental illnesses requiring extensive treatment, have all been voted out of the official diagnostic manuals. General anxiety disorder and dysthymia are currently under consideration for possible removal, while a variety of sexual behaviours, such as cross-dressing

---

[1] Blanch, Andrea et al. Consumer-Practitioners and Psychiatrists Share Insights About Recovery and Coping. *Psychological and Social Aspects of Psychiatric Disability*. Roy Spaniol et al eds. Boston: Boston University, 1997. p. 71, 69.

are being considered for inclusion.

The diagnosing of certain behaviours and experiences as mental illness, or the removal of a mental illness from diagnostic manuals, is under continued political disputation. For example, a conservative US group calling itself the Traditional Values Coalition has mounted a campaign to have homosexuality reinstalled into the diagnostic manuals.[2] They hope their lobbying will prompt the decision-makers to vote homosexuality back into existence as a mental illness. What sort of ontological status does a mental illness have which can simply be voted into and out of existence? The psychiatric 'invention' of mental illnesses, because mental illness is based on the dominant social and political environment — not to mention a confused and contradictory ontology — has been and remains deeply problematic.[3] Allan Horowitz is a professor in the Department of Sociology and Institute for Health, Healthcare Policy, and Aging Research at Rutgers University. His research into the ontology of mental illness has led him to conclude that

> "...the symptoms of most psychological dysfunctions are not direct indicators of discrete underlying disease entities. ...Culture, not nature, influence how most disorders become real both to the people who suffer from them and to those who treat them."[4]

So if mental illnesses don't actually exist as disease entities, and if the label mental illness is simply applied to emotional suffering, then it's entirely possible that philosophical counseling can be an effective treatment and even a cure.

CAUSATION

Philosophical counseling requires a shift in thinking from the standard mental illness causes misery to misery causes mental illness.

For example, depression doesn't cause unhappiness. It doesn't **cause** anything at all. Depression is only the label applied to a number of symptoms such as insomnia, lack of appetite, and unhappiness. To re-

---

[2] See the website at http://www.traditionalvalues.org/read/3645/diagnostic-and-statistical-manual-of-mental-disorders-under-attack-by-lgbt-activists/

[3] Fulford, Bill, Tim Thornton, and George Graham. *Oxford Textbook of Philosophy and Psychiatry*. Oxford: Oxford UP, 2006. p. 317.

[4] Horwitz. Allan V. *Creating Mental Illness*. Chicago: University of Chicago Press, 2002. p. 131.

ally grasp this, it requires a different way of thinking about mental illness from what is commonly believed by most people in our society. It requires a paradigm shift. Depression is not a cause. It is a name or label applied to symptoms such as insomnia, loss of appetite, and unhappiness. Depression, is, in part, unhappiness, and unhappiness is caused by life circumstances. The same applies to other so-called mental illnesses such as schizophrenia. Schizophrenia doesn't **cause** anything at all. It is merely a label given to a list of symptoms. And that list of symptoms varies considerably depending on what book or which expert is attempting to define it. This definitional vagueness and ambiguity in the treatment language of so-called mental illness has prompted its defenders in North America to reluctantly change the language from mental illness to mental distress.[5]

THE SO-CALLED UNCONSCIOUS

Freud's (and his followers) hypothesis of a dark, inaccessible unconscious and the related theories this produced about dreams, free association, and so on, have all been thoroughly disproved. Freud wanted to explain humans according to the cause-and-effect laws which govern the physical universe. In other words he wanted to explain the mind in a scientific manner—where the being is driven by causes—while the beliefs, values and assumptions of the person's mind are ignored. But there have been many books[6] written to show that the Freudian unconscious simply doesn't exist, and if it did we human beings would be no more than machines controlled by the uncontrollable. Unfortunately, the belief that there is a human unconscious still pervades western societies. And this belief still partly drives many of the most ineffective therapies, including medication as treatment.

TALK AS EFFECTIVE THERAPY

Philosophical counseling is not just talking. It is therapeutic discussion informed by a knowledge of philosophy and the skills associated with philosophising. Research has shown that the most effective forms of

---

[5] For a discussion about the problematic use of language of psychoanalysis and psychotherapy see the chapter titled The Abuse of Language in Psychoanalysis and Psychotherapy by Robert J. Stoller in *Crucial Choices Crucial Changes* (New York: Prometheus, 2000.) p. 55-77.

[6] See for example *The Challenge to Psychoanalysis and Psychotherapy* edited by psychiatrists Stefan de Schill and Serge Lebovici (London: Jessica Kingsley Publishers, 1999) and philosopher John Searle's book *The Rediscovery of the Mind* (Cambridge, Mass.: MIT Press, 1998) especially chapter 7, The Unconscious and its Relation to Consciousness.

treatment with the best overall long-term outcomes are the so-called talk therapies.[7] An examination of all the major talk therapies reveals that they are based on philosophical discussion. Therefore philosophical discussion is at the root of all the best therapies.

PHILOSOPHY IS VITAL TO TALK THERAPIES

The therapy of any psychotherapist or counsellor is poorer for not having studied philosophy. This is an obvious conclusion based on the previous point above. If counseling and therapy are based on philosophy, but the students of counseling and therapy are not taught the content of philosophy and its application to real life issues and problems, but are taught only various psychotherapeutic treatment methods, then their practice will be all the poorer for it. For example, a student can learn the method of Existential therapy without an understanding of what existentialism actually is. This is like learning how to move a pawn on a chess board without an understanding of what chess is all about. It must be remembered that some of the most famous psychoanalysts and psychotherapists, such as Sigmund Freud, Carl Jung, Alfred Adler, Aaron Beck, Albert Ellis, and Viktor Frankl were all well educated in philosophy. Their methods were based on the reasoning tools they had learned from the content and the practice of philosophical discussions.

PRACTICE INFORMS THEORY

Philosophical practice affords an understanding of actual human reasoning and responses to situations which hypothetical and classroom examples can't hope to duplicate. Theory can't address the myriad contingencies that reveal themselves in actual practice when the counsellor is face to face with a suffering human being. While theory informs practice, practice furthers theory. Teaching young people **how** to think about what they believe to be true and good is more important than teaching them **what** to think and believe. Philosophical counseling involves both the content of philosophy that has been developed by philosophers over the centuries as well as the method of philosophical inquiry they exemplified.

THE BRAIN/MIND DISTINCTION

There's a difference between the biological brain and the non-material mind.

---

[7] See for example pages 86, 99, 144, 144, and 275 in *Textbook of Anxiety Disorders* (Washington: American Psychiatric Publishing, 2002).

Changing one's mind is not the same as changing one's brain. There is no such thing as 'mental content' defined as something in the mind. The content of the brain simply is the mind. The mind is propositional, not biological. Mental propositions consist of attitudes—such as doubts, beliefs, desires, values, and assumptions, toward propositional content. For example, a person's mind may consist of the doubt that she is worthy of love and respect; the belief that she is unworthy of love and respect, the desire to be loved and respected, and so on. These can, of course, lead to unusual or even socially unacceptable behaviours. But notice that none of this propositional content—the doubts, beliefs, desires, values, and assumptions—has any material existence. While the defining characteristic of the brain is its physical structure, the defining characteristic of the mind is, what philosophers call, 'intentionality'—thoughts or attitudes about something.

Although foetal alcohol syndrome, Alzheimer's, syphilitic dementia and other biological disorders affect thinking, they are not mental illnesses. These biological disorders certainly interfere with the person's normal thinking—the ability to effectively deal with beliefs, values, and assumptions. But they are not problems caused by the individual's beliefs, values, and assumptions. This is what differentiates brain diseases from so-called mental illnesses. As soon as mental difficulty is found to have an organic cause it is no longer a mental problem; it is a biological brain problem. This is the point Thomas Szasz and other mental healthcare professionals have been making since the 1950's. But our society is so saturated with the belief that mind problems are brain problems that this message has had only minor impact.

3. What, if any, practical and/or social-political obligations follow from understanding philosophy from the point of view of Philosophical Practice?

Practical and/or social-political obligations follow from what my work has revealed about Philosophical Practice that other related academic fields typically fail to appreciate. Therefore my answers to this question are necessarily somewhat repetitive of my answers to the previous question.

First there is the obligation to counteract the pervasive biomedical model of mental illness. An understanding of philosophical counseling obliges the practitioner to make the general public aware that so-called mental disorders are not the **cause** of suffering. Mental disorders are not causes; they are a collection of symptoms caused by some other problem. This requires a paradigm shift in thinking from the idea that mental illness causes misery to the truth: misery causes mental illness.

Philosophical counsellors are also obligated to educate the public of the fact that so-called mental disorders are not endogenous—they're not the result of malfunctions or weaknesses within the individual sufferers. They are instead the result of external factors. People are not born with mental disorders; they develop due to external stressors. Here is just one example: in the book *Development of Psychopathology* the authors of one chapter state that studies indicate individuals with schizoid PD (personality disorders) are more likely than patients with other PDs to report a history of sexual abuse or childhood emotional neglect and that significant risk factors for the development of schizoid PDs are low childhood parental affectionchildhood physical abuse, emotional abuse, supervision neglect, physical neglect, and emotional neglect[8] Philosophical counsellors who understand this so-called mental disorder correctly—as precipitated by external causal factors—are obligated to see this type of client as the victims of his environment, not some biological or genetic weakness. The philosophical counsellor understands, and promotes the fact that philosophy can be more effective than medications in dealing with the actual cause of his misery: his low self esteem, his skewed self image, and the damaging relationships with his significant others. To believe that mental disorders are endogenous amounts to blaming the victim.

The philosophical counsellor is obligated:.

- to correct misperceptions such as that emotional responses simply erupt from within. They are not only learned, emotions are the result of beliefs, values, and assumptions. This means that it is a mistake to treat emotions as though they are biologically generated, that is as simply created by the brain. This leads to the claim that emotions can be treated with medications. But how can a belief, value, and assumption be treated with medication. If a person has been diagnosed with depression rather than asking which drug will alleviate the depression, the question ought to be what is making this person unhappy? Unhappiness is an emotion that results from beliefs, values, and assumptions. Medications can dull the brain to the point where beliefs, values, and assumptions are forgotten. But does that resolve the problems or issues that created the negative emotions in the first place? To keep those emotions at bay the individual must necessarily depend on the medication. How does this improve that person's situation? Beliefs, values,

---

[8] Johnson, Jeffrey G., Pamela G. McGeoch, Vanessa P. Casey, Sodoodeh G. Abhary, Joel R. Sneed, and Robert F. Bornstein. The Developmental Psychopathology of Personality Disorders. Benjamin L. Hankin and John R. Z. Abela eds. Thousand Oaks: Sage Publications, 2005. p. 448.

and assumptions are best addressed with discussion. And discussion can lead to shifts in beliefs, values, and assumptions, or even life changes, that will alleviate emotional suffering.

- to not only see people in private practice, but also to educate practitioners in the use of philosophy to counteract the overuse of drugs in treatment. Philosophical counsellors are obligated to promote the paradigm shift from the belief that mental illness is biological and primarily treatable with medication to the perspective of mental distress originates from beliefs, values, and assumptions and is treatable with philosophy.

- to teach people that the mind and the brain are not identical, and that the so-called medical model does not apply to the human mind which is a person's beliefs, values, and assumptions.

- to teach people that there is really no epidemic of mental illness in North America, despite the statistics that we hear in the news almost daily. One statistic says that 50% of the general population is suffering from a diagnosable mental disorder. Another says that more than half of working North Americans are suffering from work-related mental disorders. The reason for their so-called mental illnesses is job dissatisfaction. A newly created diagnosis for children is Oppositional Defiance Disorder (ODD) which refers to a child who talks back to its parents. One web site claims that a treatment for this childhood mental disorder is teaching the parents better child management. So why is ODD diagnosed as though it were endogenous or within the child? But then the website also suggests the child might benefit from being medicated. This is all sheer nonsense! There is no epidemic of actual mental illness in North America. But there certainly is an epidemic of diagnostic categories and wholesale diagnosing which makes it possible to label every living citizen as mentally ill.

- to teach the public that so-called mental illnesses don't **cause** anything at all. See the discussion of this point in my answers to question 2 above.

- to publicize the fact that the interpretation of psychotherapeutic test results are subjective. The so-called 'instruments' used to find mental illness are questionnaires which require the therapist's subjective interpretation and evaluation of the patient's responses. This means that test results are interpreted differently by different therapists often leading to differing and conflicting diagnoses and recommended treatment protocols. A very famous case here in Canada involved a man whose wife had fled to her mother's house because her husband was so abusive. He proceeded to strangle all five of their children while they lay sleeping, and then set the house on fire with them in it. He then drove to his mother-in-law's house, forced his wife into his truck, and drove her home to watch their house burn down. After he surrendered to the police, his defence lawyer hired one of the most respected psychotherapists in the province to evaluate his mental state. After administering a number of psychological tests the psychotherapist said the tests revealed the man to have several mental illnesses making him unfit to stand trial for what he had done. But the prosecution also hired a very respected psychotherapist to administer the same tests. This psychotherapist interpreted the same test results as indicating the man to be completely normal and therefore fit to stand trial. The fact that the same psychotherapeutic tests can be interpreted as revealing two completely opposite conclusions about human sanity shows how misleading the claim is that there are scientific tests that indicate mental illness.

- to educate the media about how they are being manipulated by the pharmaceutical industry to promote the misinformation inherent in the medical model of mental illness because it benefits their profit margin.
- to make the public aware that there is a lot of misinformation being circulated about so-called mental illness, such as that once you are diagnosed you will never recover or be cured. Treatment outcome studies have shown that therapies based on philosophical discussions, also called talk therapies, are the very effective in not only resolving seriously troubling issues, but in long-term effect and benefit. Again, a mental disorder is not an organic problem of the material brain; it is instead a problem within a person's mental narrative, within the mind's propositional content which are beliefs, values, and assumptions. So it is no wonder that talk therapies have been found to be as effective, and in some cases more effective, than medications—and without the horribly debilitating side effects.

But this raises the question, what constitutes recovery? Does it make sense to speak of a cure for mental illness? A skeptic might argue that there is no scientific evidence that will reveal a person is cured of their mental illness if they have undergone philosophical counseling. But the skeptic will then be faced with the problem that there is no scientific evidence which will show that a mental illness was present in the suffering individual in the first place. The skeptic will then ask, What about the fact that geneticists are finding the genes that cause mental illness. Doesn't that prove their biological origin? But the so-called genetic evidence of mental illness is another popular myth. More than thirty years of biological research have not been able to identify a specific [genetic] marker for any of the current diagnostic categories.[9]

One of the things a medical doctor has at his/her disposal in trying to determine if a patient is cured is simply to ask, How do you feel? If the answer is, Much better then isn't this an indication that at least the treatment is of benefit? While the medical doctor has actual biological tests at his/her disposal, the philosophical counsellor has only his/her questions. But clients require no more proof for themselves that philosophical counseling works other than that it has made them feel better. Philosophical counseling has cured many suffering individuals in this way.

4. What do you see as the most interesting criticism against your own position in Philosophical Practice?

I find it difficult to think of any interesting criticisms against my position on philosophy practice. The criticisms to which I am subjected often stem from simple denial and disbelief that philosophy can benefit people suffering from so-called mental illnesses. Lack of a comprehensive understanding of the similarities between philosophy and the talk therapy part of the various psychotherapies often leads to a dismissive incredulity. Furthermore, ignorance of the questionable science behind the medical model of mental illness leads supporters of biological psychiatry to deny much of the scientific research I have presented in my books and papers which document the glaring misrepresentation of so-called mental illnesses and the so-called effectiveness of medications in their supposed treatment. The criticisms to which I have been subjected, which stem from denial, disbelief, and ignorance, are tiresome and not very interesting to me.

I'm sometimes criticised for suggesting philosophy as a treatment for so-called mental illness because the assumption is that problems in the mind are problems in the brain. This is clearly false because the brain is biological while the mind is propositional—it's made up of beliefs, values, and assumptions. Drugs can alter the functioning of the brain, but they can't change the mind. For example, a woman is addicted to crack cocaine. When she takes the drug it makes her forget her belief that she is worthless, and it helps her to temporarily forget the memories of

---

[9] Maj, Mario et al, eds..Preface. *Psychiatric Diagnosis and Classification*. West Sussex: John Wiley & Sons, 2002.

her childhood abuse. Then one day she is taken into a treatment centre where methadone is used to help her give up her physically destructive substance abuse. But while the physical cravings for the crack cocaine have been reduced she finds her belief that she is worthless coming back, and then the memories of her childhood abuse come flooding back as well. Her brain has been changed twice—once by crack cocaine and once when she stopped taking the drug, but her mind is still full of the same beliefs, values and assumptions. This is a major reason why it is so difficult to force drug abusers to give up their addiction: they know it would be foolish to do so because the painful beliefs about the self, and the painful memories of the past will return as soon as they stop taking the drug. Another example is medications that are prescribed by medical doctors to combat anxiety. At a recent presentation I was invited to give about philosophical counseling a member of the audience asked me what drugs I would recommend to combat his sister's anxiety attacks. I asked him, What does she get anxious about? This simple question is never asked when it is assumed that anxiety attacks are a function of the random malfunction of the chemical processes in the brain. Philosophy deals with the reason for anxiety, and all other so-called mental illnesses, because what is mental is in the mind—it is beliefs, values, and assumptions. So, again, I don't find the criticism that philosophy can't help mental illnesses very interesting because it's based on a misunderstanding of the enormous difference between the mind and the brain.

I find it interesting when it's argued that the medical model is a legitimate treatment model for so-called mental illness. I find it interesting because a mental illness is never treated according to the medical model, no matter what the claims are in defence of the medical model. There are no biological tests for so-called mental illnesses—as there are for medical problems. There are no clear causes given for so-called mental illnesses—as there are for medical problems. And there are no agreed-upon treatment modalities for so-called mental illnesses—as there are for medical problems. There is no medical model that is followed in the treatment of mental illnesses.

5. With respect to present and future inquiry, how can the most important problems concerning Philosophical Practice be identified and explored?

This is an awkward question to answer. In order to decide how a problem can be identified and explored in any field there must first be an understanding of that field. For example, in order to identify and explore the problems associated with a fianchetto in chess there must first be an understanding of chess. And a practical understanding comes from direct experience, not just theoretical book knowledge. In the years I have been involved in the practice of philosophical counseling I have found that the majority of philosophers who have theorized about philosophical counseling have never had a discussion with an actual client. They have no direct experience and therefore lack a practical understanding of what it's like to talk with a distressed individual about a potentially life-altering issue. Many philosophers I have met are not even able to explain in a few sentences what philosophy is, and what it means to practice philosophy, let alone what philosophical counseling is all about. Simply put, it's impossible for philosophers to identify and explore the most serious issues in the practice of philosophical counseling without ever having experienced a single session of philosophical counseling.

After that, I believe the two most important kinds of problems concerning Philosophical Practice are, first, internal political disagreements about its formal structure and organization, and second the lack of public and professional awareness of the importance of philosophy in relation to so-called mental disorders and their treatment. How can these be identified and explored?

The main way to identify and explore political problems is to examine what motivates the politics in the first place. I am completely uninterested in political problems caused by a struggle for personal recognition, power, and control because these are organization-centered and not client-centered. A different sort of political problem concerns questions regarding the relationship of philosophy to other professions such as counseling and psychotherapy. If there are problems in this area they can be identified and explored in consultation with those professional groups and associations. In our university (University of the Fraser Valley) the Student Association of Philosophical Counseling has gained the endorsement of the university's Student Services (counseling) department after several collegial meetings and discussions.

The second problem, concerning the level of public awareness of philosophical counseling can be identified and explored through various means such as public meetings, philosophy cafés, discussion groups, and in the classroom. These venues of exploration easily help to identify the misconceptions the general public and students have about so-called mental disorders, their causes, the conventional therapies, the over-prescription of medications, and the value of philosophy as treatment.

I never deal in hypothetical case discussions. This is where someone begins an argument in favour of medication for mental illness by presenting a story like this:

But what about the patient who had a perfect childhood, wonderful parents, great teachers, a good education, a loving girlfriend, a good job, never took drugs or drank any alcohol, and so on, but then became clinically depressed and suicidal for no reason at all. Wouldn't you say his depression is endogenous, and therefore treatment with medication is reasonable?

Because this is a hypothetical scenario, it's completely unrealistic. It's a hypothetical scenario not based on an actual case. It's more like a script for a television sitcom, which is also not real life. If this person's life were as wonderful as claimed, there would be no clinical depression or suicidal ideation. The so-called 'facts' of the case are not offered as information with which to assess the patient. They are invented in such a way that they anticipate and block any possibility of a negative response to medication. That makes it a loaded question. It's a no-win situation. It's like trying to win at cards with a partner who intentionally deals you a losing hand.

So I refuse to discuss hypothetical patient cases because hypothetical patient cases are not reasonable discussion topics. They are designed to win the argument. But hypothetical cases are a favorite ploy of both psychotherapists and philosophers wanting to discredit philosophical counseling.

I hope that this book will help to educate people about the usefulness of philosophy in their everyday lives. I am very grateful for the helpful suggestions and patient editing advice given to me by Jeanette Bresson Ladegaard Knox, research associate at the University of Copenhagen, in the preparation of this essay for publication.

Bibliography

Books by Peter Raabe

1. *Philosophy's Role in Counselling and Psychotherapy.* Forthcoming. Rowman Littlefield/ Jason Aronson Publishing, 2013.
2. *Philosophical Counseling and the Unconscious.* Amherst, NY: Trivium Publications, 2006.
3. *Issues in Philosophical Counseling.* Westport, CT: Greenwood Publishing (Praeger), 2002.
4. *Philosophical Counseling: Theory and Practice.* Westport, CT: Greenwood Publishing (Praeger), 2001. Also in Italian and Japanese trans.

Articles by Peter Raabe

"Philosophy and the Sparkling" Life in *Values of the Wise*, Jason Merchey editor. San Diego, CA, 2006.

"'Mental Illness': Ontology, Etiology, and Philosophy as 'Cure'" in *Universitas: Monthly Review of Philosophy and Culture*. No. 446 (Vol. 36 no. 07). Jlu, 2011. New Taipei City, Taiwan.

"'Mental Illness': Ontology, Etiology, and Philosophy as 'Cure'" in *Haser: Revista Internacional De Filosofía Aplicada (International Review of Philosophical Practice)*. Sevilla, Spain. No. 1 (Vol. 1). October, 2010.

"Healing Words: Philosophy in the Treatment of Mental Illness" in *Monthly Review of Philosophy and Culture*. Taipei, Taiwan. No. 428 (Vol. 37 n. 1). January, 2010.

"Mental Illness, Shame, and Philosophy" in *Proceedings of HT2009. The 1st International Conference on Humanities Therapy*. Kangwon National University. Seoul, South Korea. Sept., 2009.

"Would Socrates be Diagnosed as Mentally Ill? Observations on our Mental Health Philosophy Café". *Philosophical Practice. Journal of the APPA*. New York. Vol. 4 No. 2 July, 2009.

"Philosophy in a Psycho-Pharmaceutical World" *Practical Philosophy: Journal of the Society for Philosophy in Practice*. London, UK. Vol. 9 No. 2, July, 2008.

"Reinterpreting Psychiatric Diagnoses." *Janus Head: A Journal of Interdisciplinary Studies in Literature, Continental Philosophy, Phenomenological Psychology, and the Arts*. Volume 8.2 (Winter 2005/6).

"Dragons to Windmills: A Philosopher's Perspective on Psychiatric Diagnoses". *Conference proceedings*. Barrientos Rastrojo,J.—Odoñez García, J.—Macera Garfia, F. editors. *La Filosofía a las Puertas del Tercer Milenio, Sevilla*, Editorial Fénix, 2005. Pages 283—294 (Translated by José Barrientos Rastrojo).

"The Man Who Killed his Six Children: Philosophical Counselling and the 'Problem' of Free Will". *Universitas* Vol. 31 No. 1. Dept. of Philosophy at Catholic Fu-Jen University. Wu-Nan Press, Taipei, Taiwan. January 2004.

"Morals and Ethics in Philosophical Counselling: Sex, Suicide, and Mental Illness". In the *Journal of Philosophical Practice*. E-journal of the University of St Paul, at the University of Ottawa, Canada.

"Causal Nets and the Disappearance of the Unconscious. Co-authored with Martin Hunt". In *Philosophical Counseling and the Unconscious*. Amherst, NY: Trivium Publications, 2006.

"The Relationship Between Philosophical Counselling and Psychotherapy". *Pratiche Filosofiche* (Italian philosophical counselling journal). Vol. 1 No. 2, Milano, Italy. October, 2003.

"An 'Open Textured' Case Study in Philosophical Counselling" *Practical Philosophy:Journal of the Society for Philosophy in Practice*. London, UK. Vol. 6 No. 1 Spring, 2003. 42-55.

16

Shlomit Schuster

Philosopher and Director
Center Sophon for Philosophical Practice and Counseling,
Jerusalem, Israel

---

1. First attraction

It remains a question to what extent philosophy can be differentiated from the practice of philosophy. Philosophy could be viewed as theory of thinking, reflecting and contemplating, as interacting Ideas existing in a Platonic cloud: in that case Philosophical Practice could be a type of applied theory in action. Or philosophy could exist in a subconscious manner in life itself, and in all that people do. If this is the case then only by reflecting on life and creation can philosophy be recreated from its existence. In both cases philosophy without a dynamic and dialectical relationship to actual living and thinking is a poor enterprise. So I find there to be two possible types of Philosophical Practice: an essentialist kind and an existentialist type.

My first attraction to Philosophical Practice has been through and towards the existentialist type: I first came to observe it through ethical dilemmas as presented in humanity's great literary stories, poetry, art, religion, and finally in the philosophy classroom. Basically I encountered Philosophical Practice as the human or divine drama, which can through reflection become a play with the conflicts of life in the realm of our minds. Without a love for philosophizing one cannot love Philosophical Practice, not by observing and practicing it in one's own daily life, and also not as a profession. To love philosophy just as one would love another thousand things seems as well not fitting. Philosophy must be a first and finale attraction, if not a person is liable to consent to entanglement with other disciplines and loose the vision of authentic philosophy which is meta-disciplinary, but not inter- or multi-disciplinary. It is possible to be attracted to Philosophical Practice for egocentric, or for altruistic reasons, but it can also be just for the sake of philosophy.

As a professional activity Philosophical Practice mainly appealed to me as an alternative to psychotherapy and psychoanalysis. In this way of Philosophical Practice I have been mainly inspired through the work of Dr. G. B. Achenbach.[1]

In 1981, the German philosopher Achenbach was the first one who opened as a professional practitioner a philosophical praxis. In a pleasant office, in the forest-surrounded Bergisch-Gladbach, near Cologne, Achenbach, began receiving those searching for a certain kind of guidance. Some of his clients—or visitors in Achenbach's terminology—had already tried everything that today's society offers as solace for anxieties, suffering, and existential questions. After the psychoanalyst, guru, astrologer, and the New Age workshop, they arrived for help at the praxis of a sympathetically listening skeptic. Achenbach's aim is to offer the public an alternative to psychotherapy, but not an alternative therapy. He explicitly states that Philosophical Practice is no therapy at all.[2] Clinical diagnoses and treatment, along the lines of the medical paradigm of therapy, are absent in Achenbach's approach; even so, philosophical counseling can have therapeutic results as well.

Achenbach resists turning his praxis idea into a method, and prefers to keep the style of conversation indeterminate and open-ended. Nevertheless, one can present descriptions, "road signs," that give directions to other philosophers aiming to imitate his successful and responsible advice to people searching for meaning or solutions in problematic situations. Of these road signs, four basic ones are as follows:

1. The sincere communication between the practitioner and the visitor is based on a "beyond-method" method. 2. The importance of dialogue, as that which enlivens and flows from being. 3. "Auslegen"—a looking for explanations—in which the practitioner becomes united with the problem, not by imparting his own understanding of it, but by giving the visitor a fresh impulse to explain him or herself. 4. The innovative component of dialogue, the element of wonder in Philosophical Practice, which does not allow for fixed viewpoints, standard attitudes or permanent solutions.

From the onset of Philosophical Practice in 1981 it was clear that Dr. Achenbach's approach would be attractive to people from all over the

---

[1] Achenbach, G. B. (1984). *Philosophische Praxis*. Cologne: Juergen Dinter; Achenbach, G. B. & Macho, Th. (1985). *Das Prinzip Heilung*. Cologne: Juergen Dinter; Schuster, S. C. (1989). The Philosophical Practice and Counseling Website. Center Sophon. Internet publication (Last accessed: 10. 12. 2011 http://sites.google.com/site/thephilosophicalcounselingweb) Schuster, S. C. (1991). "Philosophical Counselling." *Journal of Applied Philosophy*, 8 (2), 219-223; Schuster, S. C. (1995). "Report on Applying Philosophy in Philosophical Counseling." *The International Journal of Applied Philosophy*, 9 (2), 51-55. Schuster, S. C. (1999). *Philosophy Practice; An Alternative to Counseling and Psychotherapy*. Praeger Publishers: Westport, Conn.

[2] Achenbach, 1984, ibid., p. 29.

world because it is based in reflections on everyday life, and it is not limited to any particular philosophy. Through its openness, philosophical counseling can indeed embrace all traditions and disciplines, and while not overwhelming these by its embrace, it is neither a slave of schools and methods. Socrates, the so-called father of Western philosophy, has often been considered the ancient philosophical practitioner par excellence. Yet, long before Socrates, other men and women in possession of practical wisdom and a philosophy of life were in their own way as well helping themselves and others through philosophizing.

Over the last three decades, Achenbach's idea of Philosophical Practice has inspired philosophers worldwide, and philosophical counseling has become a global practice. There is evidence of an ever steadily growing international movement with quite a few philosophical practitioners in many European countries, Asia, North and South-America, Africa, and Australia. Since Achenbach initiated this modern day ancient practice, many and different philosophical counseling perspectives have emerged. Some of its latest inventions challenge the critical and humanistic principles of the original perspective. For example, philosophical counseling as described in Lou Marinoff's books: *Plato, not Prozac, Philosophical Practice,* and *Therapy for the Sane.* Marinoff encourages the application of any school of thought, and as in most New Ages approaches, critical reasoning and logic are absent. Madame Blavatsky, Bhagwan Sri Rajneesh, Chogyam Trungpa, and other esoterics, are described as meaningful thinkers for philosophical counseling sessions and self-help. I find esoteric wisdom and their sages beyond mainstream philosophical argument, and therefore these have not much to contribute to a common philosophical dialogue.[3]

Although Achenbach's approach is not against philosophical methods, it encourages an open-ended inquiry in the subject matters that are important to the client—while holding off becoming a method. The purpose, goal, and manner of the Achenbachian dialogue are set-forth together with the client, and the only remaining elements are the search for philosophical perspectives on the matters in question, and the supportive and humane relationship offered by the philosopher. This philosophical wayfaring together with a client can be compared to dancing to a client's tune, toward an unknown philosophical horizon.

Regardless of the profundity and success of Achenbach's approach, it has not always been understood by philosophical colleagues as helpful. Thus, some philosophical practitioners felt a need for a structured dia-

---

[3] For a critique of Marinoff's works see Schuster, S. C. (2004) "Marinoff's Therapy: A Critique of his Books on Philosophical Practice" in *The International Journal of Philosophical Practice* , Vol. 2.2.

logue. New types of philosophical counseling arose, sometimes merely shadows of the profundity of the original idea: the beyond method approach was turned into a few simple methodological approaches with particular goals, similar to psychotherapy.

It seems to me that if philosophical counselors want to be therapists it is best for them to get an additional degree in psychology or psychiatry. For philosophers to pretend to be therapists without any general accepted psychotherapeutic credentials does not add to the credibility of their practice.

As a profession Philosophical Practice is important as an *alternative* to psychotherapy, but not as just another kind of therapy. Philosophical practice and counseling without being a competent critique of the helping professions looses its most needed asset and value for today's society.

2. Other related fields

In many academic disciplines there is a lack of a philosophical meta-disciplinary stance. Academics strive to be interdisciplinary, but this is often resulting in that humanity and social science departments adopt for themselves scientific research approaches and lose their classical, creative, analytical or metaphysical methods. Instead of having a dialogue about and with science, philosophy becomes subjected to science. Freud and Jung were much indebted in their approaches to classical-philosophical and traditional understandings of human beings, and this still has influence on today's psychology. But this is changing, and humanistic thought in science may soon come to an end and be replaced by technical soul engineering. It is not through criticism of philosophers that this will happen, but through so called technological advancements in the field of medicine, which began to consider mental health problems as purely physical illnesses.

The science editor of the BBC, Susan Watts, described some of the changes in the field of mental health as follows:[4] The descriptive, superficial approach of today's psychologists will be replaced by a deep medical diagnosis of brain scans and genetic analysis. Watts quoted Professor Shitij Kapur, Dean of the Institute of Psychiatry at King's College London as saying: "There was no aid from clinical tests—lab tests or blood tests—that have been there for last 50 years in other aspects of medicine. So this is our first opportunity to take psychiatric diagnosis from the descriptive, to in some sense based on their deeper

---

[4] Susan Watts, On the brink of a mental health revolution Available on line http://news.bbc.co.uk/2/hi/programmes/newsnight/9631964.stm Last accessed 10. 12. 2011.

biology."

In the face of this ongoing mental health revolution a philosophical meta-disciplinary stance on emotions, the mind, the soul, the ethical nature of human beings, seems extremely needed. If philosophers and colleagues from related disciplines will not confront the practice of mental health as purely biotechnological medicine, then the talent of human beings to understand themselves through self observation and reflection might get lost. Thus Philosophical Practice might become an art practiced by some very exceptional individuals, who with historians and literature professors will search to grasp how human beings once upon a time had a soul or self that was beset with temptations and ethical dilemmas.

The criticism of philosophical practitioners can be helpful for psychotherapy, it may even be prophetic in its assumptions. For example, I published a paper in 2002 in which I suggested philosophical counseling as an alternative to treatment to post-traumatic stress disorder. It was my response to how in general the fall of the New York Twin Towers was reacted upon: PTSD was presented as "in many ways a normal response to an abnormal situation. The guidelines of the American Counseling Association nevertheless recommended recognition that persons were in the grip of a disorder since that would be the elementary step to recovery and treatment. If one did choose not go into treatment immediately, one was advised not to deny these feelings (symptoms) and to keep oneself, family, and surroundings in control.[5]

The American Psychologist Association recommends that when a person suffers the warnings signs of trauma related stress for more then a month, he or she should get treatment. There are also other clinical opinions concerning PTSD, but the above guidelines were authoritative the first years after the 9/11 terrorist attacks.

Ten years later, researchers who evaluated the effectiveness of the aid provided in the Twin Tower attacks showed that it was often lacking results and even wrong. Some of the conclusions in the *American Psychologist* journal 9/11: Ten Years Later are similar to my assumptions in "In Times of War and Terror: Philosophical Counseling as an Alternative to treatment of Post-traumatic Stress Disorder."[6] Benedict Carey reports in the New York Times that Experts greatly overestimated the number of people in New York who would suffer lasting emotional di-

---

[5] American Counseling Association (2001) Crisis Fact Sheet. Retrieved from http://www.counseling.org/consumers/ptsd.htm, last accessed January 29, 2003.

[6] Schuster, S. C. (2002) "In Times of War and Terror: Philosophical Counseling as an Alternative to treatment of Post-traumatic Stress Disorder" in the *Canadian Journal of Community Mental Health*, Special Issue concerned with international innovation in community mental health, Vol. 21, No. 2, pp. 79-90.

stress. Therapists rushed in to soothe victims using methods that later proved to be harmful to some.... And they fell to arguing over whether watching an event on television could produce the same kind of traumatic reaction as actually being there. . . . ." These and other stumbles have changed the way mental health workers respond to traumatic events, said Roxane Cohen Silver, a psychologist at the University of California, Irvine, who oversaw the special issue along with editors at the [*American Psychologist*] journal.[7]

In my paper on philosophical counseling as an alternative aid to PTSD, I proposed the work of Jaspers, Tillich, Kierkegaard, Heidegger, and Sartre as a modern way to affirm existence in the face of anxiety and despair. Likewise, philosophical narratives by philosophers who lived through war events, apparently without becoming the subject of pathology, can strengthen persons who live in times of war and terror. Russell, Wittgenstein, and Sartre are some modern examples of philosophers whose philosophizing was influenced by war events. I argue that in spite of war experiences, or even due to periods of terrorism, philosophers created meaningful philosophies of life. These philosophers asked the great questions of life and they also tried to answer them, and many found answers that were helpful for them. Others surrounded by terror and war may find meaning and comfort by knowing how philosophers lived during tragic times, and dwell on the questions and answers these philosophers produced. Philosophical inquiries can be helpful for people in their specific tragic situations. One does not have to accept all or any of these answers, but it is obvious that philosophical activity can provide answers and relieve.

3. Obligations

The obligation inherent to philosophy and its practice is freedom. Freedom to think, to speak one's mind, and to discuss ideas with others. This I pointed out as well at the colloquium of the Fourth International Conference for Philosophical Practice, in Bensberg, Germany, in a speech entitled Human Rights and Philosophical Counseling.[8]

---

[7] Carey, B. Sept. 11 Revealed Psychology's Limits, *New York Times*, July 28, 2011, available online:
http://www.nytimes.com/2011/07/29/health/research/29psych.
html?r=1&ref=benedictcarey Last accessed December 2011. Also 9/11: Ten Years Later, *American Psychologist*, Vol. 66, No. 6, September 2011.

[8] Schuster, S. C. (1998) Human Rights and Philosophical Counseling, available on line at
http://sites.google.com/site/thephilosophicalcounselingweb/
texts-and-documentation/human-rights-and-philosophical-counseling. Last accessed 10. 12. 2011.

Virtues in general require freedom to flourish in. The Socratic virtue was to choose freedom above anything; even preferring death above being curtailed in speech and action. This is the path of wisdom and virtue that Socrates set forth. In his final speech Socrates asked the citizens of Athens to rebuke his offspring if they would not really care about the free investigation of thought and morality, and only would pretend to be philosophers. It is a major virtue for philosophical counselors to share in this Socratic ethos. Today, unlike in Socrates times, philosophers and philosophical practitioners living in democratic ruled countries find themselves in the fortunate position of having international legal protection and support to practice their profession in freedom.

Additionally there exist the obligation to the International Declaration of Human Rights and the United Nations Civil and Political Rights Covenant. In particular I refer here to article 18 and 19 of the International Declaration of Human Rights: "18. Everyone has the right to freedom of thought, conscience and religion; this right includes freedom to change his religion or belief, and freedom, either alone or in community with others and in public or in private, to manifest his religion or belief in teaching, practice, worship and observance. 19. Everyone has the right to freedom of opinion and expression; this right includes the freedom to hold opinions without interference and to seek, receive and impart information and ideas through any media and regardless of frontiers."

Through the philosophical critique of psychotherapy, philosophical counselors add different potential interpretations and understandings of the clients' personal or social problems. By doing so a philosophical counselor recreates, upholds, and defends the individual freedom to self understanding in addition to the understandings endorsed by psychological and scientific paradigms. In today's global society, in which these last mentioned paradigms gained tremendous power and influence over persons and all areas of life, philosophers would do well to remind people of their own thinking abilities as equal, or even better, for finding solutions to their questions or problems.

It seems to me that where such standing in philosophical freedom would create a conflict with any authorities that would want to oppose freedom of philosophical thought and its practice, a philosopher has the ethical obligation to claim the rights concerning freedom of thought granted by the International Declaration of Human Rights.

4. Criticism

It is interesting that some people do not consider G. B. Achenbach's approach to philosophical counseling practical, because it is a critical and open-ended approach. By calling it impractical these persons really mean to say that the critical approach in Philosophical Practice is not commercial. The commercial value is understood as elementary, and thus Philosophical Practice has to be popularized, and made into a method that is very easily grasped, taught, and practiced. It was turned by some into an eclectic mixture. These practitioners seek to be in agreement with the other helping professions and like to present philosophical counseling as a nice package deal on the marketplace of well-being.

Achenbach's approach is not easily understood as an approach, even not by philosophically educated persons because for many persons an approach can only be a methodology. It is the profundity of Achenbach's type of Philosophical Practice that causes it to be difficult to grasp for minds that cannot detach themselves from currant fashions of thinking and demands of living. Notwithstanding these last the free philosophical practitioner ascends to new philosophical heights and dives into the depths of eternal wisdom.

I was told by a Buddhist nun that the way I practice philosophy is similar to Buddhism. Though this was not a criticism of my practice, it helped me understand better the criticisms of others. Though at first the nun's statement was very surprising to me, through some verses from the 13 century Zen Monk Dogen[9] the apparent similarity became clear to me:

"Mind itself is Buddha" — difficult to practice, but easy to explain;
"No mind, no Buddha" — difficult to explain, but easy to practice.

In a similar sense philosophical counseling is the Mind as Philosophical Practice. This is said in a few words but it is difficult to practice because of its very indefiniteness in the actuality of life.

5. Present and Future Inquiry

The most important and only problem for the present and the future concerning Philosophical Practice is for it to remain faithful to itself as a *personal* practice. With this I mean first of all that the philosophical practitioner must practice philosophy in his or her own life. Philosophical practice has to start with the lived experience. An experience that one could narrate as an autobiographic or biographical account. In my book *The philosopher's autobiography: A qualitative study* I described the practice of philosophy as it was lived and described by different philosophers, but mainly in the lives of Saint Augustine, Rousseau and Sartre.[10]

---

[9] Heine, S. *The Zen Poetry of Dogen: Verses from the Mountain of Eternal Peace*, Dharma Communication, Mount Tremper, NY, 2005.

[10] Schuster, S. C.: *The Philosopher's Autobiography: A Qualitative Study*, Westport,

As an example of life narrative as Philosophical Practice I will present here an account of such practices from Augustine's *Confessions* and from Martin Buber's "Autobiographical Fragments". These two accounts, one from the time area of Late Antiquity by a Catholic bishop, and the other from the 20 century by a Jewish philosopher, I present as open ended narratives. The aim is for the reader to self-reflect him or herself in these accounts, and thus questions may arise about one's own philosophical formation through the experience of life.

Achenbach's concept of philosophical counseling can include the investigation of the nature of irrationality and rationality, or the investigation of coherency or consistency, or the development of particular ideas, in the life of a client, if this seems appropriate to the client. Accordingly, poetic and religious expressions of feelings and concepts fall within the context of philosophical counseling, no matter if the poetic—or other artistic expressions—and the spiritual are considered rational or irrational subject matters. For example the next reflections on Augustine's *Confessions*.[11]

I briefly describe Augustine's life story through the changing concepts of rationality in his search for consistency, and his final acceptance of a particular form of irrationality (faith that cannot be explained). Augustine described his philosophical development as progressing through five stages:

1. During the first stage he becomes a seeker for wisdom and God, after reading Cicero's *Hortensius*. The *Hortensius* persuaded Augustine to examine himself. In this self, he explained, he found a need for his childhood faith. But the Catholic faith, as he had known it in Thagaste, his home town, did not blend with his philosophy-converted soul.

2. He then turned to the Manichaeans, who claimed to have rationally obtained knowledge of divine truth, namely through the Biblical Scriptures. Though being a new member of the anti-Catholic Christian sect, Augustine nevertheless continues his readings in philosophy. After a while, Augustine found the Manichaeans less rational than they at first appeared to be.

3. After nine years of Manichaeanism Augustine decided finally to make a new start in Rome, continuing his search for "Wisdom

---

Conn.: Praeger Publishers, 2003.

[11] This section on Augustine is based on the second chapter of my Ph. D. thesis: *Philosophical Autobiography: A Commentary on the Practice of Philosophy*, Jerusalem, The Hebrew University of Jerusalem, 1997; and Augustine, *The Confessions*, Trans. Watts, W., Cambridge, Harvard University Press, 1950.

itself, whatever it was," although despairing of ever finding it. Augustine's third stage of philosophical development is skepticism. After a year of teaching rhetoric in Rome he was promoted to a better teaching job in Milan, where he came under the influence of the Neoplatonic Catholic Bishop Ambrose. But his former adopted skepticism prevents him from embracing Ambrose's new promises of truth. How could he know that this was not another deception?

4. Although this Catholic-Neoplatonism, as a further philosophical intervention, helped him reconcile many contradictions in his reading of the Biblical Scriptures, the disappointed Augustine needed some "strong" proofs before he could come to terms with his childhood faith. He realized that he wanted a philosophy that could enable him to live an exemplary life. A pragmatic insight, that truth can be known through its results, brought about an inner crisis. Where up to then rationality had guided him to believe, now faith became a prerequisite for philosophical understanding of truth: Augustine first had a divine revelation of what to do and when he faithfully obeyed this revelation he was instantly enlightened on a matter that had troubled him for many years, i.e. his weakness in overcoming sexual desire.

5. The final stage is that of Augustine's own pragmatic Christian philosophy. Through this pragmatic spiritual philosophy Augustine counteracted diverging parental influences on his development, and harmonized Christian devotion with classical erudition. Augustine's eventual submission to the doctrines of the Catholic Church and his maturing in Neoplatonist-spirituality is evident in all his writings.

Just as Augustine's writings are consistent with his way of living, so is continuity a characteristic of his life and writings, which he envisioned respectively as a journey towards his own philosophical-spiritual maturing. It is clear from the *Confessions* that Augustine's search for consistency was an essential element in his final transformation. Though it might not be possible to everyone to reach the particular consistency achieved by Saint Augustine, nevertheless, we can question ourselves and others concerning the role of consistency in personal development and in daily living. How important is it to be rational and consistent within oneself? How to achieve such consistency? Can one permit the existence of irrationality in being and living?

These and many other questions concerning rationality and irrationality can be raised by philosophical counselors and their clients. Approaches that don't include irrationality as a possibly meaningful option in living, or as material for philosophical reflection, seem to me to ignore a vital part of the human inner world and the often absurd reality of life. Another example of philosophical self-reflection is found in Buber's "Autobiographical Fragments".[12]

The manner in which Buber narrates his life in "Autobiographical Fragments" (referred to hereafter as AF) poses the question to what degree encounters played a role in Buber's life and the formation of his thought. Buber opposed reductionist psychoanalytical and psychological tendencies, but was close in his psychological understandings to psychosynthesis, similar to Gestalt psychology's use of it. From this perspective it might not have been an incident that Buber called his autobiographical essay "Autobiographical Fragments".

The first four sections of Buber's autobiographical text are about Buber's childhood, his parents, and grandparents. Buber describes these memories as early moments that "have exercised a decisive influence on the nature and direction of my thinking" (AF, p. 3). Throughout the description of his childhood Buber switches back and forth from the first person singular "I" to a detached observational form, another's perspective, possibly a "Thou" view. For example, "At that time I had been brought to my grandparents on my father's side near Lvov" (AF, p. 3), and a few sentences further, "The child itself expected to see his mother again soon; but no question passed his lips" (AF, p. 3).

Buber's parents separated, but his parents and grandparents never told the child anything about what had happened. Buber gets to know a bit more about his mother's disappearance through a slightly older neighborhood girl under whose guardianship he often spent afternoons: I cannot remember that I spoke of my mother to my older comrade. But I hear still how the big girl said to me: 'No, she will never come back.' I know that I remained silent, but also that I cherished no doubt of the truth of the spoken words (AF, p. 3). At the age of fourteen, Buber perceives that the absence of a close relationship with his mother, and the absence of unrestrained, honest communication between him and other members of his family, as characteristic of all communication between people. He calls this unhappy aspect of human interaction *Vergegnung* or mismeeting. Buber believes that what he learned throughout his life about genuine meeting became possible only through those moments of

---

[12] This section on Buber is based on: Schuster, S. C. (2004) "The Autobiography of I and Thou: A Philosophical Psychoanalysis" in Journal of the Society for Existential Analysis. Vol. 15, 1, pp. 133-142 and Buber, M. ""Autobiographical Fragments" in The Philosophy of Martin Buber. Eds. Paul A. Schilpp, and M. Friedman. La Salle, Ill: Open Court, 1967, pp. 3 - 39; and Buber, M. I and Thou. Trans. Walter Kaufmann. New York: Charles Scribner's Sons, 1970.

true disclosure by his guardian and playmate.

The child Buber lived at his grandparents' home till the age of fourteen. His grandmother Adele had a great passion for reading, writing, reflection, and communication of thoughts. She introduced Buber to her life of the mind and the cultural heroes dwelling there: i.e. Schiller, Jean Paul, and many others. It seems to Buber that when his grandmother talks to people, she does that differently from how others speak: when she at times addressed someone, she really addressed him (AF, p. 5). Buber describes his grandfather as a true philologist. He daily meets him, and often helps the elderly man with translating some obscure phrases from old French to German. Translating these phrases raises in him an authentic philosophical wonder concerning language: What does it mean and how does it come about that one 'explains' something that was written in one language through something that one is accustomed to say in another language? The world of the Logos and the Logoi opened itself to me, darkened, brightened, darkened again (AF, p. 6).

Buber describes his father as a man concerned with the social and personal welfare of the workers on his estate, as well with that of the Jewish community of Lemberg. Buber attributes his early intellectual development to his grandparents' influence on him, while his father adds to the emotional, social, and spiritual aspects of the boy's education: Accompanying him . . . the growing boy learned something that he had not learned from any of the many authors that he read (AF, p. 7). A distinct influence on Buber's later understanding of interpersonal relationships seems to have been his father's relationships to others: his father understood no other help than that from person to person, and he practiced it (AF, p. 7).

Buber's relationships with his peer group at school is another break down of communication, an additional mismeeting. He had been tutored privately till the age of ten, but thereafter his father sent him to the Franz Joseph Gymnasium. There he did not encounter the caring relationships which he, nevertheless, had felt at his home. He describes the atmosphere at school to mirror the social climate at that period between the peoples of the Austro-Hungarian empire: mutual tolerance without mutual understanding (AF, p. 8).

Though a part of the Jewish minority at his school, he has to attend daily Christian morning prayers. Buber describes how severely this affected him: "The teacher and the Polish students crossed themselves; he spoke the Trinity formula, and they prayed aloud together.

Until one might sit down again, we Jews stood silent and unmoving, our eyes glued to the floor (AF, p. 8). Eight long years he experienced himself as an object in a religious ceremony. Buber ascribes to this obligatory worship the particular kind of relationship he had the rest of his life with all people who have faith with roots of its own (AF, p. 8).

The summer after Buber started to attend school, he spends at his grandparents' estate, where he has a first experience of what he later would name Thou. While stroking gently the neck of the horse he was particularly fond of, he experienced the horse as really other, yet the animal let him approach: it] confided itself to me, placed itself elementally in the relation of *Thou* and *Thou* with me (AF, p. 10).

Other fundamental encounters are during his teenage years when he meets the philosophers—mainly Plato, Kant, and Nietzsche—through reading philosophy books. And, during his student days in Vienna, his visits to the Burgtheater are more than entertainment. During these hours of dramatic leisure, it was not the play in front of his eyes that particularly fascinate him, but it was the word, the 'rightly' spoken human word that I received into myself, in the most real sense (AF, p. 14). Later, when studying in Leipzig, he becomes a regular visitor of the concert hall. A new language, the language of music, strongly affects him. Bach has an especially powerful influence on him, even to the extent that he believes Bach to have influenced his thoughts, but he is unable to understand in what way: The ground tone of my life was obvious modified in some manner and through that my thinking as well (AF, p. 14-15).

"Autobiographical Fragments" includes Buber's meetings with Theodor Herzl during the Sixth Zionist Congress in 1903. Buber is critical of Herzl's political influence and power. He finds Herzl's influence—and political charisma in general—a dark determinant. I believe that the meeting with Herzl lead to the crystallization of Buber's own charisma, which I relate to role models Buber had observed in rabbinical and Hasidic circles. Buber questioned Herzl's attitude concerning the relationship between the cause and the person: was there a place in Herzl's Zionist vision for the other as person? Buber answered this question himself through his own utopian and humanistic Zionism and I-Thou philosophy.

The last sections of "Autobiographical Fragments" are about Buber's religious development, if one may label his spiritual evolution as such. Unlike Buber's unhappy encounter with Christian religiousness at school, he recalls in a positive fashion the holiday visits with his father to the Hasidic rabbis of Sadagora. Though on the one hand he compares the centralist place of the *rebbe* with that of a dictator, on the other, he is favorably impressed with their creation of genuine community and genuine leadership (AF, p. 20). The young Buber understands the rebbe's task as a fundamental relationship of responsibility and care for the world. Nevertheless, during his childhood and teen years religion had remained peripheral and even exceptional. So much exceptional that he identifies the religious experience with what he calls the experience of otherness. Buber describes that as a child he experienced sometimes exceptional states of consciousness in which suddenly something familiar would become cryptic, and would finally be lighting a way into the lightning-pierced darkness of mystery itself (AF, p. 25).

Buber also experienced a type of conversion. But what he describes as a conversion is really the actualization of the task of responsibility he felt for the world, a moral agility he first observed among the Hasidic rabbis. Synchronously Buber rids himself of all appearances of religiosity—he gave it up or it gave up on him. Religion becomes everything: all that is lived in its possibility of dialogue (AF, p. 26). A particularly unfortunate meeting had triggered the conversion: Buber had not really been available for dialogue when somebody asked to meet with him. He met the person nevertheless, but he was not fully absorbed in the encounter, the meeting was mismeeting. Afterwards it seemed to him that he had failed the person in a way that was beyond rectification. This incident prompted the radical change in his life.

What the subjects "God," "Scripture," and "prophecy" meant to Buber, is nowhere so clearly described as in his fragmented life narrative. It seems as if only in the narration of the origins of the I-Thou relationship he can reveal the essence of these matters with extreme translucency.

In the final section of the narrative, Buber retells his debate with an observant Jew about some verses from the Book of Samuel. Buber claims here that the prophet Samuel misunderstood God. More than Buber's arguments, it is the unspoken, the intangible interaction, that causes the Orthodox dialogue partner to agree with Buber in the end.

The three short appendixes attached to the end of the narrative part of the autobiography, are literary and abstract discussions of Buber's intellectual development in dialogical philosophy. Here he traces the origins of *I and Thou* to the literature of the Hasidic tradition, and finds the dialogical principle emerging in some of his early writings such as *The Legend of the Baal-Shem*, and *Daniel*. He describes the essence of all spiritual work to exist in real encounters and relationships of genuine reciprocity with all creatures. Buber adhered to his utopian philosophy of *I and Thou*, in spite of what he considered a degeneration of dialogical principles; a lifestyle he found typical for the century he lived in. He believed this degeneration in humanistic values to have been caused by philosophical positions that people universalized.

I find particularly interesting that Buber's final meditation in "Autobiographical Fragments" is about love and a personally felt demand to love others; a concern that stands central in most humanist religions. Though the eternal worlds of words and spirituality seem pure, Buber prefers the real world which consist of less pure tousle-heads and good-for-nothings (AF, p. 38).

The autobiographical essays and incidental personal statements prove that meeting fellow human beings—but even more: all of existence—was extremely important to Buber. The narration of the fractioned story of his life, when read in the context of his major works, displays that "fundamental encounters" significantly influenced his development, his philosophy, and his life.

The purpose of this relatively long description concerning Buber's life and his philosophical formation is multiple due to the lessons to be learned by it for the practice of philosophy:

First of all it is required of philosophical practitioners to show interest in the details of a client's life and to understand it together with the development of the person's thought. One cannot easily and quickly do this; it remains a time and patience consuming effort on behalf of the practitioner. Philosophers need to develop much patience for listening to their clients problems and to understand these in the context of the client's life. Secondly, clients are likely to tell their lives to the practitioner in bits and pieces, similar to Buber's fragmented account. The practitioner then may ask questions that can unite the bits and pieces and thus receive a better inside in the context of the client's thoughts, questions, and problems. But most important, it seems to me, is Buber's reflections on the concepts of "meeting" and "mis-meeting". Through these reflections a practitioner becomes more aware of the possible positive or negative effects of a meeting.

Buber's life and other life narratives of philosophers may help philosophers and their clients to understand in depth the idea of Philosophical Practice and counseling. In *The Philosopher's Autobiography: A Qualitative Study* I demonstrated to a greater extent that there are no specific methods or circumstances needed for a Philosophical Practice to develop as a lived experience. Nevertheless, for such a practice of philosophy to be authentic, freedom of thought and practice are indispensable.

Bibliography

Schuster, Shlomit C., *Philosophy Practice: An Alternative to Counseling and Psychotherapy* , Westport, Conn.: Praeger Publishers, 1999.

Schuster, Shlomit C., *The Philosopher's Autobiography: A Qualitative Study,* Westport, Conn. Praeger Publishers, 2003.

Schuster, Shlomit C., *The return to philosophical counseling: A*

16. Shlomit Schuster *conversation with Dr. Shlomit Schuster*. In Hebrew, Interviewer and editor: Idit Parienti. Jerusalem: Beit Allim, 2005

For a list of articles see http://sites.google.com/site/thephilosophicalcounselingweb/publication-list

17

Helge Svare

Adjunct professor
Work Research Institute, Oslo, Norway

---

1. Why were you initially drawn to Philosophical Practice?

One day at the university as I had just finished my masters degree and had begun working as a university teacher, teaching introductionary courses in philosophy, I passed a small note at the message board outside the administration office at the Department of Philosophy announcing that a group was being formed dedicated to Philosophical Practice, and inviting those interested to join in. At that time, even if I had never heard the term *Philosophical Practice* before, my heart started to beat faster, and I was instantly interested.

As I originally decided to study at the university, as the first in my family to seek an education at this level, I was driven by a naïve, but still strong desire to achieve a knowledge that might somehow be useful to other people, or to the world at large as I used to think back then. Even my choice of studying philosophy was thus motivated, as I believed that it would somehow supply me with the wisdom necessary to become a good citizen and helper to the world. During my years at the university this original mission gradually faded, being replaced by the logic of academic life with its focus on exams and grades and highly detailed and technical questions of interpretations of philosophical texts, until it has almost disappeared. Now, standing before the message board, I was forcefully reminded of why I had been drawn to philosophy in the first place: This group, so I understood, was not about academic philosophy as I had grown used to it. It was a chance to re-conquer the original core of philosophy, and at the same time to revive my original intention in seeking to study it, namely, to achieve wisdom, a wisdom, moreover, not distancing itself from the everyday world of living human beings struggling with challenges, choices and ethical dilemmas, but aiming to make itself relevant to exactly this world. This is still, roughly, my reason for continuing doing Philosophical Practice.

2. What does your work reveal about Philosophical Practice that other related academic fields typically fail to appreciate?

As a philosophical practitioner, one of my main inspirations is existentialism. In particular I find it useful to constantly remind myself of the philosophical anthropology of Jean-Paul Sartre in *Being and Nothingness*, and the concept of the *human project* found here, with its radical criticism of causal explanations of human beings, and its alternative focus on freedom. Very roughly, according to Sartre's theory of freedom, human existence is always directed at a future that does not yet exist, into which the subject projects the image of the life he yearns for. In this projection, according to Sartre, we also find the basic form of human freedom, as in defining his projects, or goals, the subject is always transcending what is already the case, thereby creating something completely new, i.e., something not yet existing. Sartre therefore also rejects a psychology that thinks it possible to explain causally human thoughts, desires and actions. Such a psychology radically misunderstands both the nature of the human subject and the nature of actions and choices. Its most basic mistake, however, is its failure to acknowledge the subject as basically free.

In my work as a philosophical practitioner, one of my basic aims is to tune into this dimension of the freedom of the guests visiting my practice, and, so to say, *address this freedom* in the evolving dialogue. In my latest book, called *Livsmesting* in Norwegian, which may be translated as *The Mastery of Life*, my project is to use this idea of freedom as a basis for suggesting how the reader may enter into a dialogue with himself, in order to, for instance, clarify and perhaps revise his life goals.

I think it is essential to emphasize that Philosophical Practice addresses human freedom, e.g. that human freedom is, so to speak, the medium in which the philosophical dialogue takes place. Seen from this perspective, what makes the dialogue taking place within Philosophical Practice *philosophical*, is that it establishes a space in which the guest is able to think for himself, which for many people is not something they are used to or trained in, but which is the essence of philosophy. Philosophy is unique among university discipline in allowing its scholars not only to do what according to Thomas Kuhn calls puzzle-solving, which is what most normal science is about, but constantly to, metaphorically, take one step back with the aim of trying to get a fresh look at the world and its various phenomena, as well as seeking out new descriptions of it, which, seen from a certain position in philosophy, to which I adhere, amounts to very much the same thing.

I often feel that representatives of other academic fields fail to recognize this essential trait of Philosophical Practice. The comments or criticisms directed at us from these fields may be seen to testify to this, for instance when suggestions are being made that one ought to examine systematically the *effect* of Philosophical Practice, or when we are criticized for being just another therapy. As for the first suggestion, it presupposes a radically different paradigm from the one of freedom, as the concept of effect is analytically dependent on a causal model of the human being. Now, I do not think that all other therapies therefore involve the denial of human freedom. On the contrary, I know a number of therapists who, I am sure, are able both to create a free reflective space for their clients, and to address and enhance their client's freedom. According to the official norms and ideals of their therapies, autonomy or freedom is also something they actively pursue. However, the concept of effect introduces a logic different from this, as it implies that it is possible to induce, so to say from the outside, a certain effect in the person, which may then be measured. Also, if the measurement is to make sense, it has to focus on some effect defined in advance, for which there is operationalized criteria for its measurement. This is all contrary to the idea of freedom.

As for the second criticism, I will return to it in a moment.

3. What, if any, practical and/or social-political obligations follow from understanding philosophy from the point of view of Philosophical Practice?

I do not want to criticize former colleagues at the university who have continued to pursue academic philosophy, even if sometimes I can't help thinking that it results in a kind if scholasticism with little interest to others than the very few. Still, the point with academic research is that you never know when it may become more interesting, and sometimes it is only in retrospect that one is able to see the value of some contribution that at the time was regarded to be insignificant. There are also a number of highly skilled academic philosophers who are able both to inspire their students, and in addition to address a greater audience through lectures and books.

However, I think it is highly significant that besides academic philosophy a viable area of Philosophical Practice is being developed. The idea to start the philosophical reflection, not from some sentences in some ancient text, or some problem emerging from the technical discourse of academic philosophy, but from the experiences and challenges of ordinary life, either in the family, in friendship, in the work life, or some other domain, allows a different type of philosophy to emerge, which I am convinced that the world needs.

Exactly how this philosophy will appear, should be kept open, as it would violate the idea of a free philosophy to postulate this in advance. For my own part, however, I have experienced magnificent moments of small philosophy, i.e. when the reflection of a guest on its own doing suddenly takes a leap into what is *for her* a totally new field of insight. Whether this insight is original also in the sense of academic philosophy, meaning something new in a global sense, is irrelevant here, as the focus lies on the reflective process of the guest and its free movements. On the other hand, I have also experienced how taking part in these processes revives my own understanding of the philosophical tradition, which I will claim, is also of great value.

4. What do you see as the most interesting criticism against your own position in Philosophical Practice?

Recently Philosophical Practice in Norway has been criticized for being just another therapy, and as such, of contributing to the enhancement of a therapeutic culture that is deeply problematic. Even if this criticism is perhaps not very well founded, as it is based on the interpretation of texts, and not of any firsthand experience with Philosophical Practice, it has triggered my attention. Could it be that Philosophical Practice, in spite of its good intentions, contributes to create subjects who grow less and less independent, expecting others (such as the philosophical practitioner) to assist them through every insignificant challenge? Another part of the criticism of therapeutic culture is that every societal problem is here transformed or translated into an individual problem and an individual responsibility in a way that camouflages the real nature of the problems, and moreover, either overcharges and exhausts the subject, or alternatively inflates the ego to a caricature of itself, installing in it illusionary beliefs of omnipotence.

This criticism, I think, is not totally unfounded, as there are today tendencies of a therapeutic culture evolving in the West that has some of the features being criticized. Also, it may be worth noticing that philosophical existentialism has inspired some rather troublesome strands of self-help movements, especially in the States, which may be said to be guilty of procuring just those illusions of human omnipotence that was criticized above.

The way of addressing human freedom, is, however, radically different in those self-help movements as compared to Philosophical Practice. In the self-help movements, the concept of freedom is installed through a process of self suggestion, frequently using visualization techniques, or techniques similar to those found in charismatic religious communities, promoting an idea of unconditional and total general freedom which may certainly induce brief feeling of ecstasy, but at the same time, is strangely unfounded. In Philosophical Practice, the dimension of freedom is invoked through establishing a self-reflective space in which the guest is invited to explore his own everyday life, and step by step, learning to recognize his own authorship of this life. The freedom thus discovered, moreover, is always situated in the life already present, and far from bringing images of omnipotence, it celebrates the freedom present in the mostly smaller movements characteristic of this life.

As for the fear that Philosophical Practice should help create personalities who need the help of others to handle even the smallest challenges, I think this fear is itself a caricature. My own experience as a philosophical practitioner testifies that people mostly need the assistance of the philosophical practitioner for a limited period of time. Sometimes, also, during the dialogues with the practitioner the guest develops new reflective capabilities in a way that makes further dialogues with the practitioner less important. However, even if some should want to see the philosophical practitioner regularly for a longer period of time, perhaps even all his life, I am unable to see this as a problem. Just as people in earlier times visited church regularly and sought counsel from the priest on how to live his life, so today, when religion has become less significant in many people's lives, the philosophical practitioner might be used in some of the same function, however, now on the basis of philosophy.

5. With respect to present and future inquiry, how can the most important problems concerning Philosophical Practice be identified and explored?

One of the most pressing challenges of Philosophical Practice is to conquer for itself a place in modern society, to be recognized for what it is, and to be sought and valued for its unique contribution.

This is not as easy as it might seem. And the fact that we live in a culture that more and more develops into a therapeutic culture, makes it perhaps even harder. One problem is this: In spite of the fact that we live in a time that celebrates freedom, and in which freedom for some people is perhaps the highest of all values, the therapeutic field is, I think, far too often sought not to develop or confirm human freedom, but to escape from it. It is a field we approach when life has become too much so that we feel we cannot handle it anymore. Thus, when we seek therapy it is from a desire for relief: We want someone to take the burden from us. We want someone to *give us something* that may make things better. In this way therapeutic culture converges with consumer culture: The good things we seek in therapy become just some other merchandise that we can buy, and it should not cost too much in terms of activity or responsibility.

On the other hand we have the whole state sponsored social and health care system with its own particular logic, which, even if officially ascribes to ideals like empowerment, client participation and autonomy, is enclosed in a system logic that makes these ideals hard, or perhaps even impossible to realize. As each entity within the system is established to promote some fixed mission, based on certain norms and values set in advance, the space for free reflection and autonomous action is correspondingly limited. Now that public funding is increasingly put under pressure due to a growing discrepancy between available funding and public demand, there is also a growing emphasis on *effect*. In some sense, this is positive: One should not spend public money on a public service without checking out whether it works or not.

For Philosophical Practice, however both of these trends are disturbing. Firstly, Philosophical Practice cannot answer to the demands of therapeutic consumerism, as the activity it involves is of a radically different sort. Secondly, its orientation towards human freedom makes it incapable of being included in a system logic that demands that it has the right effect in order to be of value. The point is that the philosophical practitioner cannot promise anything in regards to what might be the outcome of the dialogues he has with his guests, except that it will hopefully increase their reflexivity and autonomy. Except from that, he cannot promise anything! To do this would compromise the very core of what Philosophical Practice is all about.

The major challenge for Philosophical Practice, therefore, is to develop a language capable of making clear to the public how it is different from both therapeutic consumerism and state sponsored therapies as found in the social and health care system. It needs to resist the constant temptation to define itself through terms and concepts borrowed from either of the two fields, and find the right words to present itself on its own terms. In order to achieve this, conceptual work is also needed. The concepts and models that are available to us in our language is always better suited to describe what we already know, than something new. And Philosophical Practice is something new. It invites people to join in philosophical reflections of a sort that few have experienced. We need to develop a language that explains to people how it is different, what they are invited into, and how it may contribute to enhance humanity.

About the Editors

Jeanette Bresson Ladegaard Knox is a philosopher with additional degrees in theatre and religious studies. She also has a diploma within Philosophical Practice and is a certified Socratic facilitator. She is a researcher at the Department of Public Health, University of Copenhagen, with a focus on medical philosophy and the practice of philosophy within health care. She serves as a clinical ethicist at the NICU at the University Hospital in Copenhagen. She is a board member of the Clinical Ethics Committee for Pediatrics at the University Hospital in Copenhagen, a board member of the Danish Society of Clinical Ethics and chairman of the Danish Society for Philosophical Practice. She has published several books and translations and contributed with articles and chapters in journals and books.

Jan Kyrre Berg Olsen Friis is an Associate Professor in Philosophy of Science and Technology at University of Copenhagen. He holds a MA in Philosophy from University of Oslo and a Ph.D. in Science Studies from Roskilde University. Presently he is Deputy Director of MeST—Centre for Medical Science and Technology Studies, Department of Public Health, University of Copenhagen. His philosophical interests include scientific observation and observer variability, perception, tacit knowledge, technologies and scientific practice. Friis is author and co-editor of several books, among these are *A Companion to the Philosophy of Technology*, Wiley-Blackwell; *New Waves in Philosophy of Technology*, Palgrave Macmillan; *Philosophy of Technology: 5 Questions*, Automatic Press.

Index

A

Academic philosophy, 2-3, 7, 48, 49, 63, 65-66, 70, 78-79, 123, 126, 132, 159, 237, 239, 240.

Art of living, 33-39, 55-57, 70, 87, 94, 112, 120, 183.

Autonomy, 6, 11-12, 55, 156, 239, 242.

B

Bildung, 90, 96-97, 105-106, 177.

C

Causal explanation, 124.

Colleague, 39, 152, 166, 204.

Community, v, vii, 38, 44-45, 52, 69, 81-82, 84-85, 91, 93, 96-100, 102-104, 109-111, 115-119, 129, 161, 172, 183, 191, 195, 205, 225, 227, 232, 233.

    Community of Wonder, 91, 106.

Critical thinking, 5, 6, 22, 35, 103, 177, 204.

D

Demarcation, 110, 196, 199, 200.

Depression, 4, 7, 46, 57, 69, 71, 206, 207, 211, 217.

Dialectic, v, 138-139, 140.

Dialogue, vi, 24, 33, 35, 36-38, 55, 77, 78, 79, 80-93, 95, 97-102, 104-105, 111-113, 118-120, 125-127, 129-139, 141, 145, 150, 152-156, 160-161, 168, 172, 174-178, 180, 188-190, 193, 196, 198, 206, 222-224, 234, 238.

    Socratic dialogue, 137, 139.

    Strategic dialogue, 153.

Dilemma training, 33.

Discourse, v, 4, 56, 64-66, 82, 91, 239.

Doubt, 55, 85, 149, 152-153, 210, 231.

E

Education, 2, 4-6, 8-9, 12, 29, 34, 44, 49-51, 55, 61, 63-66, 69-70, 74, 83, 94, 96-97, 105, 110, 149, 160, 172, 177, 187, 189, 203, 217, 232, 237.

Effect, 45, 65, 73, 126-127, 129, 139-140, 142, 176-177, 179, 185, 190, 208, 213, 239, 242.

Efficiency, 40, 126.

Emotion, 4-5, 12, 46-47, 86, 135, 138, 145, 162, 173, 176, 179, 211, 225.

    Active emotion, 173, 179.

    Passive emotion, 179.

Empathy, 62, 64, 75.

Empowerment, 35, 242.

Encounter, 58, 111-114, 116-119, 163, 172, 180, 232-234.

Enlightenment, 63, 128.

Ethics, 4, 9, 29, 35, 39, 44, 47, 50, 55, 79, 121, 140, 174, 185, 187, 196-197.
Applied Ethics, 55, 79, 185, 187.
Ethos, 197-198, 227.
Evidence based medicine, 124, 126-127.
Existentialism, 34, 110, 149, 204, 209, 238, 240.
Experience, v, 10, 18, 24, 26, 36, 38-39, 50, 62, 64-66, 68, 77-78, 82, 89, 92-93, 95-96, 99-102, 110-112, 115, 120, 128, 130-131, 133-134, 137-138, 140, 144, 152, 155-156, 171, 174-176, 179, 181, 188, 199, 205, 216, 228-229, 233-235, 240-241.

F

Fate, 68, 72, 75, 171.
Freedom, 3, 6, 11-12, 74, 109-110, 115, 119, 125, 135, 172-174, 226-227, 235, 238-242.
Free space, 133-135, 146.

G

Genetic, 77, 211, 214, 224.
Glassbead game, 136.

H

Hermeneutical, 145, 181.
Hourglass model, 133.
Human existence, 22, 68-69, 75, 112, 238.
Humanistic approach, 125, 127.
Humor, 9, 12-14.

I

Ideas, 2, 9, 11, 17, 20-24, 28, 37-39, 49, 78, 80-81, 87, 90, 94, 102, 132, 135, 139, 144-145, 151-152, 155, 160, 162-166, 172-173, 192, 226-227, 229.
Power of ideas, 162.
Intersubjectivity, 82-83.

K

Kierkegaardian humourist, 94, 96.
Knowledge, v, 2, 9, 11-12, 24-27, 29, 34, 36, 50-51, 57, 63-65, 72-73, 79-80, 82, 84-85, 90, 92-93, 96-97, 100-102, 112-113, 128, 132, 134-136, 140, 142-144, 173-174, 178, 186, 203-204, 208, 216, 229, 237, 243.

L

Life topic, 178.
Lyrical impulse, 100.

M

Medical approach, 124-126.
Medical model, 57, 205-206, 212-215.
Medication, 57, 125-127, 208, 211-212, 216, 217.
Melancholy, 69, 114.

Mental disorder, 211-213.
Mental illness, 57, 205-208, 210, 212-216.
Meta-dialogue, 152, 200.
Meta-disciplinary Philosophy, 221, 224-225.
Meta-disciplinary Philosophy practice, 221, 224-225.
Method, 9-11, 16, 21-22, 39, 63-66, 72, 82, 85, 87, 112, 116, 125, 131-133, 151-152, 178, 180-181, 188, 209, 222-224, 228.
Mind, v, 3-4, 16, 21, 24, 29, 38, 43, 56, 80, 87, 114, 127, 134, 141-142, 144, 149, 151-152, 156, 172, 188, 192, 194-196, 205, 208-210, 212-215, 225-226, 228, 232.
Models, 49-51, 55-56, 111, 113, 155, 175, 194, 233, 242.
Modern philosophy, 3, 109, 111-112, 114, 116-117.
Moral education, 5-6.
Morality, 4-6, 9, 35, 174, 227.

N

National bubble, 197-198.
Network, 184.
New Socratic, 78, 81-82, 84-85.

O

Oracle, 142.
Orientation, 54, 81, 84, 86, 172, 174-175, 177-178, 180, 242.

P

Phenomenology of Wonder, 103, 106.
Philosophical café, 34.
Philosophical counseling, 3, 18, 23, 26, 31, 33, 53, 57, 94, 106-107, 125, 160-161, 185, 190, 200, 205, 216, 218-219, 222, 229, 235.
Philosophical exercises, 37.
Philosophical practitioners, 6, 13, 17, 19, 25, 27, 30, 45, 50, 58, 72-73, 77, 88, 191, 197.
Philosophizing, v, 65, 74, 78, 81, 85, 89, 97-98, 100, 104, 113, 116, 119, 134, 151, 172, 179-180, 221, 223, 226.
Phronesis, 37, 90, 98, 101.
Plato, 13, 20, 55-56, 62, 78-79, 80, 82, 103-104, 117, 130-132, 136-140, 142-146, 164-166, 174, 188, 199, 201, 223, 233.
  Allegory of the cave, 164.
Poetic reason, 135.
Polis, 35, 56, 109, 111-112, 115, 119.
Political, 5-6, 9, 28, 43, 52-54, 57, 66, 77, 83, 90, 92, 100, 109-119, 121, 126, 151, 164, 172, 177, 180, 183, 187, 189, 190-191, 197, 198, 207, 210, 216, 233, 239.
Practical philosophy, 7, 11, 33-39, 80-81, 183, 189.

Index

Praxis, 13-14, 66, 75, 106, 109, 111, 120, 157, 171, 181-182, 222.
Prison, 51, 57-58, 154, 190.
Propositional content, 210, 213.
Psychiatry, 7-8, 57, 109, 124, 189, 192-193, 195-196, 199, 205-206, 214, 224.
Psychology, 4, 13, 21, 23, 49, 162, 180-181, 218, 226.
Psychotherapy, 50, 66, 71, 125, 199, 208, 217, 219, 222, 235.

R

Reason, v, 22, 24, 27, 35, 46, 54, 77, 80, 96, 114, 135, 152, 156, 165-166, 173-174, 177, 179, 187, 212, 215, 217, 237.
  Intuitional reason, 177.
  Poetic reason, 135.
  Practical reason, 174.
  Rational reason, 173, 174.
Reconciliation, 179, 180.
Religion, 3, 8, 37, 128, 172, 195, 198, 221, 227, 233, 241.

S

Science, 24-25, 63, 181, 200, 243.
Self-help, 223, 240.
Situation, 5, 23, 29, 35, 38, 46-47, 62, 65, 79, 86, 98, 115-116, 118-119, 121, 127-128, 138,-140, 153, 174, 176, 211, 217, 225.
Skills, 2-3, 9, 11-12, 26, 28, 50-52, 77, 92, 100-102, 111, 125-126, 130, 175, 204, 208.
Socratic dialogue, 33, 35, 37, 78, 81-82, 84-85, 97, 100, 131-132, 134, 145, 188-189, 198.
Socratic eros, 102.
Socratic impulse, 100.
Socratic method, 82, 151.
Socratic situation, 79, 86.
Socratic Virtues, 102.
Spirituality, 7, 34, 230, 234.

T

The Enlightenment, 5-6, 114-115, 183.
The New Age, 7, 222.
Theoretical philosophy, 73, 80, 189, 190.
Theory of ideas, 117, 145.
Theory (theoria), 80.
Therapeutic culture, 240-241.
Therapy, 3-4, 49, 62, 70, 74, 86, 104, 114, 123, 125-162, 178-180, 193, 204, 209, 214, 222, 224, 239-241.
Truth, v, 3, 10, 12, 21, 34, 65, 77-78, 80-82, 84-87, 90, 102, 109-110, 113, 129, 136, 143, 145, 149-152, 195, 210, 229-231.

U

University, 1, 15-21, 25-29, 35, 40, 43-44, 56, 74, 89, 91, 94-95, 97, 99, 102, 106, 109-111, 121, 123-

124, 145-146, 150-151, 159, 160, 167-168, 171, 173, 184, 186, 190-191, 200-201, 203, 206-207, 216-218, 226, 229, 243.

V

Virtue, 11-12, 39, 47, 56, 135, 138-140, 189, 227.

W

Wisdom, v, 1, 3, 7-12, 20, 23, 35, 37, 56, 65, 74, 86, 89-92, 97-101, 104-106, 161-162, 164-165, 167-168, 179, 199, 223, 227-229, 237.